THE CHILD PATIENT AND THE THERAPEUTIC PROCESS:

A PSYCHOANALYTIC, DEVELOPMENTAL, OBJECT RELATIONS APPROACH

Diana Siskind

JASON ARONSON INC.
Northvale, New Jersey
London

Production Editor: Judith D. Cohen

This book was set in 11 on 14 point Garamond by Lind Graphics of Upper Saddle River, New Jersey, and printed and bound by Haddon Craftsmen of Scranton, Pennsylvania.

Library of Congress Cataloging-in-Publication Data

Siskind, Diana.
    The child patient and the therapeutic process ; a psychoanalytic,
  developmental, object relations approach / by Diana Siskind.
        p. cm.
    Includes bibliographical references and index.
    ISBN 0-87668-494-0 (hard cover)
    1. Child psychotherapy—Case studies.   I. Title.
    [DNLM: 1. Object Attachment—in infancy & childhood—case studies.
  2. Psychoanalytic Therapy—in infancy & childhood—case studies.
  WS 350.2 S622c]
  RJ504.C54   1992
  618.92'8914—dc20
  DNLM/DLC
  for Library of Congress   91-47068

Manufactured in the United States of America. Jason Aronson Inc. offers books and cassettes. For information and catalog write to Jason Aronson Inc., 230 Livingston Street, Northvale, New Jersey 07647.

For my brother Devi,
in his memory

Contents

Acknowledgments

I thank Dr. Jason Aronson for encouraging me to write this book and for being so responsive and enthusiastic throughout the writing process. His graciousness extends to a staff whose professional expertise combines with friendliness. I thank Judith Cohen, my editor, and the entire staff at Jason Aronson Publishers for their courtesy and for their help. I thank Mrs. Barbara Frank who typed transcripts of supervisory sessions, deciphering often hard to follow dialogue with her usual intelligence and efficiency. The prospect of writing this book motivated me to enter the world of computers and here again I was very fortunate to have the staff of COLE SYSTEMS set me up with perfect equipment and then with patience and good humor initiate me into its versatile uses. The ease of writing on a computer greatly enhanced the pleasure of my work.

    This book represents many years of learning from my patients, students, supervisees, colleagues, and teachers. Two teachers who have most directly influenced my thinking are Gertrude and Rubin Blanck, and this book reflects much of what I have learned from them over the past twenty years. I am very grateful to them for their outstanding work and for their contribution to my professional growth. I thank my many friends and colleagues whose interest has added to the excitement of this endeavor. I believe that being able to write this book with a sense of enjoyment involved a confluence of forces; psychic readiness met with fortuitous external circumstances. I thank Mark Grunes, Joyce Aronson, Renee Goldman, Anne Marie Dooley, and Mira Spektor for helping to create the field of forces that generated my book-writing state of mind. I thank two dear friends and colleagues who each played a very direct and invaluable part in the writing of this book. Helen Goldstein and Beatrice Weinstein were my writing partners. Each read my manuscript chapter by chapter, raised important questions, and made astute comments. I thank them very much for their generosity of time and interest, and for having made the process of writing feel more like a collaboration than the solo project it would have been without their wisdom, and support, and encouragement.

I thank my children for their interest and confidence in the progress of this work. Over the year of book writing they began many of our telephone conversations with: "How's the book?" as if the book had become an accepted family guest who was going to be around for a good while. My husband took to my book writing with complete naturalness and exhibited consistent interest as well as acceptance of my investment of time and thought. He read my manuscript and from the point of view of a layperson made valuable and insightful comments. I am very grateful for his unwavering help and support.

Finally I would like to thank Linda Small for allowing me to use her case for this book and for the pleasure I had in supervising her work. I wish that I could use her real name but confidentiality must be protected and she knows who she is. I hope that when she reads this book she enjoys being witness to the unfolding of her professional growth as reflected in its pages.

Preface

Long ago, I had an initial interview with a 9-year-old girl who was referred to me because her mother wanted her to have the opportunity of expressing her feelings about her parents' bitter divorce and its equally bitter aftermath. The patient, Jenny, did not exhibit any particular signs of distress except for her firm insistence on spending her nights in a sleeping bag outside her mother's bedroom, rather than sleeping in her own room.

Jenny arrived for her first appointment looking perky and relaxed. She ignored my toys and drawing materials and sat down in the adult chair.

I told Jenny that her mother had been to see me and had told me her reason for wanting Jenny to see a therapist, but I was most interested in learning what Jenny thought of this idea.

"Well," she said, "I don't know much about it, but my two brothers both see psychiatrists. Joey says he spends his whole time listening to questions that he really doesn't want to answer, so he makes up lies, and lies, and more lies, and that's very boring. Rob doesn't hate it quite as much because his shrink likes to work on model planes, so Rob helps him and they don't talk much. Still, going to a shrink is not what he *wants* to do.''

"What about you?'' I asked.

"Look, it can't be helped,'' she said smiling a big smile. "My mother is under some sort of spell or something. She's been going to a psychiatrist for years and years and she does whatever he tells her. When he told her to divorce my father, she did, and when he told her to send my brothers to shrinks, she did. I guess it's my turn now, and there is no way that I'm going to get out of it, so I might as well just make the best of it. Also, you seem pretty nice. Can I show you a card trick? I mean, is it okay to do that here . . . is it allowed?''

I nodded yes.

Jenny pulled a deck of cards out of her blue jeans pocket and separated all the kings, queens, jacks, and aces from the rest of the deck. After placing the discarded part of the deck back in her pocket, she shuffled the figure cards, laid them face down solitaire style, and then randomly picked a card. It was a jack. "The jack is the queen's lover,'' she said turning up her next card, a king. "The king finds out about it and calls. . . .'' She now lifted an ace. "The police . . . the ace is the police. Let's see what happens now.''

Jenny now reshuffled and spread out the cards. Again she picked a card at random. It was a queen.

"The queen wants to save her lover, the jack, so she gets the police to be on her side and tells them not to find the jack.''

Jenny picked another card. It was a jack.

"The queen and the jack get married and the queen orders the police to chase the king out of town. The jack becomes the new king and they live happily ever after.'' Jenny sat back and grinned at me.

"How did you get the story to go that way?'' I asked. "What would have happened if you had picked different cards?''

"Well, you see the whole trick is to make up a story to fit each card as you pick it. Sometimes the king and queen end up together and the jack goes to jail,'' answered Jenny in a thoughtful voice. "You see, it can turn out all different ways. The trick is, no matter how it goes, to make up a good story.''

This engaging and precocious child is presented as an example of a dilemma particular to the child therapist. Here is a child whose ability to adapt to a difficult family situation is extraordinary. She takes pride in being able to make the best of things and conveys this in her card trick. She is unaware of paying a price for being so accommodating. She does not know that her night fears are a symptom of psychic distress. She guards her carefully established equilibrium.

The child therapist has the awesome task of upsetting the equilibrium of his or her patient in those cases where that equilibrium is impeding development. Some children quickly recognize that the therapist is a potential source of help. These children are usually aware of their distress. Others, like Jenny, do not feel their distress and their resistance to treatment is formidable.

This book is about another child's treatment and about her therapist's struggle to stay in step with her. It is about a little girl named Cleo who was very different from Jenny except in one regard: both were afraid. But whereas Jenny's fears were contained, Cleo's were pervasive and unrelenting. She lived in a state of perpetual distress and did not experience the adult world as potentially helpful. Her elusiveness made her hard to locate as she darted in and out of fantasies of mayhem and disaster. Yet, despite the chaotic climate of her psychotherapy sessions, Cleo was ultimately more accessible to treatment than the more poised and balanced Jenny.

This book is also about a partnership between a therapist and a supervisor. I believe that it took the two of us working hard together to find a way to engage Cleo in the treatment process. The supervisory process was the ballast, our theoretical knowledge the compass, and Cleo's psychic safety our destination.

In the chapters that follow, the reader will join us in a session-to-session description of what actually took place in the early phase of Cleo's treatment and how the sessions were understood in the supervisory discussions.

While this book is about Cleo, her therapist, and the supervisory process, the questions it raises are applicable to all our child patients: What do we actually do with the children who are brought to us for treatment, and how do we work with the willing ones and the unwilling ones, and what has to take place to make the child become an ally to the treatment?

1

An Introduction

The idea for this book came about quite spontaneously shortly after I received an interesting request for supervision. A psychotherapist called me after hearing me present a paper on my work with a child. She explained that despite extensive training, she had never achieved the ability to treat children with the depth and scope that she had developed in her work with adults. She found that while she enjoyed her child patients, she often felt that she was nothing more than a friendly adult to them, a benign presence with good common sense, rather than their psychotherapist. She was most eager to develop her ability to feel more grounded in her work with children. She requested intensive supervision with a dimension that resembled a tutorial. After meeting with her, I agreed to work with her on the condition that she call me when she was about to begin a new case so that her supervision could start with the beginning phase of treatment. Within a few weeks she called to say she had just completed the evaluation of a child who needed treatment and was ready to begin our work.

We began weekly supervision, and after several supervisory

sessions I realized that we were reviewing many of the basic principles of child treatment and that our work could become the format
of a book. One particularly fortuitous benefit of using such a format
was that it solved the delicate problem of confidentiality. The use of
case material, particularly extensive material in contrast to a brief
vignette, always poses this concern. In some instances patients are
asked to grant permission for their treatment to be written up, but
that can have harmful ramifications and is complicated where child
cases are concerned, for whose permission would you request? That
of the parents? But that would not be fair since the child has been
assured that the relationship with his or her therapist is private and
that the parents will not be told the content of sessions. Would you
ask permission of the child, a 6 ½-year-old child in the case that
follows? How could a child possibly understand such a request? In the
case that follows, confidentiality was protected in several ways without compromising anyone's best interests. Factual material was al-
tered where such changes did not significantly change the portrayal
of family dynamics or descriptions of the child's affective climate. As
the supervisor of this case, I was never told the child's name or the
names of any family members, thus upholding the sanctity of confidentiality by restricting knowledge of the identity of this family
solely to the child's therapist. And finally, the therapist was given the
fictitious name Linda Small, thus eliminating the only remaining
possible link to the patient.

With confidentiality protected and with permission from Linda
Small, I began to tape our supervisory sessions with the thought that
the interweaving of case material with discussions between therapist and supervisor might be of interest to others in our field. These
discussions contain the type of reflection and conceptualization that
is such a constant and necessary part of work with children, a
dimension of our work that at times is difficult to achieve without
the benefit of collegial dialogue or supervisory consultation.

Of course, analytic self-scrutiny is an intrinsic aspect of our work
with patients of all ages, but in some ways the child therapist carries
an even greater responsibility than the adult therapist, plays more
roles in the life of his or her patient, and has to deal with a variety

of extra-analytic situations that do not occur in work with adult patients. For instance, the usual complexities of transference and countertransference are compounded by the child's youth and by all that it implies in terms of actual dependency, vulnerability, psychic immaturity, and developmental state of flux. Also, therapists of young children generally have some ongoing contact with the child's parents, and this too inevitably complicates the transference and the countertransference. In regard to work with the parents of their young patients, child therapists need to exhibit a high measure of tact and skill. This can become very taxing when working with parents who are extremely anxious, or rivalrous, or openly undermining of their child's treatment. Since these parents are not our primary patients and often have their own therapists, some of their transference manifestations cannot be explored with them as they would be were they our patients.

Many therapists who work with adults are not aware of the manifold challenges particular to child treatment, or of some of the delightful aspects. I hope to gain some of these therapists as readers of my book. But most of all, this book is for my fellow child therapists, the freshmen who are beginning, the sophomores who are in the thick of it, the juniors who might need a boost, and the seniors who are teaching in addition to doing clinical work and who can use some case material, interspersed with theory, as a teaching enhancement.

One of my objectives in writing this book is to present a case that is realistic in all respects. The child can only come once per week. The family situation is very difficult. The therapist is often baffled by the material and makes mistakes. The supervisor fails to note some of the supervisee's oversights. In short, this is not model treatment, but it is "good enough" treatment. The therapeutic process evolves despite the therapist's and supervisor's occasional ineptness and lapses of insight.

One of the factors that made the dialogue between Linda Small (the therapist) and me (the supervisor) so comfortable was that we share the same theoretical orientation. References to theory appear throughout the chapters as the material stimulated discussion and review of relevant theoretical issues. Some background needs to be shared with the reader. In her child work, Linda Small is a psychoanalytic psychotherapist, that is, a psychotherapist whose theoretical orientation has as its base classical psychoanalytic theory updated by developmental and object relations theory. She is not a child psychoanalyst but relies on the same theory that is the basis of child analysis. Child psychoanalysts generally see their patients four or five times per week. Psychoanalytic psychotherapy is usually limited to three or fewer sessions weekly. This difference in frequency is not necessarily a matter of preference. Child psychotherapists tend to be willing to see children less frequently if that is what is possible for a particular family, and (ideally) they are trained to adapt their technique to these variations in frequency of sessions.

The difference between child psychoanalysis and child psychotherapy is currently more complex and controversial than it was when psychoanalysts first began to work with child patients. The distinction between these modes of treatment was sharply defined several decades ago, before theoretical explorations had probed the path and vicissitudes of preoedipal development. In those days the criterion for suitability for child psychoanalysis was analogous to that of adult analysis: a diagnosis of neurotic structure. All but neurotic patients were relegated to psychotherapy, which, in those days, was a catchall term for a variety of treatment approaches, many of them haphazard and lacking in theoretical base. As our theory became enriched and diagnostic skills deepened and expanded, some of the former diagnostic demarcations began to seem strained and at times inaccurate. For example, there is now general agreement that in some of the early examples of child analysis described in our literature, the children presented no longer fit our definition of neurotic structure. Some of these children would now be viewed as suffering from ego deficits and developmental derailments originating in the preoedipal period and interfering with the attainment of neurotic structure.

Advances in theory building gradually filter down to refinements in diagnostic understanding and eventually allow for amplification of technique. The enrichment of psychoanalytic theory over the past decades has enhanced the work of psychoanalysts and has benefited many analysands. It could have been restricted to serve this modality, but that was not the course of our history. What happened instead was a burgeoning of interest in psychoanalytic theory stemming from various academic disciplines, primarily psychology and social work. As growth of interest in psychoanalytic theory spread, so did the opportunities to pursue its study. Many hitherto nonanalytic therapists eagerly sought to improve their psychotherapeutic treatment of a population that covered a vast spectrum of diagnostic as well as economic, educational, and cultural conditions. Psychoanalytic theory provided these therapists with a theory and a structure that could be adapted and applied to their work. Eventually, these psychotherapists were able to identify themselves as *psychoanalytic* psychotherapists and to make their own valuable contributions to the evolution of theory and practice. Child psychotherapists also contributed to and benefited from this spiralling growth. Many gradually developed a technique appropriate to the treatment of children over a broad diagnostic continuum, a technique that rested on a foundation that combined theoretical precision with technical flexibility. Because psychoanalytic psychotherapy now shares a common base with psychoanalysis, some of the boundaries between these modes of treatment are less distinct than they were in the past.

Ideally, child psychotherapists would be trained to work in both modalities. That way it would be possible for us to stay in step with all of our patients from beginning to termination. Our skills would allow us to be an organizing and structure-promoting force in the life of a child whose developmental deficits required that treatment approach, and to stay with that child as the development of structure allowed for higher levels of interpretive work. Ideally as well, all psychoanalytic psychotherapists, like psychoanalysts, would undergo their own psychoanalysis, for that is one of the best preparations for attaining the depth and versatility of insight, capacity for self-analysis, and tolerance for ambiguity so essential in our work.

A brief overview of our theoretical orientation will act as a review for some and an introduction for others. Our theoretical base is that of *psychoanalytic developmental object relations theory* (Blanck and Blanck 1986), generally referred to as *ego psychology,* a less cumbersome but also less precise term.

Psychoanalytic developmental object relations theory begins with Freud and the birth of psychoanalysis. Freud's dual contribution—psychoanalysis as a scientific theory and psychoanalysis as a method of treatment—inspired countless followers, some faithful to what we regard as *classical theory,* and others taking divergent paths. Using Freud's monumental work as their foundation, a number of classical psychoanalysts enriched and expanded his contributions by investigating territories that he had noted but not been able to explore during the limits of his lifetime. One particular group of brilliant theorists became known as *ego psychologists.*

Heinz Hartmann, generally referred to as the father of ego psychology, was the first psychoanalyst to shift attention to the functioning of the ego outside the sphere of conflict. His interest in early normal development led to his speculations about the earliest reciprocal interaction between mother and infant and its impact on the adaptation of both partners in the dyad (Hartmann 1939). The concept of adaptation has added an essential dimension to our way of thinking about our patients.

Around the same time, Anna Freud wrote *The Ego and Mechanisms of Defense,* describing nine of the defenses employed by the ego, and stating that it is through our observations of the *ego* that we gain insight into the workings of the id and the superego. She was a child analyst of outstanding talent as well as a gifted teacher and theoretician. Like Hartmann, she was equally interested in normal and pathological early development (1965) and believed that insight into the one deepened understanding of the other. One of her most significant contributions to the widening scope of psychoanalytic theory and technique was her statement that the analyst "take his stand at a point equidistant from the id, the ego and the super-ego" (1936, p. 30).

René Spitz approached his psychoanalytic explorations from a direction that was novel in his time. He observed infants in institutions and used his observations to add an important dimension to his theory about early infant development. His brilliant and clinically invaluable contributions trace and describe the development of the ego in great depth, always linking ego with object. He states that development must be "quickened" (Spitz 1965, p. 99) by the object, and if the object is unavailable or lacking (as in institutions), pathology and death are the consequence. His observations also uncovered three organizers of the psyche, which, in normal development, follow a general timetable and have recognizable outward manifestations: the three-month smile, the eight-month stranger anxiety, and the eighteen-month "no." He postulated that the outward manifestations of these pivotal developmental steps may serve as indicators of whether development is proceeding or becoming skewed (1959, 1965).

Edith Jacobson's expansion of our theory regarding the development of the superego and her corresponding extension of the range of the superego's functions vastly enriched Freud's original proposition. She developed a kind of topography of the self and object world that greatly enhanced our insight into identity formation and became clinically indispensable. By proposing the terms *self representation* and *object representation,* she made an important distinction between the actual self and object, and the psychic representation of the self and object. Jacobson's (1964) definition of *self representations* is "the unconscious, preconscious and conscious endopsychic representations of the bodily and mental self in the system ego" (p. 19). The definition of object representation is analogous to that of self representation: the unconscious, preconscious, and conscious endopsychic representation of the bodily and mental *object* in the system ego. This profound refinement of theory defines both a process and the shifting states of perception that result.

Margaret Mahler's separation-individuation theory is so well known at this point that it does not need even brief introduction. Her work beautifully integrated and expanded the contributions of her predecessors. For instance, consider how her developmental timetable from physical to *psychological birth* dovetails with Spitz

and with Freud's psychosexual stages, and then goes on to illuminate new areas of psychic functioning (Mahler et al. 1975). Her
writings on the treatment of severely disturbed children (1968) are
a model of integration of theory and technique and an essential
contribution to child treatment.

This brief highlighting of some of the contributions of the pioneer
ego psychologists is meant to convey to the reader the general
orientation of the author. Ego psychology is now such an accepted
body of knowledge in our field that any further attempt to summa-
rize its history and development would take us far afield and away
from the case of Cleo. I would like to remark, though, that the *ego
psychologists* were misnamed, for each of them discovered that it
was not possible to talk about the development of ego without
taking into account the influence of the object, and neither ego nor
object can be considered without including the dimension that fuels
all psychic activity, the instinctual drives. It is precisely this interweaving of psychic forces that made the contribution of these
theorists so dynamic. It is not surprising that they sparked and
nourished the continuing evolution of psychoanalytic theory that
current generations are privileged to employ in their daily work
with patients.

Yet with all the best training at our disposal, we are all familiar
with the minute-to-minute decisions to be made in that room with a
particular patient. In this case it will be a little girl full of fears and
oblique communications. In the immediacy of these therapeutic
moments Linda Small is on her own. She, or you, or I, may arrive
equipped with our carefully won fund of learning and a readiness to
apply all our training to the understanding of our young patient's
inner life. But as we all know, what counts here for all of us is the use
that we can make of our knowledge, and that requires a high level of
equanimity, attunement, and curiosity about the known and the *not
known*.

The reader is now going to join us: Linda Small, her patient Cleo,
and her supervisor, the author. Together we will go through the
blunders and the high points, the confusion and ambiguity, and the
fine moments of the beginning months of treatment.

2

The Evaluation Process

Cleo is a 6-year-old first grader who was experiencing a period of very great fright. She was afraid to be alone in any room of her apartment and followed people around so as never to be by herself. She was afraid that the paintings on the wall would become real and that people would step out of them and talk and move like real people. She was afraid to go to sleep at night and tried to keep herself awake as long as possible. She was afraid that monsters would come and take her away to some dark and horrible place with screeching sounds and shadows of weird and unfamiliar shapes and keep her there forever. She said that maybe these thoughts came to her because they appeared in her dreams, but her dreams felt so real to her that she wasn't sure that they really were dreams. Most of all, she was afraid that she would die and go to hell because in some way she equated being terrified with being bad.

Cleo expressed some of these fears to her mother, who tried to comfort and reassure her. The mother read soothing stories to her and sang familiar songs. Some of the objectionable paintings were removed from the walls. The mother sat in Cleo's room with her at night until Cleo felt relaxed enough to fall asleep. While her efforts to soothe Cleo did reduce the intensity of the fears, this easing lasted only while she was physically present and actively helping. The fears persisted in intense form at other times as long as Cleo was at her home. Cleo appeared to be less afraid while at school and outside of her apartment. After several months the mother decided that she needed professional help and consulted a child therapist.

Cleo was the younger of two children. Her sister Tina was four years older. The family had emigrated from Argentina because the political situation there was volatile. When they settled in New York City, Cleo was a year old, and her sister was 5.

The parents were both scientists and had been university professors in Argentina. Since academic jobs were scarce in New York, the father joined the editorial staff of a company that published science textbooks, and the mother found a job teaching science in a private school. While these were certainly respectable jobs, they meant an end to the type of scientific research that they each had valued and that had comprised the basis of their scientific writing and teaching.

The mother was able to adapt to her new country. She felt safe here and that feeling made up for some of her losses. She described herself as the only daughter of devoted parents and considered herself lucky because her parents visited her in the United States on a regular basis. The mother's parents spent their summers with Cleo and Tina in a house in Connecticut that belonged to a cousin who never used it and who donated it to the family for their use summers and weekends. The grandparents also generally visited once in the winter. Both grandparents were retired academics and both spoke English and Spanish.

Cleo's father felt bitter and diminished by his loss of status and professional opportunity. He missed his friends and colleagues. He had no siblings and his parents were both dead. He had little interest in his present job and his sense of isolation was intense. By the time Cleo was 2 years old, he began to drink. At first he drank only after work. Gradually he began to stay out later and later and to make scenes when he did come home. He was contrite after these outbursts but seemed unable to control his temper or his drinking.

By the time Cleo was 4, the family atmosphere was often tense. The mother lived in fear of the drinking episodes. She could not reconcile the image of the crude, abusive, and infantile drunk with that of her brilliant and scholarly husband. For a long time she clung to the good image of her husband and made excuses for him by recounting to herself all that he had lost in leaving his native country. She felt responsible for his deterioration since she had been the one to insist on the move to the United States. She recognized that she too had had to relinquish a lot, but feeling safe in her new country compensated for her losses. She reasoned that her husband was not as capable of compromise as she was and felt very sorry for him. However, the drinking episodes mounted and he became increasingly abusive and even physically rough with her. The children were awakened on several occasions and witnessed some very angry and loud fights between the parents. It was the children's increasing exposure to these violent scenes that finally gave Cleo's mother the impetus and courage to separate from her husband.

The separation took place when Cleo was 5 ½. At the time of the separation Cleo and her sister shared a room and Cleo did not exhibit any of the fears mentioned earlier. A few months after Cleo entered first grade and turned 6, her mother decided to give the children their own rooms. It was shortly after this separation from her sister that Cleo began to have fears and sleeping difficulties.

The above is the information that the therapist was given in the first session with the mother. It was an emotional session for the mother, with some crying and then apology about crying. Here was a woman under a great deal of stress coming for help for her daughter, a mother who found that her love, devotion, and profound commitment to help her daughter did not have enduring impact and did not ameliorate her daughter's extreme distress. Here was a mother who recognized that her best efforts were not enough and that she needed to turn to a professional for more effective help.

What does the therapist need to know at this point in the first consultation in order to proceed? And what does the therapist do about getting additional information?

If this part of the case were presented at a case seminar these are some of the questions that seminar members would usually ask: What is the child like when she is not experiencing fears? How often does she see her father? Does she have friends? How is she doing in school? How was her birth? Was she planned? How does she get along with her sister? Is she bilingual? When did she walk? Talk? Eat solid food? Give up the breast? Bottle? Thumb? Diaper? What is the parents' attitude toward treatment? What is the family history of mental illness and alcoholism? Are there any important family members or friends who comprise a family network in the United States? What language is spoken at home? Why this particular symptom and why did it appear now?

These are all very important questions to consider when we are evaluating a child and assessing the need for treatment. We need a picture of the child, a picture of the child's current life and functioning, a developmental history, and a picture of the family with a sense of each family member and also a sense of their interaction.

What we need even more than the above information is an awareness of the part that factual data play in the evaluation process. I am referring here to the dual purpose of the initial interview with the parent or parents. The obvious purpose of the interview is to gather information that will allow us to form an initial diagnostic picture of the child so that we know what needs to be done and what to recommend to the parents. An equally important goal of the initial interview is to begin to build a connection with the parent or parents. Sometimes too much zeal in gathering information about the child and family can interfere with the establishment of a leisurely climate, one that allows the parent to tell the story at a natural pace. Very often, when parents are allowed to tell their story in their own way, they select what is most meaningful to them and reveal more of what is the heart of the matter than when the interview is a tightly structured one with preplanned lists of factual questions.

In the initial session with the mother, father, or both parents, we need to convey our interest in the situation and our sense of competence in how to proceed. It is in this first session that we begin to lay the foundation for a working alliance. In Cleo's case, as sometimes happens with divorced parents, only the mother was present. Had both parents been present, we would have been able to think in terms of an alliance with both parents. While that is at times difficult to achieve in equal shares, the response of each parent to the consultation does afford the therapist with a sense of who is likely to be an ally of treatment, at least at the early stage.

These considerations concerning the parents' attitude toward treatment bring us to one of the dramatic differences between treating adults and treating children. In treating children we cannot proceed unless the adults bring them to our office. The child therapist must have an ally in at least one parent in order to proceed. This need not be the type of established working alliance (Greenson 1965) necessary in an analysis. It just needs to be a situation where the parent or parents feel that the therapist represents the possibility and/or hope that the situation can get better, and has the training and competence to provide the necessary help.

The therapist saw the mother twice before seeing the child. She obtained a developmental history that provided her with enough information to speculate that Cleo was a child whose development appeared to have been even and predictable. As an infant she had nursed well, had not had any illness or digestive problems, and had patterned well so that by three or four months she had a predictable schedule regarding food, sleep, and a period of "socializing," as the mother called her playful interaction with her caretakers. The mother's affect, while describing her daughter's babyhood, was warm and affectionate. That she remembered in detail many of the ordinary happenings of life with a young infant was indicative of her emotional presence during this very early time. She took pleasure in revisiting this period of her daughter's beginning and said that Cleo was the kind of baby who made a mother feel like a good mother. Cleo was a baby who could be satisfied. When she cried and was picked up, the crying stopped. When she was hungry and was offered the breast, she sucked vigorously with smacking sounds. The mother recalled that Tina was a sickly baby who was finicky and hard to please. With Tina, the mother was not so sure that she was a good mother. The difficult time with Tina had made the mother anxious about a second baby, and some of that anxiety was always present, but because Cleo was a cuddly and responsive baby the mother was generally reassured. It was particularly fortunate that Cleo was an easy baby since her babyhood was spent in an atmosphere of uncertainty regarding moving to the United States. Once the parents made the decision to move the plan was put into effect rapidly and the family came to New York shortly after Cleo's first birthday.

The therapist listened to the history in a leisurely manner, thus giving the mother the opportunity of remembering both the developmental facts and the emotional climate that existed in those early months. The taking of a history in this manner is in and of itself therapeutic. It allows the mother to recathect aspects of the relationship with her baby that have gotten buried under the weight of the present problems. The recathecting experience takes place in the atmosphere created by the therapist, and if that atmosphere is one in which the therapist is interested in the mother's experience and affect as well as in the developmental facts, then the therapist's presence becomes a part of the process of remembering and recathecting. Something tremendously important can develop here if the therapist allows the connection to the parent to hold equal importance with the job of gaining the necessary information about the child.

It is essential never to forget the distress that parents feel when their child is in emotional trouble. With a parent like Cleo's mother, the distress is obvious and likely to elicit a supportive response. But with some parents who are angry, hostile, and combative with the therapist, it is at times very difficult to respond to the distress that the anger obscures and distorts. It requires enormous skill on the part of the child therapist to deal with belligerent parents. Yet we must at all times remember that the connection between parent and therapist is a critical factor in child treatment, and the lack of this connection is the most common cause for premature termination of the treatment of children. There is no question that the ability to work well with the parents of our child patients is the greatest challenge that faces child therapists, and the one that requires the most tact, talent, and maturity. However, there are always those extreme cases wherein parental hostility can be so pervasive that these cases can be doomed even in the hands of the most tactful and experienced therapist. Put very simply, some extreme forms of parental pathology make it nearly impossible to work with the child.

In the case of Cleo's mother, the opportunity to talk about her child was in and of itself therapeutic. Mrs. C. found the remembering of her child's early history so emotionally meaningful that it established a bond between the mother and the therapist. Thus, when the mother reached a part of Cleo's history that she could not remember well, she was not defensive about her poor memory. There was good reason for the difficulty in remembering for it was the period following their arrival in the United States. Too many things were going on in terms of looking for housing and jobs, and becoming acclimated to a new country. However, enough was remembered to establish the likelihood that despite the very disruptive move to a new country, the family unit had maintained reasonable stability.

The mother had chosen her teaching job to lessen the length of her workday and to be with the children during their school vacations. A baby-sitter took care of the children at home because the mother felt that would afford them more attention than was provided in a day care center. There had been no significant illness or hospitalization among any of the family members, and no separations between children and parents except for the normal workday hours.

In considering the developmental facts, the family history, and the mother's apparent attunement to her child, the therapist speculated that Cleo was a well-endowed child with developmental landmarks that were within the normal and average range. Her working hypothesis was that Cleo had in some way been traumatized by the father's violence. How she had incorporated this into her fantasy life and why symptoms were emerging now and in this form were unclear and would require exploration.

The therapist considered requesting psychological tests for Cleo.

This can be a useful adjunct to the evaluation of a child. However, she decided that this mother was already so burdened by her life situation and all the anxiety that she was experiencing that the request for testing would feel like an additional hardship. She decided to delay her decision about psychological tests until after her consultation meetings with Cleo. If her diagnostic interviews with Cleo were satisfactory, in terms of giving her some assurance that Cleo was accessible to being understood and did not appear to present any confusing symptom picture, she would dispense with the psychological testing. If, on the other hand, Cleo was very different from the mother's description and was the kind of child who was very withdrawn or difficult to evaluate for other reasons, then she would request psychological testing despite the financial and emotional strain this might place on the mother.

The issue of Cleo's father and his participation in the evaluation process and/or treatment, if that came to be the plan, was discussed. Mrs. C. explained that her husband was generally scornful of psychotherapy, psychoanalysis, and all therapies that involved mental health. He had been forced by his employer to attend a program for alcoholics and had gone because he could not afford to lose his job. In fact, he appeared to be sober at present but did not credit the program with his sobriety. Rather, he claimed to have stopped drinking on his own. He considered mental health professionals unscientific and did not respect the field. He was concerned about Cleo's fears and would not interfere with the mother's quest for help, but he felt that Cleo was having a hard time as children do sometimes and would get over this problem if left alone. Mrs. C. thought that he would probably be willing to come in if that was deemed to be helpful, but that he would not be likely to participate, except for an occasional session. Mrs. C. added that he would probably only come in if she presented the request as the therapist's need for his input. If he suspected that she or the therapist thought that he needed help with Cleo, he would experience this as criticism and would probably not be willing to come to a session.

Mrs. C. provided some background information about the relationship between Cleo and her dad. She explained that he saw his children on the weekends and sometimes had them sleep over at his apartment. His reliability in this regard depended on whether he was in a sober or drinking period. Mrs. C. said that one important characteristic in her husband was that he demanded a great deal of himself and of others; consequently he was demanding of his children. He was both an outstanding scientist and an athlete. Of the two children, Cleo was the more physical child and Mr. C. enjoyed promoting that part of her. In fact, Mr. C. appeared to favor her and to be proud of her daring and adventurousness. He liked to take her swimming and taught her how to dive off high diving boards. Since she was 5, he had been taking her horseback riding. In the winter he took her skiing and skating. The mother worried about the pressure that he exerted on Cleo and wondered whether some of these sports were not too frightening. Because Cleo was always enthusiastic about these outings, the mother felt reluctant to intervene.

The therapist decided to postpone meeting with the father until the diagnostic sessions with Cleo were completed and recommendation could be presented to the parents. Her decision was based on the information provided by Mrs. C. about his negative attitude toward the field and his general defensiveness about needing help. It made more sense to the therapist to see him after she had a firsthand sense of what Cleo was like, since that would probably make it easier to communicate with him. It was likely that the kind of loosely structured initial interview described earlier, which so often elicits valuable information, would not work well with this father. It was more likely that he would respond better to very specific observations and a plan of action.

Linda Small was now ready to see Cleo for the first time. She discussed with the mother the best way to prepare Cleo for her session. She asked the mother what she planned to tell Cleo about coming to a therapist's office. The mother explained that her focus had been so much on all that had happened and her wish to find help that she had not thought about what she would actually say to Cleo. Mrs. C. said that she would like some help in deciding what to tell her.

The therapist suggested that being simple and direct was a good guide. Cleo could be told that since for a while now she has been very frightened, her mother was concerned about how uncomfortable that was for her, and so she was going to take her to see Mrs. Linda Small, a woman who understands children very well and whose work is to help them figure things out so that they can feel better. Mrs. Linda Small had toys and the mother would be allowed to stay in the room.

The mother felt comfortable with this explanation and did not anticipate that Cleo would object. She did ask about being allowed to stay in the room, how long she would be allowed to stay, and should she aim at being able to leave as soon as possible? The therapist answered that there was no benefit in getting Cleo to let the mother go quickly. The therapist would take charge of asking Cleo whether she wanted the mother in the room or not and the mother could just relax and be natural and observe what was going on without having to feel responsible for any decisions.

The therapist told the mother that she would see Cleo a few times and as soon as she felt that she had a sense of what was needed to help Cleo, she would meet with the mother and present her recommendations. An appointment for Cleo was made for several days later.

The following is a summary of the three consultation interviews with Cleo.

Cleo walked right into the therapy office after being introduced to the therapist. She dismissed any need for her mother to be present. She was an attractive looking 6 ½-year-old girl dressed in jeans and a sweater. Two neat, dark braids and large brown eyes contrasted with her pale skin. Her face had a quality of stillness that was not childlike. She moved in a somewhat tomboyish manner, sat down in the adult chair, and began to tell the story of her fears. She said that she was afraid to sleep alone because she worried that people might come out of the paintings in her room and take her away and then she too would become a picture and not a real person. She said that she knew that it couldn't happen really but she worried about it a lot, so her mother sat with her until she fell asleep. She said that she wanted to come to therapy because she hated to be so scared. She added that she was hungry all the time and that she didn't have any friends at school except for two boys. She wished that some of the girls would play with her. School was okay but staying home was better. She was interested in seeing the office toys and inspected them carefully. She asked the therapist, what do I call you Linda Small? and when asked what she would like to call the therapist she said, I'll call you Linda Small.

The therapist found Cleo to be a friendly and lively little girl. Although Cleo did not enunciate well, she was communicative and spoke with good organization. She seemed intelligent, curious, and eager to have regular appointments and to be helped with her fears. On the basis of only three interviews with Cleo, the therapist was, of course, not able to form a definitive diagnostic picture. However, Cleo had been reasonably accessible during her interviews, and that, combined with a fairly comprehensive developmental history, allowed Linda Small to rule out psychotic or severely atypical pathology. Furthermore, there was no question about the need or appropriateness of treatment for this child. Linda Small felt that she could go ahead and recommend treatment. The treatment process would allow her to get to know her young patient more deeply and to refine her diagnostic understanding. The continued contact with Cleo's mother would, in turn, provide her with a more thorough early history and a better diagnostic understanding of this mother. If, after a few months of treatment, she decided that her decision to proceed without the benefit of psychological tests had been a mistake, she could make the request then. She realized that introducing psychological testing when treatment was already in motion often caused some confusion, which could affect the treatment alliance, the transference, and even the parents' confidence in the therapist's competence to work autonomously. Linda Small was aware of some of the pitfalls of not having psychological tests prior to beginning treatment, but she was willing to take that chance. All in all, she felt that she had gotten off to a good start with both mother and child, and she felt equipped to begin the work of treatment.

Her primary concern at this point in the consultation process was of finding a way to present the need for treatment to the mother in such a way that would emphasize the constructive aspect of such a recommendation. She did not know how the mother would respond. Often, parents respond to such a recommendation as indicative of their failure as parents, of proof of how inadequate they are, and then the idea of treatment represents defeat rather than the hope of growth, development, improved functioning, greater self-esteem, and a happier and more fulfilling life. Linda Small gave careful thought to how to approach the mother and came up with a simple, direct, yet optimistic presentation.

The mother was told that treatment was a good idea at this time since Cleo had suffered a setback that had caused her to lose her normal way of coping with life. The intense fears that the mother described were her symptoms. They indicated a state of psychic disequilibrium. It was important to try to get her back on track so that she could feel more comfortable, and so that her development could proceed without the current burden she was experiencing.

The mother said that while she felt both relief and distress at the thought of her child being in treatment, she found the therapist's description of the problem as a setback an encouraging surprise. She had been thinking of the problem as a morbid downward trend. It was good to be reminded that Cleo had been fine most of her life and hopefully would be fine again in the future.

The therapist suggested that they begin with weekly sessions with Cleo and monthly meetings with the mother. The mother was told that children enjoy the same rules of confidentiality as do adults but that the privacy of Cleo's sessions would not interfere with the therapist's ability to be of help to the mother. The mother agreed to the plan and it was decided that the father should be offered an appointment before treatment began.

The father accepted an appointment quite willingly but arrived 35 minutes late. In the 10 minutes left to the session, Mr. C. talked with pride about his daughter's athletic adeptness. He was not interested in hearing about the reason for treatment. He said that he did not interfere in his ex-wife's decisions. She was the mother and she did what she thought necessary, and while he did not believe in treatment, she did, and that was her right. He was a well-dressed, well-spoken, and imposing but remote man. He made it clear that he would neither interfere nor participate.

This was the information that Linda Small gathered prior to beginning treatment. The stage was set. The chapters that follow will describe the unfolding of the treatment process as described in supervisory sessions.

3

The First Session[1]

Therapist: When I arrived at my office, I found Cleo waiting in the hallway outside the office suite. She was with her new baby-sitter. I asked if she had been waiting long and she answered:[2]

Cleo: I've been waiting about 14 hours![3]

Therapist: This was the first time that she was early. This was also the first time that she did not come with her mother. The mother had just begun a tutoring job in the afternoons, following her regular day of teaching. The three of us entered the office suite together. I was the first of the therapists who use the office suite to arrive and therefore had to turn on all the lights. This was a new experience for Cleo and she asked:

---

[1]These sessions will be written in three different print styles. This will make it easier to identify the three voices: Cleo, Therapist, and Supervisor. It will also help to distinguish the two separate dialogues that run through the sessions.

[2]This print will be used when the therapist and supervisor are talking to each other.

[3]This print will be used when Cleo is the speaker.

Cleo: Where is everybody? What's going on here today?

Therapist: I commented that this was different from what she was used to. The other people weren't here yet. This was going to be her regular time but it was different from the times that she had come with her mother. I added that she had come early today, earlier than her appointment time, which was 4:15. She had 10 minutes to wait before it was 4:15. I asked her to wait in the waiting room while I got ready for her.

When I came to get her she was very animated and busy doing something that I could not figure out. I also noticed that the new baby-sitter was totally silent. I introduced myself and asked her name. She responded minimally with "Maria." Cleo walked into my office and said,

Cleo: You were interrupting my movie.

Therapist: *Would you like to continue it with me?*[4]

Cleo: No. I told the camera people to call the vice-director because he is the one who takes my place when I can't do it. The vice-director is going to take care of the movie. I might as well dig into those toys.

Therapist: She got out of the chair that she usually sits in, opened the toy drawer, started taking all of the little cars out, and said,

Cleo: Today we are going to have a train. Did you know that I didn't go to school today?

Therapist: *No, I didn't know that.*

Cleo: The bus didn't come today, and it was too cold. Thank god the bus didn't come or I would have come home with a black eye.

Therapist: *Really? Why would you get a black eye?*

---

[4]*This print will be used when the therapist speaks to Cleo or when the supervisor suggests how to phrase an intervention appropriate to Cleo at a given point in treatment.*

Cleo: Well, this boy told me that he was going to punch me and give me a black eye.

Therapist: I asked her what would make somebody say that. How did this whole thing get started? Cleo said that she didn't know. She said all of this in a serious, straight-faced way, sounding a little tough and then adding,

Cleo: Well, maybe we both started it. I don't know. You know, I've had a bloody lip twice already.

Therapist: She was talking in a tough guy manner. She sounded a little pouty, interspersed with a "la-de-da" tone. She can sound quite dramatic. I told her that I was puzzled by how all of this came about.

Cleo: Well, one day I was going up the stairs at school and this boy was coming down and he bumped into me and I had his head in my lip, and my lip was bloody. Another time my cousin told me to kiss his knee and then he went like that! and kicked me hard with his knee and I had another bloody lip. He could have waited until after dessert. I had a bloody lip for dessert and it was a yummy soft dessert that I love. I ate it anyway. It was so good. I love desserts. I'm always so hungry anyway and I love to eat. I like desserts especially, and best of all if they have ice cream.

Therapist: *This is interesting. You are telling me a story about awful things, about people bumping into you and tricking you and making you bleed, and all of a sudden you are talking about desserts.*

Cleo: Did you know that I am a very good actress? I know how to play dead.

Therapist: She then proceeded to show me how she plays dead. She flipped down on the floor and tried not to breathe and then peered up at me and asked what I thought so far. She was very cute and serious and determined doing all that. I had to work hard not to laugh, particularly since she was giving me hints on technique. She explained that you had to breathe in such a way that nobody could see, and she flipped down again and lay there saying,

Cleo: You can die with your eyes open, and you even can die with a smile, but you can't blink, so you kind of have to concentrate, and you have to look a certain way. You have to fix your eyes on something and keep them there.

Therapist: She then got up and sat down in the swivel chair and turned around and said,

Cleo: There I go daydreaming again.

Therapist: *We have room for daydreams here.*

Cleo: There's a good way of fixing your gaze, like a daydream. Then you won't blink. That helps you to keep still and to concentrate, like when you daydream. It's like looking at something and not thinking about it.

Therapist: *Gee, Cleo, you know so much about all this.*

Cleo: Let's get back to these toys now and play.

Therapist: She turned to the toys and played differently with them than she had before. She picked one of the figures to be the smoke detector. The smoke detector looked through the train tracks for smoke and asked one of the dolls what he was doing sleeping there. The smoke detector seemed to sort of be taking care of things. It was in charge of the situation.

Supervisor: The appearance of somebody taking care of things is always interesting transferentially. You might consider that the smoke detector might represent some aspect of the therapist's caretaking function—something for you to keep in mind— some early manifestation of an object representation of a good caretaking object, or one who can detect trouble.

Therapist: Yes, I will keep it in mind. Cleo played for a while in this way and then she put the character who was the smoke detector away and got up and said,

Cleo: Where's the kids? Where's the kids? I need a bunch of 7-year-olds.

Therapist: And she picked out all the small figures and said to them,

Cleo: You kids can go by yourselves on the train. Some of you have baby-sitters, and some of you have parents, and some of you are just alone, but you don't have to worry if you are alone because the subways are clean and there are no rats and no robbers or kidnappers.

Therapist: So I said to her, ***But even if those dangers weren't there, is that all that 7-year-olds have to worry about on the subway when they are all by themselves?***
She seemed to pay no attention me and just announced,

Cleo: The 7-year-olds are on the subway train by themselves. Let's see what's going to happen now.

Therapist: Cleo then had the children jumping off the train and I said, ***Goodness, what's going on here?***
She didn't respond but picked up a doll with yarn hair and pigtails and started swinging her around by the head, going faster and faster and calling her "Kamikaze Hellbound Cleo." She kept swinging her around and I didn't say anything, and then she finally stuffed her into a bag. It was now about half an hour into our session and she looked at me and said,

Cleo: I know what you are going to say now. You are going to say that our time is up and that I have to go now.

Therapist: ***No, I'm not, because we still have time, but I can see that you are thinking about our time.***

Cleo: Well, our time is too short.

Therapist: ***Maybe we could talk about that.***

Cleo: No, no, no! It's just right.

Therapist: *How can that be? How can something be too short and just right?*

Cleo: No, no, it's just right.

Therapist: She went on playing. Then I noticed that she seemed to be cleaning up and she said,

Cleo: We have to start getting ready to go.

Therapist: I told her that *I* was going to say that in a few minutes. I didn't expect her to keep track of time. That was my job. Maybe there is something about the way that I told her that she didn't like. Maybe she would like more time or less time to clean up.

Cleo: I can clean up in 14 minutes or 1 minute.

Therapist: I told her that she was telling me something but I didn't know what it was.

Cleo: You give me too much time to clean up. I only need a few minutes.

Therapist: We talked about this for a while and she decided that two minutes would be just right. I said that I would try that and see how it worked. Then, while she was quietly cutting paper, I picked that moment to tell her that I was going to see her mother for my once per month appointment with her. I said, *Remember when I told you a little about how therapy works?*

She did not look up but continued cutting circles and squares. So I said, *I think that I will tell you again because there is so much that is new about therapy that I don't expect you to remember it all. We are going to meet every Wednesday at 4:15. That is our special time to-gether. Also, once every month I am going to have an appointment with your mom. Your mom will tell me a bit about what is happening in your family and at school, and that will help our work. But remember that what you and I talk about is private and I will not discuss anything about our appointments with your mom or your dad. Our appointments are just between us and the only time that I will discuss anything that we talk about or play with is if you ask me to tell them. Sometimes you might wish to tell something to your mom or dad but feel uncomfortable saying it to them. If that happens, you can talk to me about it and if you think it's a good idea for me to speak to them, I will do that. I will always ask you before I see either of your parents whether there is anything that you would like me to say to them. I am going to ask you right now whether there is anything that you would like me to tell your mom when I see her tomorrow night. Is there anything that you are having trouble saying that I could help with.*

Cleo: Yes. Tell her that I am not ruining my sister's life.

Therapist: *I don't know what that is all about. Will your mother understand it? Maybe we should talk about that a little bit first.*

Cleo: Tell her that she can come into my room only when she wants to. She can come in when she has to put books back in the bookcase. She can come in anytime when she wants to. . . .

Therapist: She kept turning this around and getting mixed up about what the rule should be for her sister. I told her that she didn't sound sure about what she wanted to say.

Cleo: It isn't coming out right! I am getting all mixed up.

Therapist: *This might be something that I could help with if we talk about it.*

Cleo: I know what to tell my mom. Just tell her that Cleo doesn't know, and that's a joke.

Therapist: *Now, you've changed the whole thing. Now it's all a joke.*

Cleo: Yes. Tell her that Cleo doesn't know and that's a joke. Oh, I can't wait until she comes home from this appointment and tells me what a bad joke I made.

Supervisor: There is a lot of confusion in this session.

Therapist: Yes. It began with some confusion about Cleo being early and the new baby-sitter barely being mentioned. I forgot to say that I said something about the baby-sitter when Cleo was cleaning up. I said, *I noticed that you came with your new baby-sitter today and you didn't say anything about that, so I guess that you aren't interested in talking about it.*

Supervisor: That was an important issue to bring up, but the way you did it got you locked out of the dialogue. You brought up the subject of the baby-sitter, which was very appropriate, and then made a concluding comment that left nothing to be explored. You could have said, *I notice that you came with a new person today, not your mom but a baby-sitter named Maria. We didn't talk about this big change and what that's like for you. I don't know why we didn't talk about that.* Then she can either respond or not. It leaves the subject open. And by the way, how did this baby-sitter behave toward Cleo? Was she at all warm and nice to her? Did she say anything to Cleo such as, for instance, "I'll see you later. I'll be right here waiting for you"? Something caring like that?

Therapist: This person was quiet and uncomfortable. She's new to the family. The mother told me that she was looking for a graduate student, someone young who would be playful and friendly with the children. This woman looks as if she's in her late twenties but old in spirit and seems depressed. I introduced myself to her and barely got a response. When I asked her name she just muttered "Maria" and did not look up at me. Cleo acted as if the baby-sitter did not exist. I guess the lack of acknowledgment of a new sitter and of her mother not bringing her to her session for the first time set a tone for this session. It's as if she could not talk about these important things.

Supervisor: Yes, and she begins by telling you that she didn't go to school that day, right? You don't know whether not going to school is true or not, but it brings into the session her sense of danger. She presents not going to school as having averted a dangerous situation. She said that she was going to get hurt at school. In reality you know very little about her experience at school. It will be helpful to learn about that as you get to know her, but for now we have a vivid impression of her constant sense of danger. Another important theme that has unfolded today is her wish to tell and her wish not to tell. Even that is putting it too strongly. We don't yet know whether the word *wish* is appropriate. One of the most important temptations to be avoided in our work is to assume that we know when in fact we don't really know. We know that she begins to let you know how scared she is and then undoes or evades or does some maneuver to slip away. Her stories begin one way and develop a bit and then change completely. She appears to be constantly trying to make things okay. Take, for instance, the sentence about her sister. She can only come into her room if she wants to. It's so illogical that we can't help but speculate that she must have meant that Tina could only come into her room if she wanted her to, but somehow Cleo could not let herself say that and turned it around. She seems to have difficulty putting an "I" into her story.

This is such a rich session. Take the part about there not being enough time for her session followed by her beginning to clean up before you say that the session is up. It's probably very hard for her to think of her time being up, of hearing you say those words. But she can't let herself say that she wishes she had more time, or that she hates to leave, or something fairly direct. She does say that she wishes that she had more time and then takes it right back and comes up with the solution that you should only give her 2 minutes to clean up, which would give her a little more time.

She is very much engaged during her time with you. It's important to remember that this is only her fourth appointment and the first three were part of the evaluation process. During the evaluation process she didn't know that she would be seeing you on a regular basis. This was the first session that she knew to be the beginning of something ongoing, and yet, even at this beginning point in the treatment process, she certainly appears to sense that you have something useful to offer to her. Would you agree?

Therapist: Yes, it feels that way to me. One thing that's striking in terms of her evasiveness is that the first time I saw her, in the very first session of the evaluation process, she was not evasive. She talked about her fears rather freely. She did this in response to my having told her that her mother had spoken to me about her fears. She responded in a quite open manner and told me that she was afraid of certain paintings, and particularly of one in the foyer of a horse. She was afraid that the horse would come and take her to hell. She also told me that she had always slept with a bunch of stuffed animals and now she was afraid of them, afraid that they would come alive. She told me that she was too afraid to go to sleep by herself and so her mother sat in a chair in her room and read to her until she got sleepy. Then she stayed for a while longer and read to herself until Cleo fell asleep.

Mrs. C. had told me that she had arrived at this way of calming Cleo after having consulted a child therapist who told her that she should insist that Cleo go to sleep by herself and not yield to her fears. This therapist told the mother that Cleo's fears were a bid for attention and that this kind of manipulation by a child should be nipped in the bud. The mother found this advice harsh and decided to do just the opposite of what she had been told and to give the attention that Cleo seemed to need so badly. Mrs. C. asked a friend who is a psychotherapist for a second referral and was given my name.

Supervisor: The mother used good judgment in leaving that first psychotherapist and finding a constructive solution on her own. She found a way to help Cleo go to sleep without infantilizing her. She stayed with her but didn't take her into her bed or lie down with her as so many parents do when their child is in distress. These more extreme measures tend to encourage regression in children and consequently those children are prevented from developing some of their own inner resources in dealing with their fears. Mrs. C. stayed close, which is in itself an empathic act since it acknowledges the child's distress, but she did not get so close as to make Cleo feel like a baby.

Isn't it amazing that a therapist, with all the training that that should imply, would give such primitive advice? The idea that a bid for attention is something sneaky is common enough among untrained people. It misses the point of what children are up against when they are in psychic distress. Children do what they can to maintain some equilibrium, and if they need the object's help and find a way to get it, that is growth promoting. This is where the concept of adaptation is so helpful to our work. We would see Cleo's extreme measures around going to sleep as an effective way to engage her mother's help. Our developmental theory teaches us that a child's attempt to turn to an object for help, rather than to withdraw from the object world, is a hopeful sign. It demonstrates that Cleo has some confidence in the object world. She has experienced her mother's caring about her physical and psychological comfort, and because of these good caring experiences she also has the hope, and perhaps even the expectation, that her therapist can be of value in alleviating her psychic distress. We are talking about *the* essential factor in establishing a therapeutic alliance: a good-enough symbiotic phase that sets up memory traces for what Terese Benedek (1938) calls "confident expectation." But that still leaves you with a technical dilemma, because this is a little girl who also believes that children can be sent on the subway alone and should be able to manage even if there is no adult to appeal to for help and safety. So what I think I'm saying, based on the material so far, is that Cleo might at this point in her life turn to an adult only under extreme circumstances. Yet, I suspect that she would be very uncomfortable if such a thought were presented in the form of an interpretation. I am thinking of an interpretation to the effect that she is not always so sure that there is someone to appeal to who would help her when she needs help. Or that she is not sure that it's all right to ask for help except in extreme circumstances such as "rats and robbers." We know that she would hotly deny that. She even denies that rats and robbers are a threat to her. In a beautiful example of *negation* (Freud 1925b) she said, **You don't have to worry if you are alone, because the subways are clean, and there are no rats or robbers or kidnappers.** These themes appear in her play, and that is where you should probably leave them at present. The distance between you seems just right for the beginning stage of treatment. You are quietly reflective with her, you convey your interest in her in a subtle way, but you are not pushing anything or getting too close. I suspect that if you got closer to her themes you would encounter some mighty resistance.

Therapist: I think so too. Actually, it happened toward the end of this session. I said something about a character in one of her games being afraid and she said with some feeling that she was no longer afraid of anything, not the pictures in her apartment and not her toys. She said all of this with a kind of "stay away" tone. I recognize that I feel a bit tentative with her because I sense that if I get too close she will bolt. For instance, remember early in the session she talked about a bloody lip and that turned into talk about how much she loves dessert? When I questioned the sudden shift from unpleasant to pleasant, she began to talk about being a good actress. I felt pushed away and a bit stumped at that point.

Supervisor: Well, sure, it's hard to witness her constant shifting around in search of a comfortable place. She is a child who needs things to be all right even when they are not, and so she works all of the time in her effort to regulate her psychic state . . . to fend off the sense of danger that appears to always be with her. In the process, she communicates the intensity of her discomfort, and of course that evokes in you a wish to help her, but she cannot acknowledge her need for help at this point, so if you try to move closer to her she will push you away. This is where a therapist must restrain the natural inclination to be nurturing. She can't afford to have you be nurturing. She lets you know that loud and clear. Her safety, she thinks, rests on being tough. She has to be able to ride the subway alone.

As far as her talking about being a good actress, the most that you could have done with that would have been to say, *Well, as we get to know each other, we'll understand more about why it's important to you to be a good actress.*

On the other hand, it's just as well not to say anything about it because it could sound to her as if being a good actress is something negative that she should get rid of.

What is striking about Cleo is how hard she has to work all the time just to maintain some sort of equilibrium. That she can be so theatrical and charming while she does it has complicated repercussions. On the one hand, it obscures her distress and therefore is not as likely to gain for her the help she could use to feel better. On the other hand, it's a plus because children who are appealing tend to get noticed by people and evoke interest, and that at least provides some narcissistic nourishment. But now let's talk for a minute about what we are after in the treatment process. What do we want to help her with?

Therapist: I think that I want to help her to feel safe with her feelings. That's where I see so much of her energy going, into cheering herself up. She conveys the feeling that she does not believe that it's all right to have certain feelings and certain wants and certain needs. She can't be direct about having her needs met and she has to make do.

Supervisor: She feels that she can't count on the objects in her world except in the most extreme circumstances, as for instance when the fears reach epic proportions. In the main, she perceives herself as having to take care of herself.

We have to be careful to stress that this is her perception of her situation and not necessarily the reality of it. This is a headline that I cannot stress too much. Children's perceptions of their reality are shaped by unconscious forces as well as actual circumstances. Many a child therapist has undermined and eventually ruined any chance of maintaining a therapeutic alliance with both child and parents by accepting the child's distortions of his or her situation, overidentifying with the child, and becoming the child's better parent.

So here we have a child who feels that she must be super-independent and struggles gallantly to maintain this position. Of course, you must be very respectful of this need of Cleo's since her self-esteem is involved here. But look at the paradoxical position that you're in. You are offering help to a person who fiercely strives to be independent.

Therapist: Yes, but she's ambivalent about this. After all, when I asked her whether she had anything that I should bring up with her mother, at first she came up with a serious request: "Tell her that I am not ruining my sister's life," then she erased it and turned it into a joke, an absurd joke. So for a moment there she did want me to help her . . . to be her spokesperson.

Supervisor: True, she is ambivalent, and that's a great help to the treatment process. If she single-mindedly guarded her independence at all costs we would be in trouble. But what are you going to do about the joke? Are you going to tell the mother that Cleo said, "Tell my mother that I don't know"?

Therapist: I don't know what to do with that.

Supervisor: Well, you could do the simplest thing and that is to explain to the mother your custom of asking children whether they want anything brought up at the meeting with a parent, and then tell the mother just the part about Cleo not knowing and that being a joke. Then you'll find out whether there is a history to saying "I don't know." Maybe she says that a lot. Maybe it's her way of not rocking the boat, or maybe the mother will not recognize it. We'll find out. I don't think that Cleo is a child who doesn't know. What do you think?

Therapist: I think she knows. When I brought up taking a message to her mother, she looked hard at me as if to say, "Is this for real? You will tell my mother things that I have trouble telling her?" And she began right away with the business of her sister coming into her room only when she wants to, or to put her books away and so on. She got very jumbled and finally said, This isn't coming out right. And then she thought of the joke.

Supervisor: We'll have to know more about the situation with her sister. Did you have a chance to find out about sleeping arrangements during the evaluation process? It's always helpful to know that when working with children. So much material revolves around sleeping arrangements both from the point view of primal scene exposure and from the point of view of fears and/or a sense of isolation. For instance, in some homes, the child is down a long hallway, or on a different floor far from the parents. Or the child might be moved out of its room and further away from the parents when a sibling is born. We so often hear about these early sleeping arrangements in the analysis of adult patients, and without exception, the passionate feelings they caused in childhood seem to live on into adulthood.

Therapist: I did ask the mother during the evaluation process. It seemed a natural question since we were dealing with Cleo's terror of sleeping alone following that period of violent behavior by the father. I'm referring to the drunken scenes he made when he lived at home. The mother did tell me that the children must have heard him, and on some occasions seen him.

I learned that they live in a two-bedroom apartment and that the children used to share what was meant to be the master bedroom. When the mother decided that they both should have their own rooms, she took the master bedroom for herself, moved Tina into a small back room that her husband had used as a study, and moved Cleo into the dining room, which was the room that she and her husband had slept in prior to the divorce. She gave Cleo a corner of the room for her very own and that contains her bunk bed and a play table. The rest of the room is a shared playroom and contains the television and all of the books, toys, and games.

Supervisor: Well, that's helpful to know. It sheds some light on the spontaneous statement that Cleo made when you asked her if there was anything that she would like you to tell her mother. Now we can understand that the room arrangement must cause a lot of conflict between the two children. Sometimes it's helpful to have the child draw a floor plan of the apartment. You can do that at an opportune moment, for instance when she's talking about her room or about her sister's use of the room. You can tell her that it would help you to really understand how these things are for her if you knew more clearly how things are arranged and laid out in her apartment.

When the mother described the sleeping arrangement, did she seem to feel that it was satisfactory?

Therapist: I couldn't tell. She struck me as being there and not being there.

Supervisor: Depressed?

Therapist: More a sense of preoccupied than depressed. There is also a narcissistic flavor at times, as if she can't talk about the children and about herself at the same time, as if she can talk about herself or the children but not both. It will take me a while to get to know her well enough to form a diagnostic impression. She seems very burdened and depleted. I would like to see her have her own psychotherapist and will make a referral when I feel that she's ready for such a suggestion.

Supervisor: She certainly has been through a lot. Our time is almost up now. Are we almost at the end of Cleo's session?

Therapist: Yes. Cleo put toys and crayons that she had been using away in two minutes and I said, *Goodbye 'till next Wednesday at 4:15.*
And she answered,

Cleo: **See you next Wednesday, Linda Small.**

Therapist: I watched her go into the waiting room. Silently, she walked over to Maria, who stood up wordlessly, and in that cold, distant way they went out the door. I felt sad watching them go off in a state of such nonconnection, a hungry little girl who was striving hard to hold on, and a sad and empty young woman who looked as if she had given up a long time ago.

4

Cleo's Stories and the Therapist's Dilemmas

Therapist: I can see that I'm going to have to be particularly careful of my time here after my monthly meeting with Mrs. C. Today I want to discuss my session with Cleo's mother before going over my session with Cleo.

Mrs. C. began the session by saying that she recognized that she has very strong feelings about Cleo being in treatment. On the one hand, she feels terrible that her little girl is in bad enough emotional shape to need professional help. On the other hand, she's glad that help is possible. She said that she found it hard to hold on to a clear reason for psychotherapy for Cleo and tended to get muddled in this respect. She said that she found it particularly helpful to review in her mind my comments at our last meeting, the meeting that concluded the evaluation process. I had explained some of Cleo's anxieties as stemming from her lack of certainty and clarity about things in general. I had connected Cleo's difficulty in calming herself when she is upset and scared to her general sense of vagueness. I remember that this had come up in response to the mother's description of how frightened Cleo was after watching a *Sesame Street* program about fire. After the program, Cleo had behaved as if fire was an imminent threat.

I had tried to explain Cleo's lack of distance from anything dangerous as one of the issues that required psychotherapy. I had made the following formulation for the mother. Cleo was in a state of mind wherein she could lose her bearings quite easily, particularly when anything dangerous like fire was mentioned. With the loss of equilibrium, she lost her customary coping and self-reassuring mechanisms. Our job was to understand what had happened to her to cause this state of vulnerability and to help her regain the inner resources to deal with her life more comfortably. Mrs. C. told me that she had thought a lot about this and found it a helpful way of understanding why treatment was a good idea. She said that she was surprised by how intensely upset she is at the need for treatment for Cleo. She found herself constantly reminding herself that I presented Cleo as having *lost* some of her coping resources. She said that she found comfort in the idea that Cleo had lost something she had once had. She said that it made it seem less dire, more like a setback than an incipient process.

I got a chance to find out a bit about the baby-sitter. She's from Argentina and that seems to be important to the mother. Also, the baby-sitter lives in the neighborhood and that too is important to the mother. The baby-sitter is a student at a technical school. The mother didn't say anything about what she thought of Maria and I thought it best to keep my observations to myself at this point.

I got a chance to find out a bit more about the room arrangement. As I told you last week, Tina is in a tiny room in the back of the apartment and Cleo is in the larger room that's used as a playroom for both children. The television set and toys are kept there, and that is where Tina spends most of her time, both alone and with her friends. Although Tina spends most of her time in Cleo's room, she put a sign on her own door saying, "No Children under 10 Allowed and No Cleo Allowed." Cleo complained to her mother about this, and said that the sign is not fair and that it hurt her feelings. A family discussion followed and it was decided that Cleo's section of the room was off limits to Tina just as Tina's room was off limits to Cleo. The mother felt that if they each had some private territory that they were solely in charge of, that would make things equal. She recognized that Cleo can't close a door and have privacy, but from the point of view of square feet they each had the same amount of space.

Supervisor: The mother is being concrete here. She's trying to be fair but it isn't coming out right. One child has privacy and the other doesn't.

Therapist: It is a problem but I don't know what solution would be fair. . . . It's a decent-sized apartment, but it isn't a flexible layout. Let me get to my session with Cleo now.

Supervisor: Before you do that, what did you think of the meeting with the mother? Was it a good meeting?

Therapist: Yes. I got a chance to tell her a bit about why it's important for me to know something about the home, the routines, etc. I told her that there would be derivatives of life at home and school in Cleo's play and that the information that the mother provides would help me to understand what she communicates in her play more fully. I added that little children so often assume that the adult knows without being told, that they normally leave a lot of blanks. I told her, for instance, that it's helpful to know about the fear of fire following the *Sesame Street* program. I had been over some of this at my last session with the mother, but I guess certain things need to be repeated with parents because they touch on such anxiety and guilt-ridden areas in the parents that they slip out of consciousness and memory.

One thing that bothers me about Cleo's fear following the

Sesame Street program is that the program was presented in a very benign tone. I happened to have seen it with my own children, and such an extreme fear reaction in her does not seem age appropriate.

Supervisor: When you wonder whether something is age appropriate, what do you have in mind?

Therapist: The overall development of the child versus the pathological.

Supervisor: Remember that the overriding issue in Cleo's life right now is that she does not feel safe, and that lack of a sense of safety in her has such force that she's going to feel unsafe about these ordinary things that other children feel okay about. The contrast between her extreme reaction to the *Sesame Street* program and the more typical reaction of your own children is useful in highlighting how terribly scared she is and the intensity of her discomfort. You're right that such intense fear is pathological. But there is something about the use of that word that tends to distance us from our patients. We need to recognize that something is an indicator of pathology while at the same time not intellectualizing the patient's condition as a means of dealing with it in a remote or detached manner. We need to be very aware of and receptive to the particularity of the patients's condition.

Therapist: Yes. I can see that I got a bit maternal with Cleo. I didn't want her to be so scared. I felt upset about it so I got "professional" about it. I can see that I'm going to need to watch that in myself.

I got myself into a bit of a mess with the session yesterday. I was expecting a very important personal phone call at 5:00, right in between Cleo and my next appointment. Being so tightly scheduled was preoccupying me and when Cleo arrived 5 minutes early I was relieved, because it gave me the opportunity to start early and not feel so squeezed for time. When I went to greet Cleo in the waiting room I told her that we would start 5 minutes earlier than usual and end 5 minutes earlier than usual. She asked me why we were starting early and I told her that I was expecting a phone call at the end of our appointment and that I did not want the telephone to interrupt us. I told her that we would end at 4:55, and that we would have the same amount of time that we always have.

Cleo: Well, how short is our time going to be?

Therapist: *What do you mean by short?*

Cleo: I didn't say short.

Therapist: *I heard you say "short" and you say that you didn't say "short." What do you think this is all about?*

Cleo: Well, I think you heard some people outside. In my building I hear people talking outside. We live next to a building where the police always come, but the police never come to my building.

Therapist: At that point Cleo turned in the swivel chair until she was facing away from me, and with her back toward me she said,

Cleo: In my building there is only good.

Therapist: And with her back to me still, she swivelled back and forth in little movements and said,

Cleo: But in this other building, the police always go there. I'm not sure why, but bad things happen there. . . . and the police are not so good now.

Therapist: She then became very quiet and I asked, *What are you thinking about?*
    Slowly Cleo began to talk. She told me a garbled, hard to follow story about the police not being interested in babies. When she finished I said, *This is a very complicated story you're telling me. I'm having a lot of trouble following it.*

Cleo: Well, I saw a T.V. program about babies being born in jail and having to stay behind bars because the police is always in such a hurry.

Therapist: I was very unclear about what to say at that point. She was looking at me and seemed to be waiting for me to talk so I said: *Oh, dear!*

Cleo: Yes, and the police are not so good.

Therapist: *That is a very troubling idea. You are saying that the very people that we turn to when we need help are not good and caring people, and would not even help a helpless baby.*

Cleo: Let's play toys.

Supervisor: Could she have thought that you were confirming what she was saying about the police not being caring?

Therapist: I suppose she could have. I really had trouble with this exchange. I wondered whether there was a connection between the police being in a hurry and the feeling that she had that she was not getting her full session. Did she feel that I was rushing her? But I didn't know what to do with these thoughts.

Supervisor: It's very possible that she was feeling rushed and that the whole notion of her predictable time being moved 5 minutes earlier was beyond her understanding. Or, to say it a little differently, perhaps the fact that you, as a representative of reliability, changed something, was disquieting to her. She could have been angry at you and disappointed and feeling rushed and shortchanged. She talks about the police not being good, not caring about babies, being rushed. She's probably afraid of her anger, and uses denial against this unwelcome affect. Yet these are just speculations, and what do we do with them? Is it useful to explore her feeling rushed and confused at this point in treatment? I suppose that if you had a good way of doing so it might have been useful. But nothing came to you along those lines and nothing comes to me either. So let's be practical. In our work there will always be therapeutic opportunities that we miss. That's all right. The opportunities are endless and are best used when we're inspired to deal with them with clarity.

For now, for this very beginning stage of treatment, it might be most useful to stick with the basic theme that she brings to these sessions. The theme in its broadest sense consists of a fear and the solution to the fear. The fear is that the world is unsafe because there is nobody to turn to in time of need, and the solution is that one must be completely self-reliant. For example, 7-year-olds must go on the subway alone.

To put it into psychoanalytic language, if the representation of a good and nurturing object cannot be maintained, the self representation has to be of a fiercely independent self. Of course this arrangement is doomed because psychic safety depends on there being an equal libidinal investment in the self representation and in the object representation. Cleo loses the object when she is under stress. We don't understand how this came to be, but we know that it causes her intense fear and a sense of isolation. It causes her to believe that the police do not care about helpless babies. We need to understand why she cannot hold on to her objects more reliably. She gave us an important theme to watch for in this session. When she feels frustrated and shortchanged, how powerful are her destructive fantasies? What measures must she take to undo them?

Another issue arises here. She told you that she got some of these ideas about the police from a television program. Perhaps this story about babies born in jail was on the news. I would wonder about allowing her to watch the news. She's too little to do that, too little and too frightened and she needs to be protected. Imagine a child watching the news with all the horrible tales of violence, fire, and so forth, and then consider that this child could not even tolerate a benign program about fire on *Sesame Street*. I realize that it's often hard to monitor these things, especially with an older sister watching all sorts of stuff on television and an indifferent baby-sitter and a working mother. But it gives one pause to think of the effect of something as commonplace as the news on a child who is so terrified. Or even a casual comment made by an adult to the effect that you can't trust the police. This supervigilant child takes these comments very much to heart.

The child therapist has the dual job of tracking the underlying themes communicated by the child patient and working with these in the treatment situation, while at the same time noting the real day-to-day environmental forces in the life of the child. Some of the environmental factors have obvious impact on the vulnerabilities of the child and need to be addressed in the work with the parents. Of course, any discussion with the parents on the child's environmental situation requires tact and delicate timing so as to contribute to the treatment alliance with the parents, and not be perceived as criticism. That's a tall order.

Therapist: So what would a better response have been? Instead of reflecting that not trusting the police is a troubling idea, to explore what that means to her?

Supervisor: Yes, but also more personal, like perhaps, *So what are people supposed to do when they need help? Who do they go to?*

Remember that in a transferential sense you are the police. That is an assumption that you have to keep at the back of your mind. It's not something that Cleo is conscious of, or that should be interpreted at present because it's too far from the preconscious, so it would be meaningless. It's safe to assume that on some level the therapist is always in part an authority figure. That means that when the patient talks of teacher, doctor, lawyer, judge, it in some transferential sense touches therapist. You have a role in her life that has to do with protecting and regulating, and in the exchange we're discussing she tells you that the police can't be counted on, and in fact punish rather than help. That tells us that something is going wrong in the process of internalization, and this also tells us that something is wrong in regard to her object representations. Of course this too has some bearing on you, and whether she is dimly aware of that or not, it's a frightening thought and she changes the topic and says, Let's play toys.

Let's go on with the session and see how things develop.

Therapist: Okay. I then said, *I guess that you don't want to talk about that troubling idea?* and she answered,

Cleo: That's right. (pause) Guess what? Today I am going to make a rodeo.

Therapist: She got some of the toys out and commented that she had never been to a rodeo but thought that she had some idea about how it went. She said,

Cleo: I think that they catch animals there but I don't think that all kinds of animals go there. I think that dogs and lions and tigers and bears and animals like that don't go there. I think it's cows and horses that go there.

Therapist: She was looking through the toys, looking for ropes and cows and horses. She found a horse in the toy bag but the horse had broken legs. I hadn't noticed that I had a toy like that and I would have thrown it out had I known. Cleo held it up and said,

Cleo: Look. This horse has broken legs. What shall we do with it? I can't use it this way. You know, you could fix it by putting fire to it.

Therapist: Cleo said this very matter-of-factly and looked at me. I asked her how that worked, how does one fix the horse's legs with fire. She answered,

Cleo: You light a fire and you stick the leg in it. Then you put the leg into water and it's all fixed.

Therapist: *How does that sound to you, fixing the leg that way?*

Cleo: It sounds strange, but I saw it on T.V. You light the match and you put it all over the hurt. Then you put the hurt part in water.

Therapist: *Oh, the fire on the hurt makes it better?*

Supervisor: What were you thinking while listening to all this?

Therapist: I was thinking that perhaps she had seen a show for children on horseshoes, or on branding horses, and that she had retained a distorted impression of what she had seen. I was equating it with perhaps a distorted understanding of babies behind bars, or whatever she had gotten out of the *Sesame Street* program on fire that had frightened her so.

Supervisor: So we have several instances where Cleo responds to something that she sees or hears as if it were a trigger that activates the state of danger that she inhabits. I'm speculating here, but let's develop some sort of working hypothesis that we can discard if there's not much to support it. Let's assume that certain things like fire, or helpless babies, or hurt and mutilation, are so terrifying to Cleo that the word no longer just represents a threat, but becomes that threat and she actually feels herself to be on the verge of being mutilated, burned, and so on. That would explain the trigger quality of these words and her reaction to them. These words cause her to leave the context in which they appeared, and act as a magnet that draws forth her nightmarish fantasies of bodily destruction and annihilation.

   To conceptualize it in familiar terms, anxiety causes regression, and in the grip of anxiety and regression repression is weakened and she becomes flooded by fantasies. In the grip of these terrifying fantasies, her reality testing fails her as do some of her other generally adequate ego functions such as perception, judgment, attention, and the ability to organize and integrate. When a trigger stimulates anxiety, she sinks into her own story. She can't concentrate on what is being presented to her, follow it, and comprehend it. Just the beginning of anything containing some of the danger triggers causes her to panic. In her present state she is never very far from her own story.

Therapist: She believes her story and also begins to doubt it. She suddenly says that she isn't sure about the horses. And here I don't think that I handled things well. First I said, **When you're not sure, it's a good idea for us to talk about these things.**

She again repeated that she wasn't sure and then she started spinning around in her chair so that I couldn't really make proper visual contact with her. Rather than say something about not being able to tell whether she wanted to talk about it, I just plunged in with my theme and said, **When you aren't sure, it's a good idea to talk about it and to ask me questions, and as we get to know each other, you will see that it's a good feeling to get clear about these confusing things.**

She responded by saying that Sam Small would be the first rider in the rodeo. I asked, **Sam Small?** and she said,

Cleo: Yes, Sam Small, just like your name.

Therapist: She had Sam Small rope a steer and then jump off a horse. Sam got entangled in the rope and got dragged on the ground screaming for help, and here Cleo was very dramatic, calling,

Cleo: Help! Help! Help! Help! Can anyone help? A dog? . . . A rabbit? A person?

Therapist: I said, **Do you want me to answer? Do you want me to be in this play?**

Cleo: No! A dog could help, a rabbit could help, a person could help. Anyone could help.

Therapist: And she went on calling for help and finally got a doll to help, and dropped Sam Small out of the game and announced,

Cleo: The next rider is somebody else and that's an all made-up name.

Therapist: She was playing with her back toward me and I made a comment that a lot was going on and that I couldn't see very well. She nodded but didn't say anything else for a moment and resumed her play. Another rider was being dragged through the dirt, but not as wildly as the first rider. She said,

Cleo: You have to practice a lot to do something scary and you have to start very young, and then you're not so scared anymore.

Therapist: She then pretended that the doll in her hand jumped up on the couch and then had the following dialogue with the doll:

Cleo: I started at one. Doll: I started as a baby and I'm not scared anymore. Cleo: Oh yeah?

Therapist: She then pretended to put a tail on the doll and then said,

Cleo: What kind of a horse is this? Oh, I know. I'll make it a robber.

Therapist: I was getting so confused by the disjointed quality of the play that I said, *I don't know what is happening here today.*

Cleo told me to hush and just watch. She had the robber try to steal some money from Linda Small, who was now the business manager of the rodeo. Linda Small had collected all the admissions money and the robber was going to steal it. Cleo got very intensely involved in this play and with her back toward me was whispering so softly that I could not hear. I said, *Today you are being very private,* and she nodded and told me Sh! Sh!, and continued playing and saying Sh!, Sh! intermittently. Much later I had an itch and scratched myself and my nail made a slight noise on the fabric of my blouse. She said,

Cleo: What's that? What are you doing?

Therapist: *Scratching an itch.*

Cleo: Oh. I thought you were scratching a chair.

Therapist: *That's an interesting idea. What would make me scratch a chair?*

Cleo: If you were a cat you'd scratch a chair.

Therapist: She sounded a little confused at this point.

Supervisor: That's what seems to be emerging about Cleo. She gets mixed up easily and always in the direction of something unexpected, something sharp, something dangerous, something that could hurt.

Therapist: She went back to playing quietly. Our time was almost up so I felt that I wanted to make some sort of closing statement. Probably it was my need for order that motivated me. I said, *Some of what you have been playing is private and you didn't want me to see it, but you did let me hear some of the stuff that had to do with the robber. This robber needs stuff and he doesn't know how to get it, so he's going to steal it. He's going to take it from other people.*

She continued to play. I said, *Remember last week we had a talk about cleaning up and you said that you only needed 2 minutes to clean up. Well, it's now time to clean up because we only have 2 minutes left.*

Cleo: I only need 17 seconds to clean up. Just watch me.

Therapist: She began counting "1, 2, 3," until she got to 16 and then she went 16, 16¼, 16½ and by then she had used up her 2 minutes. She didn't put everything away. She left things out and glanced at me in a kind of testing way. I asked her if she would like me to help and she didn't reply. That was the end of the session.

Supervisor: Well, what do you think of the session?

Therapist: I get a strong sense of her moving into scary territory and getting caught there and trying to distract herself. I don't know how to engage her. If I say something simple and common place like, "That's a troubling idea," that might sound like a confirmation to her. To another child it might sound like an engaging statement to respond to, but not so with Cleo.

Supervisor: Do you think that "troubling" is too bland and that "scary" is closer to the affect.

Therapist: Yes, but it's too direct and when I've used that she dodges me.

Supervisor: I suspected that you went to "troubling" because "scary" carried some other problem. Of course she doesn't want you to know how scared she is. She's the kind of child who might develop all sorts of counterphobic solutions and go hang gliding and jumping off high dives and so on.

Therapist: Yes, just think of her portraying the rodeo as a place where you get dragged through dirt but you just keep doing it over and over again until you aren't scared anymore.
     Here is my dilemma. She has this strong need to be private so I must respect that, but then how do we get to work with her feelings? I was thinking that I could at least begin to address some of her confusion. There's a timing issue here that's very delicate and I just don't know how long to wait.

Supervisor: I think you have to wait. Right now a great deal is happening in her treatment. She's letting you witness so much that goes on in her fantasy. Don't underestimate the value of her being able to share this with you. She's sharing both her fantasy of danger and her determination to master the danger. She has a tremendous stake in fighting her fears and a mistimed interpretation could easily feel to her as if you want to take her mode of defense away from her. It's hard to witness her struggle because it appears so futile to us. She evades, acts macho, changes the subject, but she cannot really master the danger. As she continues sharing all this with you, you will gradually be able to connect a bit more to her scared part. Eventually you will say things like, ***Wouldn't it be terrible if you really couldn't trust the police when you were in trouble? Who would you turn to? What would you do? What a scary thought that is!***

Then as treatment develops you will take it into the transference and present yourself as a good kind of police who works with helping children feel safe in their minds. She does not yet have a concept of inner danger. She does not understand that most of her sense of danger stems from projecting her scary thoughts onto external reality. She thinks that external reality is the problem. Eventually you will be able to say something like, ***The minute you see or hear something that makes you feel scared, you don't stick around to find out how the story goes. You get so scared that you make up your own story, and your own story is the scariest of all.***

One of the things we're noticing is that she lets go when she should hold on. When scared she seems to withdraw from her objects and try valiantly to cope all by herself. So at some point you will have to address her loss of connection to a good object representation when she feels scared.

Also, here is the point where we have to play that dual role of working with the child on her internal psychic distress, but also work with the actual environmental reality, and that is part of our work with the parents, in this case just the mother for now. In working with the mother you will have to find a tactful way to enlist her attention in protecting Cleo from too much stimulation. You can tell the mother that you've noticed that at this point in her life Cleo does not seem to tune out very much of what she is exposed to. Consequently, such ordinary things as the news on T.V. can frighten her very much. This places a burden on the parent, who has to screen some of that unmanageable stimuli.

Therapist: Then there's the problem of Cleo *wanting* to be tough and *wanting* to watch horror movies. During the consultation process she told me with great pride that she had watched the movie *Friday the 13th*. One problem that I find as a parent is the lack of discretion that so many parents have about what their kids are allowed to watch. Horror films are a common staple at birthday parties for children of Cleo's age. It makes it very hard for some of us who have strong feelings about raising our children on more wholesome stuff than horror movies. For a child like Cleo who is both terrified and wants to be tough, it's hard for her to leave the room when something is too much for her.

Supervisor: Yes, we have this combination of inner terror and environmental overstimulation, as well as her wish to be brave and master danger. But you will be able to help her with all of this. She's already letting you in. Look at how clever she was with her rodeo. She didn't want to assign you an active role in it, but then made you a villain, a victim, and a powerful figure, a manager.

Therapist: Who got robbed.

Supervisor: Yes, who got robbed. That's what she does. The minute she finds a comforting solution to being so alone, she undoes it. So your biggest and most delicate task is to connect to that very scared part of her without that becoming a new source of terror and humiliation for her. She has an older sister who teases her, and a father who was violent in the home and who promotes scary activities with her. Much as she feels frightened, this must also be very exciting. We see circumstances that could form a masochistic trend in Cleo.

Before we stop today, just tell me what happened with the mother in regard to Cleo's message to her, "Cleo doesn't know."

Therapist: Oh, I told Mrs. C. about my custom of being a message bearer between child and parent. I told her what Cleo said, and the mother smiled and said that Cleo does often say that she doesn't know, and that it's now something they joke about.

Supervisor: That's a pretty interesting thing to joke about, isn't it? There's probably a lot that she would like to "unknow" if that were possible, but there's a lot that she would like to know better. She's a child whose curiosity is strong and active, and that's generally something we welcome in children, and in adults as well. For Cleo though, her curiosity has not been a comfortable or safe area in her life.

5

Toys and Play in Child Treatment

Therapist: On this day, for the first time, Cleo saw a patient come out of my office. Until now, Cleo was my first afternoon appointment. When I came to the waiting room to get her, she jumped right up and led the way to my office, but when she got to the door she said,

Cleo: Oops! I forgot to take off my jacket.

Therapist: I told her that she could do that in my office if she'd like to. She came in and took off her jacket, threw it in the chair, and said,

Cleo: Do you have a T.V.?

Therapist: *You want to know whether I have a T.V.?*

Cleo: Yes, do you have one? Do you have one here in this office?

Therapist: *Do you see one here?*

Cleo: It could be in the closet.

Therapist: *I don't have one but would you like to look in the closet for yourself?*

Cleo: Yes.

Therapist: She carefully checked out the closet, looked in some of the boxes, and then said,

Cleo: I guess there's no T.V. here. I'm missing my favorite T.V. show right now. It's called *Roaring Racers.*

Therapist: I'd never heard of that program and didn't know whether it existed, so I said, *Can you tell me a little about it?*

Cleo: Oh well, it's about racing cars.

Therapist: She started making racing motor noises and pretending to race cars around with her hand, and then she hummed a little and said,

Cleo: And they have these California kids singing "do do do," you know, surfing music. What's their name, oh, yeah, the Beach Boys. Do you know them?

Therapist: *Yes, I've listened to the Beach Boys.*

Cleo: Well, this is my favorite Beach Boy tune.

Therapist: And she started humming, trying to remember the words, stumbling over them, saying that she couldn't remember, and then remembering a bit. I knew the song and like it, so I just said,

Therapist: *From the way you are humming, and some of the words, I think that you're trying to sing "I Get Around."*

Cleo: No, that's not it.

Therapist: She hummed some more, and it was no longer the one I had mentioned, but it was one that I knew well, so without really considering what I was doing, I just joined her and together we hummed a Beach Boy song.

Cleo: That's my sister's favorite.

Therapist: I was very unsure about all of what I had just done: acknowledging knowing the Beach Boys, humming with Cleo, humming what she said was her sister's favorite song, but it felt as if there was no time to stop and think. Cleo then pointed to the toy drawer and asked,

Cleo: What do you think? Do you think the toys can sing?

Therapist: *Toys? Can toys sing? I'm not sure. It depends on what you decide to pretend.*
      And she opened the drawer and picked out a little boy doll figure and pretended that he was singing.

Cleo: I gave him my voice because he has no mouth. See, he has no mouth.

Therapist: I was thoroughly confused at that point because to my eyes that doll had no nose, but it had a mouth.

Supervisor: What do you mean "to your eyes"? You have very good eyes. Do you see how confusing she is? It's startling that you would begin to question what you see, your sense of reality.

Therapist: Yes, I sound as if there's room for different interpretations of what we saw. In fact it was a nose that was missing on that painted doll face and my discomfort with her mistake made me try to minimize the implication of why she might have reasons to eliminate the mouth. I said, *Oh, I thought that what you were pointing to was a mouth and you say that it's a nose.*

Cleo: Oh yes! That's a nose, not a mouth. These dolls have no mouth and no teeth.

Therapist: Then she suddenly got up and announced that she had to go to the bathroom. She was in the bathroom for quite a while, about 5 minutes, and when she came back she went over to the play table, picked up a round basket that I use for some small figures, emptied it, and said,

Cleo: See this ride? This is a very, very scary ride. It's a ride for teenagers only. Teenagers can go on it, and adults too. It's much too scary for kids.

Therapist: Then she picked up the smallest child doll, put it on the ride, and said:

Cleo: This ride is too scary for kids and there is a kid on it.

Therapist: She then spun the kid very fast on the ride, going around and around as fast as she could. I said, *My goodness, what is going to happen to that child?*

Cleo: Oh! Mommy, Mommy, Mommy, Mommy! Help me! Mommy, Daddy help!

Therapist: And then Cleo pretended that someone tried to help the child but then somebody else told the child that it had to stay on until the ride was over. I asked, *How long is that scary ride going to last?*

Cleo: 17 ½ minutes.

Therapist: *Is that a long time or a short time?*

Cleo: It's a very long time. It's longer than 15 minutes.

Therapist: *Isn't there any way that this child can get help?*

Cleo: All right, all right!

Therapist: And she took an adult figure out of the toy drawer who said,

Cleo: All right. Stop the ride, I'll help you.

Therapist: She then pretended that the man who operated the ride stopped the ride. Then she had the adult figure who had offered to help say,

Cleo: All right, now I am going to help you. I'll get on the ride with you.

Therapist: *Is that the kind of help that child needs?* She didn't answer right away, she just started spinning the wheel. Then in a deep voice she said,

Cleo: I can make this ride go faster and slower. I can make it go as fast or as slow as I want.

Therapist: And she started spinning it slowly but soon she had it going faster and faster, and then she said in a thoughtful, almost wistful voice,

Cleo: Once, when I was at a dude ranch I was on a ride that was called "lightning spin." Tina and I went on it, and you went around and around and then you went up and down and sometimes you were upside down. It was real scary. My mom didn't know that it was so scary. She said that if she had known she wouldn't have let me go on.

Therapist: Now the session became choppy and hard to follow. She got the child off the ride and the man who was the operator of the ride did something that "wasn't right" so that something happened to the two children. Then Cleo said,

Cleo: This kid has a very dumb father. This father doesn't know what to do. When these kids fight, the father always says the wrong thing.

Therapist: Then she took out another adult figure, one that was very plain looking, and she took this figure and handled it as if it was somebody very special, a hero, and she made it very clear that this hero person was in charge. This person now took care of the kids. He spoke softly to them and acted protective but I couldn't hear what he was saying. It was not real words; it was just sounds that had a tone of protective caretaking. I waited a bit and said, *Well, now you have someone really helping*. But as soon as I said that, the helping stranger was discarded and the two children were with their father and the father was shopping for a car. She got out all of the toy cars and had the father looking through them. Then the discarded hero figure returned and got into what she called The Horse Car. She commented that the cars were going very fast and The Horse Car was the fastest of all.

I was having a hard time following this. It was much more disjointed then it sounds in my description. I also felt as if I was very much of an outsider and I wanted to place myself back into the session so I said, *The cars are going very fast. Is that very important? Is it very important for a car to go very fast?*

Cleo: Well, that isn't the only important thing about a car. It's also important for a car to be safe. Now the horse car, it can go zoom here and zoom there.

Therapist: Now she was suddenly acting the part of the salesman who was telling the father what some of the attributes of the cars were, and the father was trying out all of the different cars. Then the father and the salesman began to try to make a deal and were talking about numbers, and then Cleo looked at me and asked,

Cleo: Do you know how much $20,000, twenty hundred, and three hundred is?

Therapist: *Do you want me to tell you?*

Cleo: Well, I know how much it is. it's $23,000 and that's a lot.

Therapist: Then, without any transition she had the father in the playground with the children and they were going down a slide. She then had the father tell the kids,

Cleo: Come on kids, it's time to go to school, let's go! You're going to miss the whole school day if you don't hurry up.

Therapist: *Boy, these kids are supposed to be in school, and instead they're shopping for a car and playing in the playground. What is that about?* Then I paused and blew my nose.

Cleo: Why are you crying?

Supervisor: I sensed that she was going to say that! It's that trigger response again.

Therapist: It fits, doesn't it. I said, *I've noticed this about you. You hear a sound and you make up a whole story about it.* Then I had to blow my nose again.

Cleo: What is that sound? Is there an elephant here?

Supervisor: She has to be humorous to undo a real feeling. She cannot be reflective about your intervention. Not at this point in treatment. She has to play the comic.

Therapist: Yes. My intervention was too much for her. Our time was up at this point and when I said that to her she answered,

Cleo: Instead of cleaning up I feel like breaking this thing.

Therapist: And she held up the father doll. So I said, *When I said that it's time to stop and put the toys away, you say that you feel like breaking things.*
      She picked up another toy figure and said:

Cleo: And I feel like breaking this one too, and this one.

Therapist: And she was squeezing and bending these dolls. I said, *When I tell you that our time is up you have some strong feelings and you feel like breaking things. It's better for you to put these feelings into words so we can understand them. Breaking things doesn't help our understanding work.*
      She didn't say anything, but just put everything away.

Supervisor: She didn't say anything about not wanting her time to be up?

Therapist: No. That stays unsaid. Does she even let herself know that she doesn't want her time to be up? I know that at some point I will have to interpret those "breaking" feelings, locate them as coming from inside her, and address the conflict they cause within her. I will have to again introduce the notion that putting them into words is a way to have control over them. But we're not yet at that point in treatment. So she left on what I experienced as a very unsatisfactory note. I felt that I had sounded a touch teacherish. I was unhappy about the way the session ended and so she left.

Supervisor: How do you handle the leaving? Did you walk her back to the waiting room?

Therapist: I walked her out the door. I can't see the inside of my waiting room from the hall outside my door, so I didn't see her baby-sitter. I waited until I was sure that she saw her baby-sitter but I didn't take those few extra steps to see them together. I went back to my office and just as I was to cross my doorway she called out,

Cleo: **Goodbye Linda Small!**

Therapist: And I called back, ***Goodbye Cleo!*** She always calls me by my full name, Linda Small.

Supervisor: What do you make of Cleo calling you Linda Small?

Therapist: I don't know. She calls me that in her play. She says my full name a lot. At her school the children call the teachers by their first name. Her teacher is Susan. Could she enjoy the formality of my full name? Is it perhaps like a title? Something official? I just don't know.

Supervisor: Your not knowing is the leitmotif, isn't it? You don't know whether "Linda Small" is an expression of affection, formality, possessiveness, a combination of many moods and affects or what. Remember the message that you were to give

Cleo's mother: "Cleo doesn't know"? Well, not knowing is an important theme in this child's treatment for both of you.

What about the rest of the session? Did the content of her play make you anxious?

Therapist: I did feel a little disturbed. The comment about the father being out of touch with his children for instance. That was so blatant.

Supervisor: It seemed to come out so suddenly, didn't it?

Therapist: Yes. There was also something very sudden about her having to go to the bathroom. It followed the business about the doll having no teeth. I had trouble understanding her at times. Her speech is still immature and her enunciation is at times poor, so I find myself saying things like, *Could you repeat that? I didn't understand.* Sometimes she talks very fast and then her speech becomes really indistinct. Then it gets to be a strain to follow what she's saying.

Supervisor: And then there is her humor, which can be sophisticated, for instance $17\frac{1}{2}$ minutes, that type of thing.

This was, as usual, a very interesting session. More and more Cleo is getting the idea that this is a special place where all sorts of feelings can be expressed. I don't mean that she is consciously aware of this, or of the degree to which she's revealing her feelings. She isn't, and what child is? What is happening is that a process has been set in motion, the process of treatment. I don't want to sound mystical. That would be inaccurate and not helpful. Very simply, she has understood the specialness of this place and time, and that it is solely for her benefit. Perhaps because she senses this already, she is less defended and her feelings take over to the point of bringing her to the edge of feeling too much anxiety, recovering from this precarious position, and getting close to the edge again, and so forth. . . .

In this session more than any before, I sensed that you were constantly trying to anchor her in a more reasonable reality than the one she kept creating in her play. It's because I noticed how eager you were to improve the reality she portrayed that I asked whether you felt anxious during parts of the session. You must have felt uncomfortable with the world she created, a world where children are placed in dangerous situations by their parents, and are left to fend for themselves most of the time. I sensed that you wanted to tell her that the world is not supposed to be that way, that it's supposed to be a good, safe place. I understand why you were taking that position. After all, Cleo is revealing something of the chaotic nature of her actual life, as well as of her fantasies. It's difficult to accept and endure the fact that this little girl, with her still immature speech, lives in such a frightening place.

Here is the technical dilemma. You, the therapist, want to provide a safe place in the therapy room, but if the whole therapeutic hour is spent on scary and dangerous escapades, how is this going to happen? Will her experience of the therapeutic hour be any different from her general experience of being alone with her fears? Yet how can you interfere with her self-expression?

I have a hypothesis here that might help you. I think that Cleo has already found a way to bring safe figures into her danger situations and I assume those to be transferential. For instance, the person that you described as the least unusual, the most ordinary, I'm assuming that that was a transferential figure. Did you make that assumption?

Therapist: No. (chuckles) I think I was too caught up in the play to think that clearly. I was relieved to think that she had it within her to know that some safe figures exist.

Supervisor: Well, she does have an ego that can regulate and regain some equilibrium, but that does not exclude the transferential aspect.

Therapist: I think that you're saying that I was directing her too much.

Supervisor: I think you were very eager to snuff out some of the danger and the affect connected to danger, the excitement of the danger. It felt as if you wanted to shorten the dangerous ride, and to tone it down.

Therapist: Yeah, I guess I did. (laughs)

Supervisor: Your mommy side came out, and you felt protective. That's pretty understandable, but in our work we sometimes have to dull that maternal urge so as not to place an obstacle in the path of treatment.

Therapist: So I could have said **Oh my** or **What is this about** or maybe not have said anything at all?

Supervisor: Well, yes, some of those very neutral things like that, like **Oh dear,** the kinds of bland things that confirm that we're listening but are not directive at all. The point here is that you want to see what she will do on her own. If you step in you will not know whether she (her ego) will be able to regulate the anxiety. Look at what she did on her own. She got the owner of the ride to go on the ride with the child. That might not have seemed such a great solution but then she went on and had the owner announce that he can make the ride go slower and faster. So here she has established some sort of regulatory functioning. You do need to know what her capacity to organize a chaotic situation is like. Then your interpretation can be a dynamic one and not just a description of the content of her play. Remember, the same rule applies to children as to adults: we interpret defense first, not content (Fenichel 1945). So you could at that point say, **I can see that when things get really scary, you can think of a way to make them a little safer.** That's an interpretation that can be very helpful and can open up the way for a series of interpretations that could go like this:

   Do you sometimes wait too long? Do you sometimes allow it to get a little too scary before you stop it? Do you sometimes like it to get so scary?

Remember what she does is both scary and exciting. Something made her have to go to the bathroom very suddenly. It followed the part about the doll having no mouth.

Therapist: No mouth and no teeth.

Supervisor: This little girl frightens and excites herself a lot. She is unable to sufficiently regulate the frightening fantasies or the states of excitement. It's going to be our job to help her in this regard. I'm talking about strengthening the ego. Her ego is not up to the job of dealing with her drives, reality, and her superego.

Let's get back to the beginning of the session. She said that she was missing a television program called *Roaring Racers.* Does such a program exist?

Therapist: I don't know. I'll have to ask my kids or look it up in the paper.

Supervisor: It's useful to know things like that. If there is such a program it would be helpful to know what it is so that you can talk to her about it in an informed way, and if she made it up, that's also important. Some kids make things up a lot and we can become devalued if we let them fool us too successfully. If a child patient tends to fool us a lot we can ask, whenever we're unsure, *Are you pulling my leg again?* If we can be too easily fooled we are not perceived as strong and reliable. When we're uncertain, just to simply ask whether this is a fooling time is a perfectly good approach. It clarifies our position as being neither mind readers nor accusers, nor fools. It's just right and helps the therapeutic alliance.

I wasn't clear about her question about your having a television set. How did you understand that?

Therapist: I was unclear too. I sort of jumped ahead of her and let her look in my storage closet. I thought that maybe she wanted to watch television with me and perhaps I let her look in my toy and storage closet as a substitute treat. I guess that I worry a little about not having enough supplies for her. In fact, I have wanted to discuss with you the toys that I have and whether I should buy more. What I have now is some puppets, a bunch of play figures, paper, crayons and Magic Markers, scissors, tape, paper clips, and a box for her pictures.

Supervisor: Are any of the figures babies?

Therapist: One baby doll, and one plastic figure is a baby.

Supervisor: Do you have any blocks?

Therapist: I was wondering whether I should get blocks and more baby dolls.

Supervisor: Let's talk about toys in both practical and conceptual terms. Let me tell you what I have because I find that it fills all play needs very effectively.

I have a sturdy wooden box full of miniature blocks of various shapes. All of my cars and trucks are picked to fit the blocks so that the building of roads and bridges and garages would all work well together. Then I have a collection of plastic people of all ages that fit the blocks so that the building of houses and rooms and furniture also all work well together. I have a nice box full of bits of fabric and a needle and thread so that blankets and pillows and clothes can be cut and sewn for the people and animals. I also have a collection of small animals, wild and domestic, also of the size to go with the blocks. I have cowboys and Indians with weapons and a dozen finger puppets of firemen, nurses, doctors, policemen, and other kinds of people who are a part of children's lives. I have a basketful of snowflake-shaped plastic pieces that can be fitted together to make various shapes. I have a small Lego set, a set of dominos, and two decks of cards. I also have very good yet safe scissors, rubber bands, toothpicks, scotch tape, a very good stapler, pens, pencils, erasers, Magic Markers, crayons, and typewriter-size paper.

I keep all of the toys in a cabinet next to the play table. The cabinet has doors on it and those doors are always closed when the child arrives for a session. The only exception to this rule is the first session with a child. Then the doors are left open so the child can see where the toys are kept. After the first session, it's up to the child to seek out the toys.[1] I would, of course, remind children that they can use the toys whenever they wish.

The guiding principle is to provide the child with tools for self-expression through play but to provide a minimal amount of these tools so that the play can be used for the purpose of therapy and does not become so entertaining and gratifying that it becomes a form of resistance to the work of treatment. Our goal is to use the play on the way to verbalization. When the child can put into words what the play signifies, then the observing ego and the experiencing ego are working together. I'm describing an aspect of a child's treatment that is analogous to a point in adult psychoanalysis, when the analysand begins to *really* listen to his or her own free association and use the insight so gained to deepen the analytic work and promote self-knowledge.

You might have noticed that I did not mention books or board games on my list of toys. I do have a board game and a couple of books locked away that I sometimes used with a psychotic boy who occasionally experienced overwhelming panic attacks during his sessions. Reading to him was soothing and helped him regain his equilibrium. I think that it was the familiarity of the book and of my voice reading those well-remembered words that had the restorative effect. This often was followed by the equally familiar and structured board game, and the combination aided him in maintaining his calmed emotional state. But in most cases I find that books and board games are counterproductive. A book tells the author's story and we want our patient to tell his or her story. Board

---

[1] I am grateful to Eva Landauer of the Child Development Center for suggesting this very useful approach to the presentation of toys in the treatment situation.

games often require one's entire attention and very little therapeutic work can take place under the structure of the board game with all of its rules. But I also know that some therapists find board games useful. Maybe they're just better at transforming them into a useful adjunct to the play aspect of treatment. I feel more strongly about the negative use of books in the treatment room.

I want to explain the purpose of leaving my toy cabinet doors closed in all but the first session. I always ask parents of very young children to tell their children prior to the first session that I have toys and that they will be able to play if they wish. The open toy cabinet is intended to serve as a transitional offering that affirms their sense of anticipation to this otherwise unfamiliar place where there is going to be a "Mrs. Siskind who knows a lot about children and who has toys." The reason that the toy cabinet is never open in advance again is because while I have toys, playing with toys is not a requirement. It's voluntary, and having that toy cabinet open with all of the attractive baskets holding all sorts of toys is suggestive and even seductive. There is an implied expectation that the child should go over there rather than begin where he or she might have begun were those toy cabinet doors closed. The child should begin his session in the same way as the analysand begins a session—with absolutely no interference or suggestion. Any directives from the therapist, however silent and indirect, are a form of interference.

To continue with the subject of play materials, I have a group of stacking boxes so that each child has his or her own place to keep special toys that are not part of the general toy pool, as well as pictures and other projects that are completed and/or in progress. There are many reasons for that private box, which was the creation of Anna Freud at the Hampstead Clinic. There, each child had a private cubby that was locked between sessions. My version is not as elaborate and does not lock, but I believe that it fulfills some of the same purpose.

Now, let's talk a bit about that private box that nobody else can open and that stays in the therapy office between sessions. First of all, all of my child boxes are identical but each has an identifying symbol that is devised and executed by the child but does not include a name, for the children have been told about the confidentiality of treatment. I impose certain rules of treatment. One sacred rule is that you cannot take any of the therapy toys into your private box. The therapy toys always stay the same. What can go into the private box are things the child has made or is making. These things can only go into the box as confidentiality prevents them from being displayed in the office and another of my rules prevents them from going home. I do not let children take things home except in special circumstances. Things made in treatment become part of treatment history and stay in the office. There are many good reasons for this rule. Some of the things made in treatment would receive a not-so-welcoming reception were they to go home. Many a parent has looked at highly valued pictures and exclaimed, "Is scribbling what you do in treatment? Is that what I pay all of that money for?" Another good reason for this rule, and the really important reason, is that things that a child makes during a session are communications to his or her therapist. That communication is private therapy business and not something to be shared with anyone else.

This has been a digression, but one that I hope can be useful to you. To get back to Cleo, it might be nice for you to get some blocks so that she can create a setting for all sorts of situations that she might want to show you and play out in your presence. But remember, this child needs your attention and the quiet structure you provide. She is bombarded by inner and outer stimuli. She does not need a playroom with easels and basketball hoops and pinball machines. She has a vivid imagination and she is very resourceful. She needs a quiet office and a chance to sort things out. She needs an "average expectable environment" (Hartmann 1939). Look at how much she can create with the toys you have right now.

Now let's discuss a point in technique. When Cleo wanted to

break the doll, you asked her to put those feelings into words. I thought that maybe you could have been a little more encouraging of some elaboration of those feelings. Maybe you could have said, *What are those feelings of wanting to break the doll? Could you tell me what that feels like?* Had she been in treatment a longer time, you might have tried to connect those feelings to her time being up. I think that it's too early in treatment to do that. She is much too proud to admit that she cares that much about her session being up.

Therapist: I felt that I was making an attempt to connect when I said, *When I say that it's time to clean up you say that you want to break things.*

Supervisor: Yes, I forgot that. That is just about perfect because you are offering a connection but not imposing it on her and she can ignore you if she wishes.

Therapist: This discussion is helpful. I realize that my main effort has been to help Cleo contain her feelings. The idea of allowing more of her state of chaos to emerge in the treatment situation is outside of my thinking. If I allow more to come out here . . . it's hard to imagine. This child thinks that a match is a fire. How do I deal with the inner chaos?

Supervisor: Very carefully. Very slowly. For instance, in the play where she has a child go on a ride that is not for children, you can comment, *That child does not say that she doesn't want to go on that ride, that the ride is too scary.*

Therapist: To comment on the controls of the child?

Supervisor: Well, yes. It could go like this: *You told me that the ride is for teenagers and adults only because it's too scary for anyone else. Then the child goes on it but you didn't tell me how that child feels about going on that ride?* Then, if she says, Oh, this kid is so tough, this kid can go on any adult rides. If she says that, I think you would have to leave that alone for the time being. That's the macho part of speaking and keeping you at a distance. But if she says, Oh, this kid is really scared, then you can say, *Well, but I notice that the kid just goes on the ride and doesn't say that it doesn't want to, that it's too scary and stop it, or anything like that. Why doesn't the kid speak up?* These interventions would be aimed at trying to engage her observing ego in addressing the situation with some awareness that she had regulatory capabilities at her disposal.

There is in Cleo that tricky combination of toughness and compliance. We can safely speculate that the toughness is a pseudotoughness that covers extreme vulnerability. She does sound tough though, doesn't she?

Therapist: Yes, but also delicate. My goodness, I don't think I've ever looked so closely at what it means to treat a child.

Supervisor: Even the word treatment sounds odd in this context. What are we treating here? This is a little girl who lives in a state of anxiety; she feels unsafe. How do you treat somebody who feels unsafe? What are you treating? You're treating a state of being.

Therapist: An internal state.

Supervisor: Yes. You are treating an internal state, so you have to help that child become aware of that internal state in a conscious way. Then you have to help that child's ego deal with it and that takes a long time, a lot of attunement on the part of the therapist, and a lot of trust on the part of the child!

Therapist: Well, she's not near to trusting this process, but I think she knows that something is being offered here, something she wants. And maybe her not being so compliant and wanting to break things is a good sign. At least she can test me a little to see what I'll do if she's rebellious and not so ready to put things away and leave.

Supervisor: Yes, I agree. Before we end for today I just want to mention the fact that she saw another patient leave your office for the first time and that it didn't get addressed. I'm not saying you should have addressed it, or when and how. I'm saying you should be aware of any major change of routine like that. It doesn't go unnoticed. It's significant and has an impact. Just keep it in mind.

I think we got a lot of mileage out of this session. It's so interesting at this stage of treatment. We just don't know how it's going to go, but we seem to be moving along, and with Cleo it's sure to be unpredictable. I loved that little touch of hers at the end of her session when she calls out, **Goodbye Linda Small.** She was being proprietary about you. She was already outside of your office but she still owned you.

6

The Many Roles of the Child Therapist

Therapist: Cleo rang the bell at 4:10 and when I came out to greet her at 4:15 she said:

Cleo: Where were you, you bad girl?

Therapist: *Oh?*

Cleo: Where were you? You are a bad girl!

Therapist: *Gee, what makes me a bad girl?*

Cleo: You kept me waiting!

Therapist: *Oh my! What is that like, that feeling you have while waiting? What is that feeling like that makes me into a bad girl?*

Cleo: You kept me waiting a long time and I had to listen to that stupid music and I got so bored. I had to fire those singers and hire new ones.

Therapist: This became very garbled and hard to follow and I had to tell her that I was having trouble understanding her. She tried to explain but I had to fill in a lot and what I could finally make out was that she had gone back to last week's waiting room fantasy of making a movie, so I said, *Oh, I didn't know that you were making a movie in the waiting room last week.*

Cleo: Yes! I was. And today you made me wait and wait.

Therapist: *I guess you felt that you were waiting a long time.*

Cleo: Forever!

Therapist: I felt that I had to check out her reality at this point yet I hated to interrupt the fantasy. Still, I chose checking out the reality and asked, *Do you know at what time our appointment is?*

Cleo: It's at 4:30 a.m. I've been waiting since 4:30 this morning and you didn't come.

Therapist: *Oh, my goodness!*

Cleo: And you'd better be here when I'm waiting. I had to miss school.

Therapist: *Oh dear, why did you have to miss school?*

Cleo: That was a joke.

Therapist: *Now you tell me that that was a joke. But having to wait, that part wasn't a joke, was it?*

Cleo: Do you want to hear me count to one hundred?

Therapist: *I think that you are changing the subject.*

Cleo: Yes. One, two, three. . . .

Therapist: And she counted to a hundred. So I said, *Well, you counted to a hundred all right.*

Cleo: Now do you want me to count to a hundred by tens?

Therapist: She didn't wait for an answer and began, but she couldn't do it and stumbled about a bit and then said,

Cleo: Let's see how those toys are doing. Let's see if they can count.

Therapist: She got the toys out and found the figure that had been the father the week before and started having him sing a song. Cleo pretended that she was a ventriloquist. She said,

Cleo: He's singing a song. Can anybody make toys talk?

Therapist: *That's an interesting question.*

Cleo: I can. See, my lips aren't moving and he is singing a song. Do you know this song?

Therapist: She was humming a song that I recognized and I asked her, *Do you want me to sing that song?* and she nodded a yes and I was reminded of last week when I sang a Beach Boys song. Feeling unsure of what I was doing I sang the song. In the meanwhile I was noticing that her nose was running and that long strands of mucus were on her upper lip and so I asked her whether she might like a Kleenex and pointed them out on the table. I felt sort of motherly doing this. She took one and wiped her nose and threw the Kleenex in the wastebasket. She put some toy cars in a row and called that a train, lost interest and picked up a toy person and facing it said,

Cleo: It's time for you to get a haircut and it's hard for you to get your hair cut. Come, sit in this chair and let's get these scissors.

Therapist: She picked up a toy fish that had a tail like scissors and said to the toy figure,

Cleo: I'm going to use these big scissors on you.

Therapist: She pretended to cut the hair and lo and behold announced,

Cleo: The boy turned into a girl. The boy was really a girl.

Therapist: Then she dropped that subject and said that she wanted to go back to the cars.

Cleo: Let's go back to those cars. Where are they? Oh here they are. Here is the horse car. Oh, it isn't going very fast this week. I'll have to go buy a faster car. Let's see. How about the rabbit car, and how about the turtle car and how about the chicken car. . . .

Therapist: She had the figure of the person who was shopping for a car get on each of these animals and there was something very comical about all of this and I had to try not to laugh, but also things were happening at lightning speed and changing without warning and she was suddenly talking about Harrian Tuckman. Now I happened to know that the preceding month had been Black History Month and that many schools had been studying the biography of a celebrated black woman named Harriet Tubman. I assumed that Cleo was either mispronouncing or deliberately playing with that name. She announced that Harrian Tuckman has a broken neck and has to go to jail, and then appeared to completely drop that subject and had a man on a horse trying to decide whether to go to a party or go swimming. She then looked directly at me and asked,

Cleo: What about you Linda Small? What would you like him to do? Go swimming or go to a party?

Therapist: *Well, this is your play and you are the one who makes the decisions here. What would you have him do in your play?*

Cleo: I am asking you, Linda Small, for your opinion.

Therapist: And then she seemed to drop that demand and said,

Cleo: My boss says that I have to go to my job. I have to go to the party and save my job. I can't be with you people here. I'm going to the party.

Therapist: Then she pretended that the boss was angry and asked the man why he was so late getting to the party, and the man answered that he had been deciding. There was a lot of whispering and I was trying to stay in there and follow so I said, *Oh, it's secrets time?*

Cleo: We are not letting Linda Small know.

Therapist: *Some things I can know and some I can't?* But she didn't answer. She was off again making a movie about Harrian Tuckman. By then it was time to clean up and I said, *What a day this has been. Did you notice how first there was the part about how long you had waited for me, and then the part about the haircut and the boy who turned into a girl, and the car shopping and Harrian Tuckman?*

Cleo: I notice that it was all pretty weird.

Therapist: Now the session was over. I had been trying to do what you suggested last week, giving her more rope to go wherever she was going. It got pretty choppy. I wondered whether her anger at me at the beginning of the session was what made it so jumbled.

Supervisor: The anger that she had to wait the 5 minutes that she was early?

Therapist: Yes. It was my hunch that her anger at me was the reason that the play was so disjointed. This was the most extreme I had seen it. I really couldn't follow her most of the time. She seemed to jump from one thing to another.

Supervisor: It sounded that way to me too. During other sessions she seemed to have had a fairly developed scene, and then something would go too fast or some disaster would happen and then there would be a resolution, but this was not like that. This was really a jumble as you said.

Therapist: I couldn't even find a way to talk to her affect. I didn't know what to do at all.

Supervisor: Well, a session like this is very hard on the therapist. Our whole training is aimed at finding the patient's track and staying with it and not imposing our ideas on where the patient is heading.

Still, when a session gets very fragmented we can try various ways to connect to the patient's state of mind. For instance, at the beginning of the session she is talking with a lot of feeling and then suddenly she says that she is going to count to one hundred. At that point you did make an intervention. You asked her whether she was changing the subject. I think you could have done a little more with that. You could have said, *Sometimes when you feel stuck you just change the subject.* Then when it happens again you can refer to it and say, *I think this is one of those times that you got stuck and changed the subject. I have been noticing that you do that when you get stuck.* Then the next time you can refer to it again and add something like, *Feeling stuck is not such a good feeling. Maybe we can figure out why you get stuck sometimes.*

You sort of begin some line of observation about her and share it with her and set a precedent of referring to it and build on it in small and careful doses, all the while respecting her need to be tough and her reluctance to admit to something as vulnerable as feeling stuck and needing help. Right now she doesn't think that she can admit to being stuck or needing help. I think it was after she couldn't count by tens that she dropped that attempt at recovering a sense of mastery, and did so abruptly and without comment. She then switched to singing, which is a more reliable solution to her state of discomfort. It's interesting to look at these shifts so closely. The switch to singing was not just an abrupt change of subject at a stuck point. It also was a return to something that happened between you the preceding week. She got you to sing last week. You knew her song. Now she called on you again. This time again you knew her song. She used her memory of a good experience between you to make herself feel better. She is building a history of what happens between you and is making use of the good feeling she must have had during the singing episode. You see, you were so unsure about the singing, and I can well understand that you would question such a spontaneous act on your part. With hindsight we can see that it provided a way of being together with Cleo that was just right for her at that time. Not too close and not too far away. The experience was cathected, remembered and called upon at a time of stress. Because of it she was able to seek a soothing experience. I'm curious about what song it was. You recognized it right away.

Therapist: Oh, it's an old Perry Como song that was used in the movie *Moonstruck.* It goes: "When the moon hits your eye like a big pizza pie, that's amore." But she was singing it differently. She was singing, "When the light's in the sky, that's amore." She was lighting up the dark and saying that that is love. I guess that would be love to a terrified little girl who wakes in the middle of the night alone. Maybe she's still awakened by frightening sounds in the middle of the night and she calls her mother but her mother doesn't hear her. I'm curious as to whether that really is part of the song or whether she made it up. I'll look it up.

Supervisor: Now she knows that a song is something she can have with you. She knows in a general way that you have something to offer her but she isn't quite sure what. So far she knows that she can have her 45 minutes every week and sometimes a song with you. But where were you at 4:30 in the morning? So you see how things begin to make a little bit of sense when we search around that way. She is reaching out in her oblique manner. But she is so far away from being able to say, "I'm so scared when I wake up in the middle of the night. I wish you could be there to make me feel better."

I also want to discuss your reaction to her needing a Kleenex. Why did you think that you were being maternal to offer her a Kleenex?

Therapist: Some kids pick at their mucus, smear it, eat it, just let it drip. I didn't want my offering her a Kleenex to sound as if I was telling her, *Come on, clean up your act, blow your nose.*

Supervisor: Well, you can say, *Did you notice that I have Kleenex? If you need any you can just take them. You don't even have to ask.* You can say something like that so that you're informing but not imposing. It certainly is okay for you to mention the Kleenex. After all, she is a little girl and as her therapist you have a responsibility to be concerned about her comfort and safety. It's more comfortable for her to have a dry nose and upper lip and clear nasal passages. There is a delicate and perhaps gray area for child therapists in regard to their young patients and the kind of caretaking that might arise during a session. For instance, if a young child cuts herself during a session, of course you would have to take care of washing out the cut or supervising the washing of it, and covering it with a bandaid. A child therapist has to play the dual role of being both a therapist and a caretaker. We do not allow our young patients to do dangerous things, for instance leaning out an open window or using a sharp knife. We don't allow our young patients to mess up our offices or destroy any of our property, or hit us, or do any other thing in our offices that would make us angry at them and wish to be rid of them. I have a simple rule that I think covers all of these situations and that is that the child is not allowed to do anything that's harmful to either of us or to the room and its contents.

   That was a very detailed response to your concern about being maternal. I'm very glad you raised that issue. I think it's a complicated issue and one that causes a lot of confusion. I have seen children come out of their therapy session soaking wet from playing with water or covered with paint because the therapist was reluctant to set ordinary, commonsense limits for fear of interfering with the child's free expression. I see that as poor judgment. But sometimes it's hard to know when to step in and set limits and when to wait to see what happens. This is another one of these areas where working with children becomes complicated in a way that adult treatment is not. Our caretaking responsibility with adults does not usually include physical care and safety. With children it does, and so in our role as therapists with a caretaking responsibility we have to find a way to present our caretaking function in a way that differs from parents, teacher, baby-sitters, and such. For instance, in this session with Cleo you can make the educational-informative statement about the availability of your Kleenex, and you can also at some point begin to address the lack of attention that she grants to her physical comfort. Her inattention to her physical comfort and safety is after all one of the primary themes of her play. In this way your caretaking function can result in deepening the treatment.

That is only half of what we have to address. What about the less conscious and less obvious layer? What's Cleo telling you when she lets the mucus drip as it did? Is she showing you that she's a messy girl? What did it do to you countertransferentially? If a child were to cut herself during a session we would have to take care of the cut, but we would also have to try to analyze the timing of the cut. We always have this dual role with young children.

All in all, the extreme disjointedness of this session probably is an indicator that treatment is thickening. As I make a statement like that and realize how oblique it sounds, I am struck for the millionth time with how unusual our work is insofar as it does not follow any obvious pattern. What do you think about this?

Therapist: I know what you mean and also wondered whether something was heating up in the treatment. I wondered whether she felt more exposed.

Supervisor: Yes, I think so. She was less guarded. But she was still extremely guarded. If she weren't so guarded you might have asked her, *What happens at 4:30 in the morning?* But she was much too guarded for that and so you were right not to ask her at this point. That will come later.

Therapist: Her ambivalence about how much to tell me is also more evident. There was that "secrets time" part in the session when Linda Small wasn't supposed to know, and whispering at some other point. She really isn't sure how much to let me know.

Supervisor: That's very clear. She might also be showing you the secrets that have been kept from her and playing out her parents' role against you. Another theme that we have talked about before was very evident in this session. That is her habit of picking up a lot of information in a fragmented way. For instance, you can't tell whether Harrian Tuckman is a play on words that she deliberately made up, or whether she really misheard and could not remember Harriet Tubman's name from her study of black history at school.

Therapist: I did ask her who Harrian Tuckman was and she said that it was just the name of a person. You're right. I couldn't tell.

Supervisor: Another example of that is the part about the boss. Again, she picks up bits and pieces and carries them around. Some children ask for clarification and some just walk around in a state of confusion. Cleo is certainly an example of the latter and that is not a comfortable state to be in. Eventually you will be able to address that with her. She also has us in a perpetual state of confusion. Take for instance the opening dialogue. She thinks you kept her waiting but then she announced 4:30 A.M. as the starting time. Does she really confuse 4:15 and 4:30, or is it just her way of dodging away? You did tell her 4:15, right?

Therapist: I think so. Listen to me, I'm becoming unsure. I certainly have told her at several points. I don't remember about today.

Supervisor: That's because she gets you onto a different track before you know it happened. Look for instance at the fantasy about the haircut. It came about so abruptly and it was so startling in content, a boy turning into a girl. You had just offered your help if she needed it. She ignored you and then suddenly came the haircut. And what was she bringing up out of thin air? How confused is she about boys and girls and the difference between them? How confused is she about her own gender? We know that clarity about one's gender is an intrinsic aspect of one's sense of identity. Is this a gray area for Cleo? Is she really confused, does she feel that her female equipment is damaged, or both?

Therapist: I wondered about her confusion. She is almost 7 and she's confused about something that most children ask about at 3 or 4 and earlier. They worry about it, get clarification, and stop talking about it.

Supervisor: That's right. According to our theory, the repression that takes place after the final phase of the oedipal process allows for the move into latency. That would mean that these highly charged issues are repressed and the anxious affect they evoke is quieted until the turmoil of adolescence. So when things go well, children of Cleo's age don't talk about these things in a serious way. They joke and whisper and giggle. It becomes contained in a different way, but still, the anxiety and lingering confusion live on in the unconscious. If that wasn't so we would not have overt castration anxiety as a universal phenomenon. But Cleo's ability to repress is very shaky. We have known that from the beginning. The symptoms that brought her to treatment revealed that to us. We know that her defense mechanisms are not so wonderful; therefore it's difficult for her to forget selectively. Consequently, everything stays in her mind in a fragmented jumble.

In this session she again demonstrates some of her attempts to soothe herself. We see her attempt to deal with anxiety by using an obsessional defense (counting) and avoidance (making a joke). These are typical of children her age. But mainly we see maneuvers that fail her over and over again. For instance, at the beginning of the session, while in the waiting room, she creates singers to listen to, presumably to feel less lonely. However, since her anger is great, the anger combines with and overbalances the wish for union. So we see that she has to fire the singers. In this instance the libido–aggression balance is tilted on the side of aggression, and so her need to connect is foiled. This is what constantly happens to her. Perhaps the paintings coming alive in the middle of the night are another example of a desperate attempt to be less alone, in this instance by animating the inanimate, but again her creation becomes a new threat, rather than the comfort she sought.

This characteristic of hers reminds me a little of some much more disturbed children I have worked with who walk around reciting disconnected jingles composed of bits of television commercials, weather reports, shopping lists and such. . . . You hear them singing or reciting something they heard about Ajax, and Hamburger Helper, and Pepsi, and so on. These children live in primary process states and it seems as if even these jingles offer some tiny measure of something familiar and therefore safer than their chaotic inner state. Of course these jingles are not object related and it's probably their inanimate nature that makes them tolerable (Ekstein 1966). As you know, ordinary children sing about more meaningful stuff and do so for pleasure as well as for reassurance and soothing. Cleo seems to fall somewhere in between. She picks up the bits and pieces and she neither discards nor integrates them. She stores them and uses them in an idiosyncratic manner.

Let me use our theory to conceptualize what I've been saying descriptively. Let us think of two ego functions, the synthetic function (Nunberg 1930) and the integrative function. The synthetic function binds things together, but not necessarily with accuracy. The integrative function is a higher and more developed ego function which not only binds things together but attempts to do so by first gathering together all of the necessary information in order to arrive at a conclusion that makes sense. Do you see where Cleo fits in here?

Therapist: Yes. Our hypothesis is that the anxiety level is very high because the defensive structure is not very good. Because she is so scared she collects bits and pieces of information, but then she can't put the information together in a way that would help her understand the world with clarity. That's where the integrative function fails to operate. She puts things together impulsively and carelessly and scares herself even more. In the process she also excites herself a great deal, which increases her anxiety even more. But her style of not getting the whole picture is probably indicative of her fear of knowing. But she's also hyperalert for all and any information.

Supervisor: She puts things together according to fantasies that she holds onto from her past. Many things in her environment encourage this to take place. It's no wonder that she's so vigilant.

Therapist: Isn't that a peculiar kind of vigilance?

Supervisor: Not really. A lot of very anxious people are that way. They can't help themselves, and of course, it doesn't work to make them less anxious. They just live with their internal state of danger and watch the external world with apprehension and anger and it just goes on and on and the vigilance is useless.

Therapist: Cleo doesn't know what she's watching out for; she just watches.

Supervisor: It seems as if she doesn't know what to watch for because she doesn't distinguish between internal and external danger. But she senses that you are not a dangerous external presence. I think she knows that. I just wish she could come more than once per week.

Therapist: I'm reluctant to bring it up with this very burdened mother. When we talk about Cleo this way she sounds more disturbed than I like to think. I'm sorry that I didn't get a psychological during the evaluation period. Do you think that I should try to get one now?

Supervisor: No. You are at the beginning of treatment. This is not a good time to bring in another professional. It would undermine the treatment alliance and complicate the developing transference (Tyson 1978). We still don't know whether Cleo is a "borderline" (Rosenfeld and Sprince 1963, 1965) child or whether she has neurotic structure and has suffered traumatic regression. We will know more as you move along with her treatment.

Child therapists are often reluctant to see serious disturbance in children and tend to minimize the severity of the problem. That is what parents do as well, but they have an excuse; they are the parents. We have to be very careful not to do that since our treatment technique depends on a reliable diagnostic understanding. What you know about Cleo so far is very adequate to doing a good job with her.

Psychological tests are nice to have but right now they are not essential and could cause complications. Maybe a time will come when we will have to reconsider, but I don't feel that now is the right time. On the other hand, you have mentioned several times that her speech is at times hard to understand. I wondered about that and about her hearing. I thought that you might ask her mother whether she too noticed that at times Cleo's speech was not very clear. I wouldn't mention her hearing at this point. I think that is checked in the schools routinely, but of course, I don't know how well. Have you told Cleo that you're seeing her mother again?

Therapist: Not yet. What do you have in mind? Do you think I should tell her about it in a special way?

Supervisor: No. I was wondering what it would mean to her now that she's been in treatment on a regular basis. You and the sessions have become more valued. Is she going to mind having to share you with her mother? Those were my thoughts. As far as telling her about it, I would remind her of the plan that you outlined at the beginning. Tell her that it's that time that comes along every four weeks when you see her mother, and if there is anything that she wants you to bring up with her mother, to tell you. I'm thinking of you building that "average expectable environment" (Hartmann 1939) with her.

In line with that, I want to address the issue of her thinking you were late for the session. For children and many adults as well, it doesn't matter too much whether you're late or they're early. That period of waiting feels bad regardless of the reality of whose fault it is. Waiting evokes all sorts of fears of abandonment and loss as well as other painful fantasies. When we understand the pain that waiting can cause and keep that in mind, it's easier for us to deal with our patients' anger at us when we are right on time and accused of being late. The experiences that our patients have in the waiting room eventually become interpretable in most cases. Timing is, as always, very important in this regard. The one thing we don't want to do is get into an argument over who was late and who was early, which can easily be done under the guise of giving the patient an exercise in reality testing. Yet with Cleo I would show her on the office clock what 4:15 looks like and what 5:00 looks like.

Therapist: You mean, show her again the beginning and end of her session?

Supervisor: Yes. You could tell her that you thought that she might like to know how things work, and that she might enjoy seeing how the clock is supposed to look at the beginning of her time and how it looks when the time is over.

Therapist: You think I can be that direct and informative with her?

Supervisor: I think you can be that direct about something like that without undermining her need to go into a fantasy mode. You could say something like, *I thought that maybe even though you like to make up stories about when our appointment is and how long it lasts, that you might like to know when it really begins and when it really ends and how many minutes it really lasts, and then we can still make up stories about it. This is the kind of place where you can talk about how things really are, and you can also talk about wishes and movies and that kind of stuff.*

She invented a wonderful way of talking about fantasy by introducing the notion of a movie. She doesn't know the concept of fantasy, and movie is a terrific metaphor. You will find a right moment to say some of these things to her, and of course in your own words. You have to be comfortable in the way you go about doing your work. We are discussing the beginning phase of treatment, and what I'm doing is suggesting ways of building a foundation. With Cleo, I am putting a lot of emphasis on the predictable and reliable aspect of the sessions and of the therapist who provides that safe climate.

Before we end, let me just remind you that Cleo did use her memory of a good experience with you when she got stuck. That she has the capacity to have already formed a good object representation of you, and to have called upon it at a moment of frustration and stress is prognostically hopeful.

7

The Therapist's Focus and Selection of Themes

Therapist: Cleo rang the buzzer 2 minutes after her appointment time. I buzzed her in and as she walked into the waiting area, and before she even saw me, she called out,

Cleo: I know I'm late!

Therapist: *You are a bit late. Let's look at the clock together. It reads 4:17 and your appointment is at 4:15. That means that you are 2 minutes late. We have until 5:00. Sometimes you pretend about our time together and tell stories about it, so I just wanted to make sure that you know for sure when we begin and when we end and how much time that is. From 4:15 to 5:00 is 45 minutes. Today we are going to have 2 minutes less than usual. Two minutes is a short time to miss. We have until 5:00.*

Cleo: I know that. We have 17 hours until 5:00 o'clock.

Therapist: She was sitting stretched out in the swivel chair, swinging back and forth. I asked, *How much is that, 17 hours?*

Cleo: Oh, that's a long long time.

Therapist: *So you feel that we have a long time today?*

Cleo: We have a long, long, long, long, long time together, a long time until I'm dead and we're together.

Therapist: I was so startled by Cleo's comment that I could not think of what to say. Before I recovered my composure Cleo asked,

Cleo: Do you know that I can turn a cartwheel?

Therapist: *No, I didn't know that.*

Cleo: Well, that's my joke 'cause I can't, but my friend can and he's only 6.

Therapist: *Would you like to be able to turn a cartwheel?*

Cleo: It's much too dangerous.

Therapist: *Oh?*

Cleo: If you turn a cartwheel and you fall, you hit your head and break it open. I have another friend who split her head open. It's much too dangerous. I don't do that.

Therapist: *What does that mean, split your head open?*

Cleo: Oh, it's not like you fall on your head and it cracks open and your brains come pouring out. It's not like that. It's like you split some of your skin, like a scrape on your forehead, and you go to the doctor and he looks to see if it has germs. I think it's like that. Let's see if some of these toys can turn cartwheels.

Therapist: *You think you know what happens with a scrape on the head but when you want to be sure that what you think is right, you know that you can talk to me about it and check it out.*

Supervisor: Very nice, very, very nice!

Therapist: She got the toys out and picked out a little figure and sort of arched its back and flipped it on a horse and the horse went riding off with the little figure flipping about on the horse. I said, *My goodness, what is going on here?* Cleo didn't answer me and suddenly flipped the horse over, the rider fell off and fainted, and the horse took a bow. She did some other stuff with the horse that was not clear and therefore hard to describe and then the horse fainted. She said,

Cleo: I know where the school kids are. It's time for soccer so let's play soccer.

Therapist: I was feeling pretty confused at this point and assumed that she must be even more confused. I wondered whether getting the "school kids" was going to be an attempt to organize herself after the wild and disjointed horse and rider play. But she didn't get the "school kids," but switched to the family figures and became somewhat frantic because she couldn't find the figure that she uses for her father. She called softly:

Cleo: Where's my father! Where's my father! Where is he, my father?

Therapist: Finally she found him and said,

Cleo: Oh, there you are.

Therapist: And tossed him away and said,

Cleo: We are going to have soccer now.

Therapist: Then she got the child figures and organized a soccer game with four girls for a girl's team and four boys for a boy's team. She had the girls kick a ball around while the boys did nothing and then said,

Cleo: Where is that teenage cousin doll?

Therapist: She then picked the doll that we had thought of as possibly being the transferential figure, the steady and organizing doll. Cleo called it the cousin doll. She held the cousin doll, pretended that he was talking, and said in a deep voice,

Cleo: I've got to go to the dance, dad. I'm going to get dressed up and wear this bow tie, and where is my car? Oh, here's my car.

Therapist: Cleo got out a toy wheelbarrow, and, pretending that it was the car, had him drive off in it, but then he had car trouble and he said,

Cleo: Oh, my father's going to kill me. Oh, my mother's going to kill me.

Therapist: Then she went back to playing soccer and began telling me about sports cars.

Cleo: Do you know how fast a Lamborghini can go? It can go 300. 300! And a Maserati and a Ferrari. All those cars are junk. They're really junky 'cause they're made of fiberglass. A neighbor at my country house has a Corvette and it really goes fast.

Therapist: Then she went back to playing soccer but changed her mind and said,

Cleo: Are you ready to play basketball with a chicken?

Therapist: *Basketball with a chicken?*

Cleo: No, maybe it's baseball time.

Therapist: And she began to whistle and asked me,

Cleo: Did you know that I can whistle? Listen, I can whistle high, and I can whistle low and I can even whistle loud, but my sister can't whistle at all.

Therapist: *Oh, that's very interesting. You're telling me that your friend who is younger can do cartwheels and your sister who is older can't whistle while you can. So maybe you're noticing something about how different people can do different things and that it doesn't all have to do with how old they are.*

She was not interested in this communication. She returned to her play, which became incomprehensible to me. A pig was running around the soccer field trying to play and then all of the children had to get on a school bus to return to school but it was the wrong school bus.

What I have just described is so much more organized than what was going on that it doesn't really convey the jumble that went on for about 10 minutes. I finally just barged in and said, *All of these things are going on today, and what I notice is how hard it is to know how things get decided and how you get to go from one thing to another. How do you know what's coming next, when you go from soccer with children, to basketball with a chicken, and then to baseball? What's happening is not clear, and when things are not clear, when they're hard to follow and to understand, that is not a comfortable feeling. That's the idea that I got from not understanding what was happening, that when you don't understand, it's hard to feel comfortable.*

By now our time was almost up. I told Cleo that it was the time of the month when I always saw her mother and that I would be seeing her the next day. I asked her whether there was anything that she wanted me to tell her mom. While I was talking, Cleo put a cape on the toy rabbit and said,

Cleo: Tell my mother that I have a super rabbit.

Therapist: *I wonder why that's the kind of thing that you would like me to tell her rather than tell her yourself?*

Cleo: **Oh, I want it to be a surprise.**

Therapist: ***Fine, I'll tell her.***
  Then I told Cleo that it was time to clean up and she looked at the clock. It was the first time that she had ever done that and I was pleased that I had gone through that little demonstration about our time at the beginning of the session. There is also something that I forgot to mention. When the cousin was going to the dance she mentioned that the cousin was even older than Linda Small. When I asked her what it meant to be older than Linda Small, she said that it meant that you die sooner. I know that there are a lot of different ways to explore a communication like that but what occurred to me in light of what we're addressing with her is that I should perhaps discuss how long she and I are going to work together.

Supervisor: I agree that it's a good idea. She also mentioned dying at the beginning of the session. Did you notice that?

Therapist: Well, yes, she said that she wanted "a long long time together, 17 hours together and then we die." So something about how long we are to be together beyond our session did seem to be on her mind. Then I know that I've discussed the length of her sessions with her several times, but never before today did I do it so systematically, with a clock. So now I'm beginning to see that it makes a difference when I really get her attention as I did today. As you have pointed out, she picks up things in a tangential way. That's her way, and maybe I can get through that mode by really mobilizing her attention in regard to matters where I can provide clarity. Of course I can't say things like, "Listen to me, this is important and it will help you." But maybe I can find other more appropriate ways of capturing her interest and curiosity.

Supervisor: You did a lot of good work in this session. You sensed her readiness to take in some of what you offer and she let you know that she registered some of your *organizing function.* She made good use of you. She looked at the clock at the end of the session and saw that something in her life was predictable; her session ends at 5:00. That's so nice for her. Small as it may sound, it's a beginning out of her whirlwind of anxiety! Here is where our treatment technique is so difficult. There are so many directions one could take in this and other sessions.

Let's review some of the themes that have appeared in preceding sessions that we haven't addressed and talk a bit about why we chose to let them go unaddressed at this time.

For instance, take the section about her cousin. That must be the same cousin who gave her a bloody lip, correct? Yes, well, her rivalry with him is powerfully expressed and her ambivalence about him is unmistakable. He is used as a condensation of father–boy, as object of penis envy and oedipal wishes. The father–boy object representation is powerful and can do things that she cannot do, and he's glamorous with his bow tie and fast car. That adds up to a wondrous phallic figure. But the object of her admiration and envy also has that other side of being a failure. He cannot do anything right and things constantly break down for him. She wants him to be the awesome powerful figure, the prince of her dreams, the oedipal hero, but at the same time, and this is the most troubling aspect, the men in her life are also objects to be feared. The father is violent and we don't know that much about how the male cousin is with her. She wants to be more powerful than he is so that she can be safe, and probably so that she can command the mother's love and admiration. She asks you to tell the mother about her rabbit-phallus so that her mother will find her as good and better than the men.

In this session Cleo is expressing some of the oedipal themes that she struggles with, but even more important is her constant struggle to deal with primal scene and the terror and excitement that it evokes in her. We know that she saw and heard her father be physically and verbally abusive with her mother. We know that little children often experience witnessing or hearing the primal scene as violent. Even when it's loving, it is after all an exciting encounter and the excitement seems wild and dangerous to little children. In Cleo's case the presence of violence was unmistakable. The father was out of control in a vicious way and the mother was the victim. These violent episodes became incorporated in the primal scene realm of experience, and she can't forget this so it comes up in fantasy and we see it in her play. While it's essential to note and register all of this so as to understand her inner world, what we do with it is to store it for a time later in her treatment when we might be able to use it with her in a growth-promoting way.

In using our developmental object relations scheme, we are, for the time being, leaving alone defense and fantasy material. Instead, we will concentrate on strengthening the working alliance, promoting the therapist as a reliable object as well as a transferential object. We do this to facilitate her gradual ability to identify with and thus internalize a reliable object, so that the object representation will be one of safety and predictability. We have been making this technical choice with this particular child from the beginning of her treatment and will continue in this vein for as long as we need to do so. Cleo cannot afford to know that she has hostile destructive wishes toward the very people on whom she depends for survival. Her structure is too wobbly to accommodate that kind of insight. It will take a very long time before her observing ego will be up to the task of experiencing that type of interpretation as useful rather than critical and dangerous. As I mentioned earlier, she witnessed actual paternal violence, and that, combined with primal scene experiences or fantasy, has probably given her the sense that little girls and women can be damaged. She revealed a bit of that fear in the section where a person can split his head open doing a cartwheel, or get into trouble from riding a horse or driving a car. Castration and death fears weigh heavily on her in this session. Fear of dying (annihilation) and object loss contribute to extreme castration anxiety. She believes that little girls are boys who have had a haircut, and in this case haircut stands for castration. She lives with all these fears and when she wakes in the middle of the night or thinks the therapist is late, she develops unbearable anxiety because she suffers object loss.

In this session you did not ask about the significance of the rabbit and that was just as well in light of our goal for her. We can assume that he represents phallic strength. Instead you asked why she preferred you to tell her mother about the rabbit rather than telling her herself. At first I was puzzled by your question. It sounded as you made the offer to be the message bearer to her mother and then were in a sense retracting that offer by questioning why she couldn't do it herself. But in thinking it over I believe that you were placing the emphasis and focus on your working alliance. You were highlighting that she wanted you to do something for her that perhaps she could have done perfectly well herself. She didn't need you to do it because she couldn't do it herself, but because she needed to have you do for her, give to her, be connected to her. So I think that was a good intervention. The working alliance is a particular type of selfobject representation. You are her average expectable environment as represented by specific day, specific time, specific place, and some hazy yet perceptible offer of help.

Therapist: It's interesting to consider that some other therapists would have focused more on the rabbit as a phallic symbol. It never occurred to me, since the rabbit appeared so fleetingly and suddenly. Yet the rabbit appeared with a cape, and that certainly conjures up phallic and magical, but to me that has the ring of primary process and it didn't occur to me to make direct use of it.

Supervisor: Well, sure, it's her unconscious. A rabbit with a cape. That's double magic since both cape and rabbit represent magic. A magician in a cape can make rabbits appear and disappear. That's wonderful and terrifying at the same time and the last thing that she needs at this time is a therapist–magician who reads her unconscious. On the other hand, continuing the theme of being more sure of things is good for her, and in that regard I would let her know that you saw her look at the clock. Now that she knows that her time is up at 5:00 o'clock, how does she like being sure of the time? She will probably not answer, or give a fanciful response, but I would ask her anyway. It's so amazing that the treatment is taking such shape despite the short time that Cleo has been coming.

Therapist: It's amazing that these very disorganized sessions where nothing stays still and everything changes from minute to minute can still provide us with such clear technical decisions.

Supervisor: Our developmental base does give us a great deal of clarity in terms of the order of things. You are giving these disorganized sessions a degree of organization by being clear about what needs to be done. At present, her unconscious fantasies, her shaky defensive capabilities, and her anger all need to be left uninterpreted. To address these issues would only increase her already intolerable anxiety and subject her to even greater fear of object loss. Right now, nothing stays the same except for Linda Small from 4:15 to 5:00 on Wednesdays, and Cleo's endless quest for equilibrium.

8

Technical Problems of Child Treatment: The Use of Information Provided by Parents; Food during Sessions

Therapist: Cleo was sitting in the waiting room eating corn chips. She had never brought food to a session before and I wondered what this was going to be like. How was she going to use the bringing of food and the act of eating in her session? What was she going to let me know through this action? I was also a bit uneasy about the notion of Cleo eating during a session, and reassured myself by taking the position that the important thing is to see what happens. Cleo came in, sat down in her usual chair, popped a corn chip into her mouth and said,

Cleo: I had only half a day of school today and so I had my snack at school real early. You'll never guess what we had for snack today. We had brownies. Usually we have muffins like banana muffins but we complained and complained and so finally our teacher got us brownies. Our teacher loves chocolate but she doesn't eat it and so she didn't have any brownies.

Therapist: *What do you think about that?*

Cleo: I think she waits until we go to recess and then has her brownies.

Therapist: *Oh?*

Cleo: I went to my country house this weekend.

Therapist: *Your mother told me that you would be going there. How was that?*

Cleo: Do you know about dinosaurs?

Therapist: She then went into a long discussion about dinosaurs, during which time she finished all of her corn chips and placed the empty bag into the waste basket. She asked me various questions about dinosaurs, for instance, which dinosaur was my favorite. I told her that I really didn't have a favorite dinosaur but I felt a little funny saying that because I really do have a favorite dinosaur.

Supervisor: I'm glad that you didn't tell her.

Therapist: I did ask her if she had a favorite and she said that it was the pterodactyl. Well, the funny thing is that that's my favorite also.

Supervisor: Do you see why it is important *not* to tell her?

Therapist: Because it's a distraction from where things would go without that sort of interference. It would turn the communication into something social and ordinary everyday, rather than the special quality of treatment.

She told me that what she liked about the pterodactyls is that they have big wings and a long peacocky tail, and they really aren't a true dinosaur, but rather a reptile that can fly. She said that what she loves most about the pterodactyl is the way they can swoop up and swoop down. She said that that was really neat. She asked me if I knew the largest dinosaur of all and chattered in this manner, not really waiting for answers to her questions. Then she asked me whether I knew anything about rattlesnakes and this time did wait for an answer. I told her that I did know a bit about snakes, and was there something special she wanted to know?

Cleo: **Does a rattlesnake really have a rattle inside or does it just go s-s-s-s-s?**

Therapist: *Do you know anything about that? Are you asking me because you want to see whether I know, or do you really not know and want me to tell you?*

Cleo: **I really don't know and want you to tell me.**

Therapist: So I went ahead and told her all that I know.

Supervisor: Tell me too. I don't know about rattlesnakes and let's hear what that story sounds like in light of Cleo's treatment.

Therapist: I said, *Every year a rattlesnake sheds its skin, and since it has grown during the year, it exposes the end of its bone, its skeleton. The rattle is the sound that it makes when it shakes that skeleton tail.*

Cleo: **But what makes that rattling sound?**

Therapist: *The bones kind of rub against each other.*

Cleo: **Yeah? They kind of go like this?**

Therapist: And she demonstrated with her hands. I said, *Yes, that's right. You know a lot of things about dinosaurs and reptiles and today you want to learn even more with me.*

Cleo: Well, I've been going to museums and the zoo and learning about this stuff at school and I'm really interested. I want to know a lot. Do you know how dinosaurs came to an end?

Therapist: *I'm not sure. I don't think anyone knows for sure how it happened.*

Cleo: Scientists know for sure.

Therapist: *That sounds important that they know for sure.*
Cleo then talked quickly, explaining how dinosaurs came to an end and she used words like meteorites and man-eaters and how meteorites came and changed the weather on earth so that it was hot and snowing at the same time, and how that formed volcanos and quicksand. She talked rapidly and intensely but she enunciated so poorly that it was difficult for me to follow. When she paused I said,
It sounds like that was a time full of dangers from all over. It sounds like an unpredictable time, a time when you just couldn't know what to expect next.

Cleo: Want to see how the dinosaurs died?

Therapist: She then lay down on the ground. Lying there very still with her arms at her side she said,

Cleo: They got stuck in the quicksand and they just sank down into it until they were buried in it and you couldn't even see them any more. After a long time they turned into sand and they were just gone forever. I bet those toys in there would never turn into sand.

Therapist: *I guess you are ready to see those toys now. You've been talking about some pretty dangerous and unpredictable things happening to those dinosaurs. Maybe it's a safe feeling to know that those toys are there.*
Cleo went over to the toy drawer and had trouble opening it all of the way. She tugged and tugged and it stayed stuck. Then she stuck her hand in and felt around until she found the item

that was causing the drawer to be stuck. Then the drawer opened. I said, *I noticed that when you were having trouble with the drawer, you didn't ask for help.*

Cleo: I didn't need help. I could figure out what to do all by myself.

Therapist: Then Cleo started playing and it was the kind of play we have seen her do so often. It was so jumbled that it's hard to describe, but the general theme was that some children were put on a school bus with a driver who was not a good driver so the children had to take over driving the bus. I noticed that it was extremely stuffy in my office and I got up and opened the window. She didn't seem to notice so I just told her that it was warm and so I had opened the window. She didn't respond. She was playing with her back toward me and she was talking about something, but I couldn't hear her very well, just a word here and there and a tone of voice that sounded as if her play had to do with scary things. I said, *I can't hear what you're saying too well, but it sounds like something scary.*

Cleo: Oh no, that's not scary to me.

Therapist: Then she changed her statement around so that I couldn't tell whether she now was saying that it was scary. She was so unclear that I cannot even remember what she said exactly but I finally said to her, *I have a feeling that right now if I say yes you will say no, and if I say no you will say yes.*

Cleo: Well, maybe it was a tiny bit scary.

Therapist: I couldn't tell whether she was just humoring me or whether she meant it. It was time to clean up and I felt as if the whole session had sort of gotten away from me. Cleo and I were putting the toys away together and she picked up the rabbit and said,

Cleo: **Here's my super rabbit.**

Therapist: *Yes, remember, you were playing with it at the end of our last session and you asked me to tell your mother about it?*

Cleo: **Did you tell her?**

Therapist: *Yes, I did tell her.*
Our session was up by then so we said goodbye and she left. There was so much left hanging in this session. For instance, the whole business of the country house was an issue that was left untouched. I learned about that during my meeting with the mother. It seems that both parents still use the country house even though they're divorced. As you know, the country house belongs to a cousin who never uses it, and while it's the mother's cousin, the father sometimes, although very rarely, uses the house on weekends and during the summer. The mother told me that she was going out of town for several days for a conference and that the father would be taking the children to the country house for the weekend and then home with him for one school day until the mother came home. This was going to be the first time that the children would be in the country house with the father since the divorce. Cleo's mother had told me that Tina was very excited at this prospect but she didn't say anything about Cleo in this regard, except that Cleo has been worried about her hair and who would take care of combing it. It seems that once when Cleo had stayed with her father overnight there was a big blowup because her father would not braid her hair. He wanted to just pull it back into a pony tail and Cleo wanted her braids. Cleo got so upset and so inconsolable that he ultimately braided her hair. By then half the morning was gone and they got to school very late.

Supervisor: How extraordinary. Is there anything unusual about her hair?

Therapist: It's very long and thick and she wears it in two long braids, so it takes some work to do that right.

Supervisor: That doesn't explain the father's peculiar behavior. Is her hair attractive?

Therapist: Yes, very. She has dark hair, neatly cut bangs, big dark eyes, and those imposing braids. She looks very nice.

Supervisor: So this might be something that she's proud of in herself, something highly valued.

Therapist: She has never mentioned anything about her hair or the difficulty in combing it. I've gotten all this from the mother. Cleo did mention having been to the country house at the beginning of the session, and I said that I had heard that from her mother. I feel that was a mistake. I probably should not have mentioned that I already knew this piece of news. I probably cut her off in some way.

Supervisor: But you had a reason for telling her that you knew about it. What was your reason?

Therapist: I felt uncomfortable not letting her know that I knew something that she was telling me. But by telling her that I knew I got a complete change of subject. She asked me whether I like dinosaurs.

Supervisor: Had you not been burdened by having information from the mother before being given the information directly by Cleo, and had you not been taken aback by her very marked change of subject, you might have thought of saying something simple like, *I guess you don't want to talk about your country house.*

Therapist: Had I had my wits about me I would have been very comfortable saying something as simple and direct as that.

Supervisor: It's often hard to think of saying the most obvious thing. Some day we can talk about why that's so hard to do. But look at how well it works. First you just observe what you see: *I guess you don't want to talk about your country house.* Then you can follow it up by saying something like, *You can always tell me if you don't want to talk about something that I bring up. Just because I ask you about something doesn't mean that you have to talk about it.* And then when that occurs again at a later date, you can say, *Here it is again. Here is one of those times that you don't want to talk about something and you forgot that you can just tell me that you don't want to talk about it. One of these days you will remember that, and you will see how much easier things can be for you when you let people know what you want and don't want.*

I think we should talk in a general way about an aspect of child treatment that might be confusing to you and to child therapists in general, and that is the handling of information provided by the parents. However, before we do that, let's talk a bit about what happened just before the topic of the weekend was introduced.

The session began with Cleo bringing her corn chips into her session and eating in front of you for the first time. While eating, she told you that her teacher eats her favorite food in private. I'm sure that you will agree that was a very provocative communication and that whatever was to follow such a loaded comment would be a continuation of the same theme. What followed was her statement about going to her country house. You responded by saying that you already knew about that from her mother. That was most likely a mistake in timing on your part. It might have felt like a real invasion of her privacy. As you described the beginning of the session, I was struck by how comfortable and close Cleo must have felt toward you to eat her snack and chatter about real things in her life. It had the quality of a child finding Mom in the kitchen after school and talking about some aspect of her day. She was eating and being verbally intimate with you. She wasn't like her teacher who eats her favorite food in secret. Then she introduced going to the country for the weekend. We don't know where that might have led because you told her that you knew that from her mother. Your bringing up her mother at that point took away from the sharing quality of the moment by bringing a third party into the room. We don't know what was happening to Cleo transferentially at that moment, but her very abrupt change of topic to something so remote certainly constituted distancing and withdrawal. We know that Cleo has difficulty in dealing with strong feelings in herself, and that such affects as frustration and anger cause her to dart away very sharply. So she ran away to prehistoric times and the fate of dinosaurs, and, as always happens, the escape is no escape at all because the dinosaur becomes a metaphor for disaster, unpredictability, and death.

In the meantime, you, the therapist, are thrown off track and choose to get back on common ground with Cleo by joining her in the discussion on dinosaurs and reptiles. That was an okay solution under the circumstances. It did get you back together and it demonstrated to her that you are someone who is interested in what interests her and that you are also someone who can be asked questions. While it worked out well in this instance, you might have to use a bit of restraint in sharing some of the information you have, for instance how the rattlesnake's rattle works. The sharing of information can take you away from the treatment process into something educational that other people can provide. What you have to provide is unique. What you have to provide is how to help children who feel scared feel safe.

Now let's go back to that difficult topic of what to do with information that we gain from someone other than the patient. We know that a basic rule of adult treatment is to allow the patient to select the material that is going to be explored during the course of a session. We also know that the therapist must refrain from interfering with this basic rule by making premature interpretations, by asking questions that might distract the patient, or by introducing "practical" issues at a time in the session that will interfere with the patient's production of material. Now here is the question: Does that same rule apply to child treatment? If it does, then how does the child therapist make fruitful use of some of the information that is provided in sessions with the parents? Let's stick with the second part of the question regarding the use that the therapist makes of information provided by the parents. This is obviously a very tricky question, since if the therapist does not make overt use of it, in other words lets the child know that she has this information, then the therapist is burdened with knowing something that the child does not know, or knows but does not know that the therapist knows. This is as distracting in child treatment as having information about our adult patients gained from a source other than the patient. Some adult therapists refrain from discussing their patients with colleagues who are treating other family members because they feel that such extra-analytic discussion interferes with the fundamental confidentiality, singularity, purity of the therapeutic relationship. Other therapists feel that so long as they have their patients' permission, confidentiality is not breached by having such discussions. In other words, in the treatment of adults, therapists have differing philosophies that determine the use of extra-analytical contact. In treating older children, say children over the age of 10, the contact with the parents can be adjusted to fit the situation and ranges from frequent to minimal. But in working with little kids like Cleo, it's hard to imagine having no contact with the parents, and therefore time and time again you will be faced with how much to share of what the parent tells you about the home and school background of Cleo's life. Here is where a child therapist has to use her judgment, but that judgment has to be grounded in good common sense combined with the theoretical anchoring that gives shape to all of the clinical choices that we make in our work. We have to preserve the purity of the therapeutic relationship, while at the same time sharing with the child information we have gained that the child can manage to hear and make use of to further the treatment process. So here is our criterion for what to tell and what to not tell: would this information be useful in furthering the treatment process? In order to assess the possible usefulness of information we would have to be pretty clear about a young patient's ability to deal with anxiety and frustration, as well as being pretty clear about the state of the working alliance. Obviously, we would not share information that would cause intolerable anxiety. I was once working with a child whose father had been diagnosed as having a slow but irreversible disease that would cause him to be an invalid within a few years. This was not information that a 4-year-old patient would have been able to assimilate and so, of course, it was not shared with the child. That's an extreme example and hopefully not one that most therapists will have to deal with. But take a more commonplace situation. A parent tells you that the family will be moving to another country in a year. The child has not been told and the parents don't want him to know. You have to respect the wishes of the parents, but you notice in the child's play that he knows that something is going to happen and he is anxious about it and doesn't know how to deal with this mystery. We know that children do not thrive in an atmosphere of secrets and we also know that even the kindest parents can be discreet on the one hand and then talk on the phone to a friend and be careless about preserving the very secrecy they are promoting. You, the therapist, are in a position to work with the parents in conveying to them that their child is apprehensive about some unpredictable unknown, and helping the parents explore their approach to the problem with the purpose of finding a better solution.

At the other extreme, we are often faced with children whose parents tell them too much, and by too much I simply mean that they are given information that is beyond their comprehension and that can be quite disturbing. Parental overstimulation of children is a big subject that we can discuss some other time. However, it does have some bearing on our topic since a child therapist can succumb to his or her discomfort at holding information that the child does not know, and tell the child in order to become unburdened, rather than considering the child's ability to deal with such information.

In summary, the sharing of extra-analytic information with a child patient is guided by the same principles that direct any and all clinical decisions: diagnostic considerations, the state and stage of the treatment process, careful self-examination on the part of the therapist for countertransferential factors regarding the child and the parents, and, as I said before, the simple question as to whether the sharing of this information is likely to help the treatment. We have been talking about some aspects of working with children that present complications that are not encountered in working with adults.

Now let's get back to where we left off. When Cleo told you about her forthcoming weekend with her father, you felt uncomfortable about having learned of this from her mom, and felt a pressure to let her know that you were aware of this plan. Do you know what it was that made you uncomfortable?

Therapist: On the one hand I felt the pressure of the mother's visit and having been told about such a big event in Cleo's life, and I felt that I had to let her know that I knew, but I was also worried about some element of trust between Cleo and me. It felt not right to know this about her from her mother so I confessed, so to speak, that I already knew her news about the weekend in the country. I just don't know how she can trust the concept of confidentiality if I know things about her that she hasn't told me. And if she doesn't believe that the confidentiality is real, then how can she trust me?

Supervisor: If you learn things from her mother you wonder how she can really believe that you are *her* special person, and that the allegiance is to her, and not to any one else in the family?

Therapist: Yes. I can't tell what it's like for Cleo to know that I talk to her mother. She doesn't seen to mind. But how can she understand confidentiality if I share things the mother tells me?

Supervisor: This has to be discussed and explored with Cleo. You can ask her how she understands it, but very likely she will change the subject. But you can also go over it with her. You can say something like, *I see your mom every month because she might have things to tell me that she thinks are important and that might help me understand what your life is like when we are not together here in this office. She might tell me things that she thinks are important that you might not think are important, or that you might just not think of telling me, or don't even want to tell me. Your mom might want to tell me some of these things because she thinks they might help our work together.* You could say that to her, and if you thought she needed to hear more, you could add the following, *When your mom tells me about your life outside of this office, she knows that I am going to tell you about it. She knows that I am your special person and that what you and I talk about is private. Therapy rules are different for your mom. What she and I talk about is not private unless she asks me to keep something private. The rules with you are that everything is private unless you ask me to tell your mom something, like for instance, about the super rabbit. That's the way the rules work here. And just because I bring up something that your mom told me, you don't have to talk about it if you don't want to. You are the boss of what you talk about here.*
You can say something like that to her, and you might need to say it more than once. On the other hand, there is also the issue of feeling pressure to take something up with her just because the mother brought it up with you. I think that must have been a part of what made you interrupt the flow of the

session by telling her that you already knew about the week-end. There was nothing to be gained by telling her and some-thing to be lost, but not a serious mistake, just an ordinary blunder. This is where you have to use your clinical judgment and allow the sharing of information to have an organic quality, rather than being something outside of treatment. We are talking about very complicated issues here.

Did you feel pressure from the mother because she was worried about the weekend?

Therapist: No. She was surprisingly comfortable about it. She fo-cused more on what a nice place the country house is than on the fact that they would be alone with the father for several days. Her concern was around Cleo's hair and her solution was to have bought her an easy-to-handle hairbrush and to teach her how to braid her own hair, and to show Cleo's sister how to help her do that so that the father would not have to get involved.

Supervisor: There was a session recently where Cleo pretended to cut a doll's hair and the boy turned into a girl. Having this information about Cleo's father acting so inept about his daughter's long hair sheds some light on what a hot subject this is. However, this is not information you can use with Cleo right now, but it certainly is an important fact to keep at the back of your mind to use when appropriate.

Therapist: Oh, I had forgotten that haircutting incident. That's interesting. The mother also mentioned concern that the baby-sitter was not sufficiently attentive to Cleo. She finds that disturbing, yet the sitter is reliable and honest and she is reluctant to change sitters. She is concerned that Cleo might feel lonely with such an uncommunicative sitter. I asked the mother whether Cleo had play dates and she doesn't, but the mother thought that was a good idea.

Supervisor: With all due respect for your idea, it isn't exactly an original idea. How come the mother hasn't thought of it herself?

Therapist: It's hard for working mothers to arrange these dates since it means that the visiting child has to be picked up and taken home in the late afternoon. A lot of parents find that hard to do on the way home from work.

Supervisor: So what if it's a little hard? Besides, the baby-sitter can be asked to do that. It's better for Cleo not to spend her after-school time in the company of a baby-sitter who acts as if neither one of them is alive. But let's get back to something you raised at the beginning of the session regarding food during a therapy session. You had some question about that.

Therapist: My dilemma had to do with the place of food in treatment. Was Cleo's snack a snack or was it meeting some other need? Should I have allowed a snack during her session?

Supervisor: What was your inclination?

Therapist: My inclination was to let her eat it. Kids are often hungry after school and need their snack, and usually she has hers before her session. This day was different and I didn't think of exploring this with her. I was too caught up in the dilemma.

Supervisor: You probably could not have explored this with her in the way that you might explore a similar occurrence with an adult patient in therapy who might, for instance, bring coffee to a session. But you might acknowledge that something new is happening and say something like, *I see that you brought a snack. Do you want to eat your snack during therapy time?*
You can find out something about the snack as communication, or you can at least respond to the snack as if it is a communication. Remember, most likely it is not a conscious communication, so if you do as little as just let her know that you are responding to her wanting to have a snack with you, you are doing a lot more than it appears. You are mobilizing her observing ego to notice something that maybe was without

shape or form. You were probably bothered by the fact that this silently slipped into the session. If you just say the little bit I suggested, then if she brings a snack again, you can follow up and say something like, *Oh, I see that today is another one of those days that you feel like having a snack with me. Is there something that you like about doing that? Does it feel nice to be able to eat here?*

I am demonstrating a form of exploration. I know that what I'm suggesting sounds so simple and obvious that to describe it as a form of exploration sounds a bit pompous. Yet, if you think about it, it's a very gradual and delicate attempt to engage her observing ego to recognize desires and to give then acceptable expression.

Therapist: I can see that, and in fact she was struggling with something about the snack. Actually, she said quite a bit about the snack. More than she usually has to say about anything so reality based. She talked about the teacher loving chocolate but not eating the brownie.

Supervisor: That the teacher loves chocolate but doesn't eat it in public but waits until she is alone is something we ought to make note of for the future, for it certainly sounds like a metaphor for something else. A lot of very provocative themes slipped into this session. The part about the dying of the dinosaurs in quicksand was really striking. They were doomed and there was nothing anyone could do for them. She also let you know how much she knows about these things and tested out how much you know. It's a very rich session that leaves us in the dark quite a lot however, which means that *she* probably is in the dark quite a lot. It would be so good to see her more often. What do you think?

Therapist: I agree that it would be good to have a second appointment, but I hesitate to mention it to the mother just yet because she feels so burdened by everything and this would put an additional strain on her.

Supervisor: Well, you sound very reluctant about a second appointment. Keep it in mind anyway. The mother might be willing if
she thought that it would pay off in terms of her daughter's
well-being. Remember that you are in a better position to judge
the impact of frequency of sessions than the parents of the
children you treat or, for that matter, of your adult patients as
well. Look inside yourself and think of countertransference as
a factor in your reluctance. The mother can always say "no" to
such a recommendation. At the same time that I say all of this to
you, I also bow to your judgment. You know the mother
directly and I know her only through you. You are the front
player and I am the observer who makes order and disorder by
challenging and questioning what you do and why.

Before we stop, I would like to say a little more about food
and child treatment. It's an issue that comes up in every child
technique seminar and causes pretty heated discussions. There
is a great deal of disagreement about it among child therapists.
Many child therapists provide food for their young patients and
some even consider feeding their child patient to be an important part of their work. I have heard this custom explained as
the repair of early oral deprivation. I have an adult patient who
remembers that as a child she went to see a therapist every
Friday for lunch. On Fridays her school day ended at noon and
her nurse picked her up and they went straight to the therapist's office where my patient and her therapist had lamb
chops, string beans, and baked potatoes. She remembers the
two years of therapy as a pleasant time but all that she
remembers of the experience is the food. She does not remember the therapist as anything other than the provider of
lamb chops. I am presenting this as one end of the spectrum. At
the other extreme end is the attitude that holds that the
presence of food, no matter whether provided by the therapist
or by the child, would be breaking the abstinence rule (Freud
1915) which, as you know, is one of the fundamental principles
of our work. Because of this view, some child therapists would
not have allowed Cleo to bring her chips into the session and

would have regarded and interpreted this action on her part as "acting in," in other words expressing an unconscious wish through action rather than working on bringing the unconscious wish into consciousness and expressing it verbally.

Now that I have placed the extreme positions on the table, let us look to our theory for a position that fits the total picture. Let's see whether we can conceptualize something that covers the greatest range of considerations, from the most practical to the most theoretically sophisticated.

To begin with, let's take food as grist for the mill in the same way that we would view any other communication from the patient whether it be tears, silence, a runny nose, a story about an event, a request for some particular therapy material, a dream, refusal to leave at the end of a session and so on. If we look at food that way, we would no sooner provide our young patients with a cookie than we would suggest what they should talk about, or what mood they were required to experience. To go a bit further in viewing food as no different from any other issue, if a young child wanted to bring a favorite toy to a session we would permit this, but we would also explore the wish that this gesture represented. Now to turn a bit more practical, what if your child patient brings an eclair stuffed with whipped cream and it's going to get all over your nice upholstered chair? That too is a communication, but so is spilling ink on the rug or kicking the therapist, and we have a rule about that and that rule is that the office has to be a safe place where neither the people nor the furniture are hurt or damaged in any way.

In summary, food may be handled as any other issue is handled in child treatment. It needs to be understood as a form of communication and the meaning of the communication needs to be gradually and delicately put into words. I agree that it can be viewed as an "acting in," but that does not mean that it should be banished from the room. It should, on the contrary, be accepted and used to further the treatment. It should not become a simply practical issue any more than it should become a completely theoretical issue.

We are protected from mishandling this and similar situations that arise in the course of treatment by remembering some of our basic rules. The "abstinence rule" (Freud 1915) protects us from overgratifying our patients. Freud's concept of listening with "evenly suspended attention" (1912b) protects us from being overly rigid and cerebral in the way we process information. Our awareness of countertransference heightens our attunement to our patients and hopefully allows us to treat them with empathy and courtesy. These are the forces that so heavily contribute to a working alliance and provide the patient, child or adult, with a safe and therefore growth-promoting climate.

9

Ego Supplies and the Capacity to Extract

Therapist: When Cleo rang the bell and I buzzed her in it was 8
minutes before her appointment time, and I was with a patient.
Cleo is generally my first afternoon patient and has only once
before seen someone leave my office. This time I registered this
fact as a potentially important event.

When I got to the waiting room I was again struck by the
coldness and disconnection between Cleo and Maria, the baby-
sitter. It's remarkable that no warming up has taken place in the
2 months that Maria has been with Cleo. The emptiness between them is painful to witness.

Cleo had been waiting for a full 10 minutes by the time I
came to greet her. She had been early and I was 2 minutes late.
When I greeted her she said,

Cleo: **Hello and goodbye.**

Therapist: She said this and stayed in her chair and made no sign of
moving. The baby-sitter didn't look up from her stare into

empty space and I said, *Hum,* for lack of anything better to say. Then I noticed that Cleo was sitting there holding a bag of chips on her lap and I said, *I see that you brought your snack again today.*

She nodded. I asked, *Would you like to bring your snack into the office like last time?* She jumped up and said,

Cleo: Yes, I want to bring it in and eat it because I'm starving.

Therapist: I was standing in the doorway to my office waiting for her to come in as I always do. She came right up to me and then slowed down to barely moving. She stayed very close to me but didn't pass by me and enter the office as I expected. I didn't understand what she was doing. It felt very odd, so I said, *What is happening here right now?*

Cleo: I'm in a real hurry.

Therapist: *You're in a real hurry but you're moving very slowly. What could that mean? Could hurry mean something different to you than to me?*

Cleo: No. This is just an experiment. I'm moving all the time but I'm taking tiny steps.

Therapist: *Oh? What is the experiment about?*

Cleo: To see how fast I can get there.

Therapist: *Oh my! First you tell me "hello and goodbye" and then you tell me that you want to get here fast and then you move slowly. What could be going on today? The only thing that I know that's going on is that I was two minutes late coming to get you. It was 4:17 and not 4:15 when I came to get you. See the clock. It was 4:17 when I went to the waiting room for you and now it is already 4:19 because we're spending another two minutes just getting into the office.*

She looked at the clock and said,

Cleo: 4:15 plus 2 is 4:17 and 4:17 plus 2 is 4:19.

Therapist: She sat down in her chair and began to eat her snack with a kind of urgency that was different from the eating quality of last week. She was pushing the chips into her mouth and licking the salt off her fingers and doing this with a quality of intensity that made me uncomfortable. She was breaking the chips into little pieces as if to make them last a long time. And while she was doing this she was staring at me head on. Something about her seemed very different, so I did what I so often don't think of doing. I said the obvious. I said, *You seem to be in a different than usual mood today. Is today a different kind of a day for you?*

Cleo: Yes. Today I had no school and no violin lesson. But today I have Linda Small.

Therapist: *That's right. You have me every Wednesday. Every single Wednesday.*

Cleo: What would happen if you got sick?

Therapist: *If I ever got sick I would call you up and tell you that I was sick and that I would not be able to see you that day.*

Cleo: And what about vacations Linda Small? Don't you ever go on vacations?

Therapist: *Yes. Those are the two times that I will miss our Wednesday. If I am sick or on vacation. I will be on vacation this summer and I already know what days I will be away and I'll tell you what they are.*

Cleo: Tell me now because I'm afraid that you aren't going to see me on my birthday. My birthday is in August.

Therapist: *Oh dear, you're right. I'm going to be on vacation for a week in August and it's the week that your birthday falls on. Your birthday is August 15th, right?*

Cleo: Yes. And I'm going to be in my country house then.

Therapist: She was quiet for a minute and I was very unclear about where to take this. It sounded as if she was expressing a very overt wish that I be part of her birthday and I was worried about acknowledging that and risking getting too close to her, so I just waited while she was quiet and then she said,

Cleo: I have to concentrate on my not sleeping. Last night I didn't go to sleep until 11 o'clock, or maybe it was 12 o'clock, or maybe 1:00.

Therapist: *That's a very long time for a child your age to be awake. What happened that you were up so late?*

Cleo: You know something? Sometimes my sister sits up with me. Most of the time my mother does but sometimes if she can't my sister does. Yesterday my mother wanted to watch something on T.V. and she asked Tina to stay with me. Then my father called and my mother had to talk on the phone to him. Tina hurt my feelings. She yelled at me and told me that nobody likes to sit with me and that I'm a pain in the neck. It hurt my feelings very badly.

Therapist: *I can see that your feelings would be hurt by something like that. What did you do?*

Cleo: I went and told my mother and she said that she had to talk to Tina in private, but I heard what they said. She told her that I was very scared and that she had to sit with me when mom couldn't do it because it wasn't good for me to be so scared and she said that Tina should tell me that she was sorry that she had hurt my feelings. Tina came in and said that she was sorry, and my mother came in and asked me if I really believed that she didn't like to sit in her cozy chair and read her book until I fell asleep.

Supervisor: In these situations her mother consistently gives to her with kindness and generosity.

Therapist: Yes. Her mother had told me that she arranged a small light right over her reading chair so that it doesn't bother Cleo, but makes for a very peaceful, quiet place for her to sit and read and, at the same time, know that she's helping her daughter.
Then Cleo went on:

Cleo: But I'm still mad at Tina even though she said she was sorry 'cause she asked me why I went to therapy, and she made signs with her hand that mean that somebody is crazy. She watches T.V. in my room all of the time even if I ask her to leave and that's not fair. But she isn't allowed to come to my sleeping corner and I cleaned it up and boy does it look nice. It's great! I made a sign that says "kids under 10 only!" and I spelled it myself. I did it because Tina made a sign on her door that said "Cleo not allowed in here." I'll fix her, I will!

Therapist: She talked a little more about keeping Tina out of her sleeping corner and then she said,

Cleo: Let's see if those toys in there have their sleeping corner.

Therapist: I was afraid that she was going to get away from me at that point. I wasn't sure whether she was continuing her territorial theme, which was now going to be transferred to the toys, or whether she was changing the subject. So I barged in and asked, *I wonder whether Tina hurting your feelings and your getting really angry with her made it hard for you to fall asleep? Do you think that's possible?*

Cleo: Yes. Well, maybe.

Therapist: She then got very busy with her toys and it turned into her usual kind of play. A test was being given to all the children. They had to get on a bus and stand on their heads. Then the bus was going around very fast to see if the children flew out of the window. If they did, they had to land on their heads, not on their bodies. It was an extreme of the kind of disaster-oriented drama that Cleo so often plays out at some point in her sessions. The adults were introduced as the protectors of the children and then were turned around to do just the opposite. First they would call the children in kind voices and promise to take good care of them. Then they would manipulate them into fighting with each other and with the adults. The adults would call the children over and say, "Come here, let me help you," and then the adults would hit them and yell at them, or at other times give prizes for fighting. I didn't really know what to do with all of this so I made comments like, *Gee, this man says, "don't fight" and then he gives prizes for fighting. That's very confusing.* Or I would say, *What's going on here? It's hard to know what's going to happen next. People who promise to help you turn around and hurt you.*

Cleo didn't respond verbally to my comments, but went on playing. She had a child call 911 and say that she needed help for an emergency, but the operator hung up on her. I thought about our many discussions about Cleo and that we always return to the observation that when anxiety overwhelms her she loses her objects. I tried to feel this out by asking, *Does that mean that the people at 911 don't listen to kids?*

Cleo: No!

Therapist: *There must be someone who listens to a child.*

Cleo: Oh, there is. There was someone there.

Therapist: And then she just left that hanging and went on to something else. I noticed as I had last week that the office was very stuffy and that I was getting sleepy. I have to take the sleepiness as a signal that Cleo and I are getting very far apart. I think that it's the feeling of no connection that makes me sleepy. I was yawning.

Supervisor: She left you. She was so much with you during the early part of the session. It was by far the most personal discussion she ever had with you, and it lasted a long time. Do you agree?

Therapist: Oh yes. She did by far the most talking directly to me ever. So what happened?

Supervisor: Well, let's try to understand what happened. Let's go to the beginning of the session, back to the waiting room. You notice the distance between Cleo and the baby-sitter. We've established that the sitter is a very depressed and uncommunicative person, yet some children would try to engage her and as far as you can tell Cleo doesn't even try. Isn't that right? When she leaves the waiting room for your office she doesn't say anything to Maria like, "See you later," nor does she say "Hi" when she returns to the waiting room. Does she ever complain to you about her?

Therapist: Well, no. When her mother used to bring her, she would put shows on for her in the waiting room, and she did that a bit with Maria the first couple of times that Maria brought her. But she stopped. It's hard to know what part to play in Cleo's shows, so I can imagine that this sitter, who is so uncommunicative to begin with, didn't have any idea of how to respond. The shows make me sleepy and I am completely invested in paying attention. But to answer your question, no, Cleo made no ordinary attempt to engage the sitter. Some children would be more demanding and more insistent. Cleo is all too ready to give up and move away into a withdrawn position.

Supervisor: Cleo has a waiflike quality. It makes me think of a useful concept introduced by Margaret Mahler (1968), which she named "the capacity to extract." It addresses a capacity that some children have to get emotional nourishment from the people around them, even from people who are not particularly attuned to them or even interested in forming a connection. These children just have a talent for engaging people and of making use of whatever spark of contact they can ignite, however much or little that may be. At the other extreme are those children who lack that capacity to engage, make use of, and feel nourished by even very loving and attuned adults. Consequently they feel poor all of the time. This is a useful concept to consider in our work. It certainly plays an important role in the establishment of a working alliance.

So let us think a bit about Cleo in light of this construct. Clearly, she has given up on the sitter. Granted, Maria is an extreme of lack of interest and unavailability. Yet we agree that some other child, who maybe is more talented in getting his or her needs met, would have tried harder and maybe might have made a little inroad. Perhaps Maria is not a good enough example. But what about you? In this session she told you how much she values you. Then she told you the most that she has ever told you about home and her mother and sister. Her mother sounded very kind and generous in the situation she described. Her "pain in the neck sister" was told off, and you were completely attentive. But she left you behind anyway.

I'm going to be speculative here and suggest that Cleo might be the kind of child who doesn't get the most out of what is offered to her. I could be quite wrong here. She might feel so abandoned by her caretakers and perhaps so worried that she will be dismissed and told that she's a "pain in the neck" that she's given up trying. That would be different from a lack of ability. That would be a defense against the anger caused by frustration and disappointment, and the sense of badness she feels when angry.

But let's go back to the first speculation, that she lacks the ability to get the most out of what is available. If that's the case, her therapist will have to do the lion's share of offering emotional supplies. Let's be very clear about this point, for it's an area of great confusion in our field. When I talk of supplies, I'm talking of ego supplies. I am not talking of gratifying id needs by giving praise, presents, or food. For instance, when you ask her whether she thinks that there might be a connection between her anger at her sister and her difficulty in falling asleep, that falls within the area of ego supplies. You are alerting her to note that her affect, anger in this case, can be the cause of not sleeping. Making connections is not something she does very well, nor does she even seem to try to make connections in situations in which many children her age would strain to understand cause and effect in an effort to comprehend how things work in their world. One of the remarkable things about her play is that so often the sequence of events appears so arbitrary and therefore hard to follow. This is one of the reasons you get so sleepy. You find it hard to stay connected to her when she appears to be floating so precariously in a wild ocean full of debris. So when you make the connection between anger and sleeplessness, that's a form of ego supplies. You are aiming at mobilizing her observing ego to attend, to perceive, to think and reason and synthesize and integrate. She has all these capacities, but sometimes she loses them very easily, while at other times she can make use of her strengths.

Just consider what Cleo did at the beginning of the session. She was mad at you because you were with another patient and kept her waiting, and she let you know that she was angry by saying **Hello and goodbye**, and by moving without moving. Then she found a way to tone down her anger by adding up the minutes past the customary starting time of her session. Perhaps because you were physically present she was able to express her anger at you without fear of severing the connection between you, and was able to use such high level defenses as displacement and intellectualization to deal with her negative affect. I'm making a bit of a leap here when I mention displacement. I'm thinking of her expressing anger at her sister rather than at her mother in the story she told you. It was her mother who left her and who kept her waiting, and I'm making a connection between you who kept her waiting and her bedtime mother.

Let me continue this discussion, keeping in mind the concept of "capacity to extract" as a possible area of weakness in Cleo, and the technical consequences of this speculation. Let me repeat, because it is so important, that when the capacity to extract is weak, the therapist has to be the major provider of ego supplies, at least until the child has been sparked to use her own resources more consistently.

I am not saying anything radical here, but I am placing great emphasis on our developmental framework. I am paying close attention to the fact that Cleo at 6½ is not 6½ all the time. When she regresses, the regressive floor is a great distance from her chronological age, much more so than the normal regressive fluctuations of latency age children. So when she loses equilibrium and begins to tumble back into chaos, the therapist has to offer ego rescue. For instance, when she calls 911 and they don't respond, you could inject yourself and say, *I notice that you didn't ask me to pick up. Does that mean that you don't want me to pick up?* That is not making an offer. An offer would not elicit intentionality, which, as you know, is an ego function. An offer would not be an ego rescue because it would not tap her decision-making capabilities. An offer misses the point and could be an intrusion. After all, she wants you to know that in her world, 911 does not always help. In fact, she might be experiencing something like that at that moment, in the office with you. The interpretation I'm proposing makes a demand on her, while the intervention that you made, which was to ask whether 911 doesn't help children, described what she had already portrayed. It doesn't require her to take it any further. It allowed the disconnecting from you to prevail, and that is one of the factors contributing to your sleepiness.

Let me try to organize this more clearly. At this point in her life, for reasons that are still unclear to us, Cleo is not talented in getting her needs met. Possibly her capacity to extract from the environment, which is an ego function, is an area of weakness. In this session we saw that when her level of frustration is not too heavily taxed, as in the beginning of the session, she can, in her own oblique style, allow some of her affects expression. With mounting difficulty, for instance when faced with a depressed and withdrawn baby-sitter, she gives up and doesn't even complain. As her therapist, you have to serve as an auxiliary ego for her and draw on her strengths when she cannot summon them within herself.

For example, it is essential that you take up the situation with the baby-sitter. The situation with the sitter is extreme. For you to ignore it might be viewed as an acceptance. I know that that isn't so and that you are concerned about the bleakness of that situation, but Cleo doesn't know that. Her lack of complaint about Maria is cause for concern. Since Cleo isn't going to bring up something that has become invisible to her, you must do it. We can address emptiness, silence, and omissions of all sorts without leading the patient. You could say something like, *You know, when I come into the waiting room and see you and Maria sitting there so quiet and far apart, if I didn't know that you were together, I would think that you didn't know each other. What is it like for you to be with someone who doesn't talk to you?*

You can wait and see where something like that takes you. Talking of the waiting room, did she ask about the person who walked through? You made a mental note to yourself at the start of the session that this was important and then I don't believe that you brought it up with Cleo.

Therapist: No. She didn't ask and I didn't say anything. I noted either her lack of curiosity or curiosity that remained unspoken. I felt that it set a tone for the session. But despite my resolve not to let it slip away, I was at a loss as to how to bring it up. After our discussion today, I realize that I could simply mention that she hadn't said anything about someone leaving my office. I was very much affected by her silent sitting with the sitter, and the lack of questioning about the other patient, and then the urgent eating.

Supervisor: What was that like? The eating made a strong impression on you.

Therapist: The quality of desperation was so evident. She said that she was hungry, really hungry.

Supervisor: If we think of that kind of hunger and combine it with what we've been saying about her use of the object, or more accurately, her meager ability to extract emotional supplies from the object, we can understand the profoundness of her hunger. She is a very lonely child.

Therapist: I remember that in my first consultation interview with Cleo she told me that she was hungry all of the time. But she seemed so lively and playful that I didn't get the flavor of this hunger, which has been emerging over time. Now the bravado is less apparent and her play is so chaotic that I no longer see her as so lively and full of ideas. What I see now, and probably that is part of what makes me sleepy, is the sadness, the depression, and the desultory quality of her play.

Supervisor: What you're beginning to see is what lies beneath Cleo's desperate attempts to distract herself: her sense of isolation, her tenuous and unreliable object connections, and her inability to soothe herself. What probably makes you sleepy is the unbearable sadness and pathos of her psychic state, her state of being. What makes it so particularly difficult is that you have to temper a natural wish to rescue and nurture. Instead you have to approach with caution, and offer help that will strengthen her from within. That will allow *her* ego to become a better regulator of her wishes and affects.

10

Diagnostic Observations Concerning Ego and Superego Development

---

Therapist: Cleo didn't have school this week. It was spring vacation. I bumped into her on the street at the entrance to my office building. She was with her baby-sitter, but I noticed that her father was sitting in his car at the curb and watching us. I said: *Hello Cleo.*

Cleo: You're late!

Therapist: *Oh? Actually we're both early. We're 10 minutes early.*

Cleo: My father brought me here today.

Therapist: *I thought I recognized him sitting in that blue car.*

Cleo: It's so hot today that when I get home I'm going to put my shorts on.

Therapist: When we got into the waiting room I said, *I have to get ready for you, and that will take me a few minutes, but I might be able to start a little early. See you soon.*
   I returned to the waiting room to get her 5 minutes before our time, and instead of following me as she usually does, she walked into the bathroom. The bathroom is next to my office. She just walked in through the bathroom doorway and stopped and said,

Cleo: Wow! What did you do to your office? How come you have a sink and a toilet and a shower?

Therapist: She was pretending that the bathroom was my office, and before I had time to say anything she said,

Cleo: Oops. I made a mistake.

Therapist: And she turned around and walked into my office and I said, *Gee, did you think that was my office?*

Cleo: I just made a mistake.

Therapist: There was no humor in her manner and I really couldn't tell whether she had made a mistake or whether this was a joke. It was one of those many times that I didn't think of saying something simple and obvious, like that I couldn't tell whether she was joking or not. There was something odd about the whole little episode.

Supervisor: Really? To me, listening to the way you tell it, it sounds as if it was a joke. Yet that wasn't clear to you, so the affect that one would expect to accompany a joke was probably not there.

Therapist: That must be what threw me off. I was confused as I so often am with Cleo. Then Cleo came in and sat down and said,

Cleo: I have to tell you about something with my mother and her teachers. I was at my mother's school, and when I went to her bathroom, there were filing cabinets in the shower. Did you ever hear of filing cabinets in a shower?

Therapist: Her mother's school is housed in an old brownstone building. I guess the faculty bathroom doubles as a storage area for files. Cleo calls the people that her mother works with "my mother's teachers." Before I could respond to her question, she went on.

Cleo: I thought that was really weird. I asked my mother about it. I asked her what happens when you turn the shower on. She said something but I don't remember what she said.

Therapist: *So you still have your question unanswered. Do you still think that it's something weird?*

Cleo: Yeah.

Therapist: *And you walked into the bathroom here. Did you want to see whether I had files in the shower? Did you think it was like your mother's bathroom at her school?*

Cleo: My best friend Eddy isn't my best friend anymore.

Supervisor: She just switched subjects that abruptly?

Therapist: Yes. She was swiveling around in her chair at this point and just made the comment about her friend. I said, *Oh?*

Cleo: He always tries to get me into fights with the other kids. He especially tries to get me into fights with this girl I like, Jodi, and with her friends.

Therapist: *How can someone else get you into a fight?*

Cleo: He tells me that I'm scared to fight.

Therapist: *That must really bother you, to be told that you're scared to fight.*

Cleo: Well, sure. I hate that. He calls me scaredy cat! Scared to fight! I don't want him to say that to me.

Therapist: *What do you think about children feeling scared?*

Cleo: Well, kids can be scared sometimes.

Therapist: *But it sounds important to you to show Eddy that you're not scared.*

Cleo: I'm just not going to be his friend anymore. I'm just not going to let him get me into trouble.

Therapist: And then, just as abruptly as before, Cleo dropped this subject. Now she seemed to be pretending to be on a television show. She was not talking in her normal voice and I couldn't hear what she was saying so I asked her, *Are you doing an imitation of somebody on a television show?* She nodded, and I went on, *You know, I'm not clear about what you were doing. Could you tell me what show you're doing so that I can understand what you're telling me?*

Cleo: I want my new best friend to be Mike. He's a good friend. He says goodbye to me when I get off the school bus.

Therapist: *That sounds important to you.*

Cleo: Yes, and when he says "no" to me, he says it in a nice voice. And you know what? He liked the lucky Easter egg that I gave him.

Therapist: I didn't know what she was referring to and asked her to explain. She told me that there had been a school outing before her Easter vacation and there had been an egg hunt. The eggs were little plastic eggs with toys inside them, and Mike liked some of the toys inside the egg that she found, so she gave it to him and he liked that and took the gift and thanked her. It seemed hard for her to explain all this to me. I could tell that it was a big effort. When she finished I said, *It sounds as if Mike is a very reliable kind of friend. He notices you, he says goodbye to you and knows how to say "no" without sounding mean, and he knows what he likes and can say so. And he can appreciate your giving him something he liked and wanted. I think that all these things about him are important to you.* Cleo nodded in response to my little summary speech and went over to the toys and began her customary disaster-oriented play.

I was mindful of our discussion last week about Cleo having difficulty in engaging the people around her. I thought Cleo might feel spent after her exchange with me and she was now going to move away from me and enter her solitary world. I found it very difficult, as usual, to stay with her, to move in, to join her on any level. A couple of times she asked a question of a character in her play, so I finally said, *I notice that you don't ask me.* I got no response by asking that way so the next time she asked a character a question I said, *Are you asking me?*

Cleo: No.

Therapist: *I notice that you ask the people in your play questions, but you don't ask me.*

Cleo: I notice that too.

Therapist: *Well, what about that? Do you wish you could find a way to include me? Would you know how to do that?*

Cleo: I've been thinking about that and I don't know.

Therapist: I didn't know what to do with that. There was such confusion in my mind. I couldn't tell whether she was just joining what I was saying without meaning it, in a kind of compliant way, or what. At that point in the session I was beginning to feel that debilitating fatigue that I regularly feel when I'm with her. It's a kind of lethargy, an emptiness. It's a difficult feeling to describe. I even began to question our communication. I wondered what the mistake about the bathroom was about. I found the way that she agreed with me to have an echolalialike unreality.

Supervisor: Could her compliance be her way of trying to make contact with you? To stay connected to you?

Therapist: Yes, I wondered about that too. I wondered if the only way she could be with me was by saying "yes" to anything I said.

Supervisor: Okay. Listen to what you just said. You said that in her play and in response to your statements she has difficulty in connecting. She doesn't know how to get you into her play or to engage you, but there's a suggestion that she wants to be able to connect. Therefore, when you volunteer something, she no longer necessarily pushes you away. She latches on to it and imitates you in a kind of lifeless manner that's disquieting, because it's a forced and faked connection. It makes you tense and fails to provide the nourishment she craves.

On this same theme, when she talks about how nice and reliable Mike is and how she wants him to be her new best friend rather than Eddy who challenges her to do dangerous things, do you hear that as transferential? You're shaking your head "no." After all, you represent the kind of reliability that she attributes to Mike. Listen to what he says to her. He says "goodbye" and "no" in a nice way, and appreciates the toys in her egg. I hear in that that he's predictable and values her. She is the egg with nice things inside her.

Cleo is hungry for connection but not adept at getting her needs met. Consequently, her object hunger is rarely satisfied, and the people who want to respond to her and connect with her are often left feeling frustrated.

We've been trying to understand why she feels so scared, so unsafe. She illustrates the nature of her fears in her typical fantasies, for instance the one where little children have to go on the subway alone and face all sorts of dangers without adults to care for them and protect them. She lets us know over and over again that it's hard for her to feel and *stay* connected to objects who are protective. We have also noted that she tolerates that awful distance with her baby-sitter, and if she did make some attempts to engage her at the beginning, she gave up and makes no further attempts to rouse some response out of Maria. Nor do we hear any complaints about the sitter's neglect. She is so unlike some children who would work hard to get a smile, a comment, no matter how grudging, or who would rebel, object, complain, make a fuss when thwarted. In Cleo we see passive surrender and dismal resignation. That is not an engaging characteristic, so while you and I often find her appealing and fascinating, we have to wonder how the world sees her. When we first talked about Cleo we had a very different impression of how people might respond to her. At the time we thought her to be much more engaging. Now it seems likely that she's not visible to too many people. Chances are that she falls in the cracks.

Therapist: I do wonder how others experience her. It's true that during the evaluation process I saw her as much more playful and engaging than in the more recent sessions.

Supervisor: Well, she has that theatrical manner, that mimicking of an on stage personality. But then she runs out of steam and there is not much to follow. It kind of begins and then drops off, as if it has a faulty generator. She can be playful, but it isn't object related, is it? For instance, she doesn't exhibit much reaction when she sees you, does she?

Therapist: No. On this day, for instance, when I went to get her in the waiting room, and said, *Hi again, Cleo, we can start now,* and she answered in a whisper,

  Cleo: Hi Linda Small.

Therapist: It felt as if she was pushing me away. And then off she went into the bathroom. And remember last week? When I went to greet her she said, Hello and goodbye.

Supervisor: She is very tentative, and it's helpful to think of her that way because it fits with all the other things we say about her, like elusive, not connected. What we need to do with the

notion of tentative is to put it to use, to apply it in understanding her unique combination of traits and mannerisms.
What I mean here is that we have to transform an observation
into something that is of diagnostic and therefore technical
usefulness.

Let's assume that being in a tentative state is another version
of not feeling grounded in the world of reality. I'm talking
about a world that's ruled by secondary process, or to put it in
everyday language, by a state of order where cause and effect
follow a logical and predictable course. So if Cleo does not
consistently feel grounded in the world of reality as you and I
know it, then her ability to anticipate is at times blocked.
Anticipation, as you know, is one of the earliest ego functions.
Now obviously, this ego function is not absent in Cleo or she
would be an extremely regressed child. Nor is Cleo's sense of
reality seriously impaired. Rather, under stress, there is ego
regression causing the boundaries between reality and fantasy
to blur, and the use of some of her ego function, like anticipation, to be temporarily shaky. Also, as you've noticed, many
situations that seem fairly ordinary, like beginning a session a
few minutes earlier or later than usual, are stressful to Cleo.
This might be an indication of her particular sensitivity about
being disappointed by you. Remember that this is a child who
has been grievously disillusioned by her caretakers. Just think
of her out of control father, her devalued mother who could
not cope with him, and her half-dead current baby-sitter Maria.
No wonder she's hypervigilant about any further disappoint-
ments. In fact, we could even consider that the tentativeness I
spoke about before is indicative of fear of disappointment and
abandonment rather than a suspension of the ego function of
anticipation. In light of Cleo's sensitivity, I would suggest that
you do not alter the appointment time or anything else that has
to do with the structure of her sessions. If an alteration is
unavoidable, then in addition to giving her an explanation, be
very sensitive to her reaction and to your reaction to her
reaction.

Therapist: I did give her an explanation about starting earlier and ending earlier, but still having the full 45 minutes. In fact when we ended at 4:55, she looked at the clock and added up the time and seemed satisfied that it was correct. I commented to her that it seemed to make her comfortable to have the clock and to know how to figure out her time.

Supervisor: So it appears that she took it in stride, but we don't know what went on below the surface reaction. As a general principle I would volunteer a little more at this early point in treatment. I would tell her that since both of you arrived early and since you didn't have much getting ready to do, you decided to start early. I would show her the clock at that point and show her when you are beginning and when you are to end. I would tell her that the reason that you're explaining all that to her is because you know that she likes to know what to expect and feels comfortable when she is clear about things. I would make this a primary theme at this point in treatment. I would return to it over and over again. I would make it a point of reference and a special mission that you share. You must provide a predictable environment par excellence. What I'm stressing here is the significance of the structure of predictability as a background factor that allows you to talk about her needs and to define them when she can't do so for herself. Is that clear?

Therapist: No. I don't understand structure of predictability as a background factor.

Supervisor: I have stressed some of the external and concrete factors used in creating the structure of an average expectable environment, such as the regularity of the day and hour and length of the sessions. This structure is important in and of itself, but its primary value is in communicating something about the climate of the treatment relationship. When you begin working with a child, you are a stranger to that child. You can't say, "I'm your therapist and you can really trust me to pay complete attention to you, to try to understand you, and to help you understand yourself. When I'm with you I will be totally attentive to you and your needs and not talk on the phone and think about my own troubles or what movie I want to see on Saturday night. Furthermore, you can rely on my strength and steadiness. If you collapse, I will not collapse with you. I will stay strong and level and help you get back on a better footing. I've had a good analysis and extensive training and that equips me to help you in a way that nobody else has been able to help you in the past." You can't say that to Cleo any more than you can tell her that you will create a predictable and reliable environment for her. But you have to convey something of the spirit and essence of what this situation is going to be about from the very beginning of treatment. By presenting the reliability and unwavering regularity of the appointment as something that is good and helpful to her because reliability and predictability are antidotes to fear and panic states, you are setting the stage and creating the climate. The regularity is the background structure. That you are the provider of that background structure *because it will help her* is the heart of the matter. Is that clearer?

Therapist: Yes. The structure is necessary in and of itself but it is also a metaphor for an aspect of the treatment relationship.

Supervisor: Exactly. Now, to move back a bit, let's talk about Cleo's "mistake" of going into the bathroom rather than into your office at the start of the session. I think that was important. What did you make of it?

Therapist: I had several thoughts. I wondered if she wanted to know whether I live in the office apartment. Also, she obviously was trying to find a difference or similarity between my place of work and her mother's school setting. I was struck by the fact that she didn't remember what her mother said about files in the shower. I thought to myself that this child usually doesn't ask questions, and when she does ask for clarification, she forgets what she was told. What is that all about? Why does she forget? Why can't she know? And when I tried to make a connection between my bathroom and her mother's bathroom, she changed the subject so swiftly that I felt as if a gate had been slammed shut. As you can see, I am very confused by her kaleidoscopic movements.

Supervisor: You made a statement that is at the heart of the problem. You said, *Why can't she know?* Let's try to organize and conceptualize our discussion around that issue. The most obvious hypothesis we can make is to say that she's very curious and that she's terrified of satisfying her curiosity. Our theoretical training teaches us to think of curiosity in sexual terms, like curiosity about the primal scene, anatomical difference, and the accompanying excitement around voyeurism, exhibitionism, masturbation and so on. Since Cleo is 6 ½, and since we know that generally applies to all children of that age, we can assume that it is so for Cleo. But how do we use this particular piece of theoretical knowledge with her?

Here again, developmental theory can deepen our understanding. It provides us with a general schema of pivotal psychic landmarks. With these in mind, we can track early developmental deficits and derailments in our patients when it's clear that certain critical developmental steps did not follow in optimal sequence. This knowledge provides us with invaluable information about preoedipal development. We know, for instance, that little children become aware of anatomical differences as early as 12 months of age, and to varying degrees can suffer castration shock and/or penis envy at that very young age (Roiphe and Galenson 1981). We also know that inhibitions against curiosity are, in the main, an outcome of the oedipal situation. So while we can assume that some aspects of Cleo's inhibition against her curiosity stems from oedipally related issues, we can also assume that that is only the latest part of the story. We have two parts of the story to consider here, the preoedipal and the oedipal, and how the early part shaped the subsequent stage. Furthermore, the oedipal phase is not necessarily our primary concern at this point in Cleo's treatment. Do you have any thoughts about that?

Therapist: Well, yes. We know that the oedipal phase must have been much more highly charged for Cleo than it is under good environmental circumstances. By good environmental circumstances I'm thinking of parents who are neither particularly seductive nor rejecting, and who are reasonably reliable and predictable. In Cleo's case, by the time she was of oedipal age, say age 4, her father was already drinking and making scenes of a violent nature and was physically abusive to the mother and Cleo was exposed to all this wild behavior. Her parents were locked in very destructive interactions until her father moved out when she was 5 ½. How does a child negotiate the normal difficulties of the oedipal period when they are exacerbated by paternal violence and abandonment? At 5 ½ she should have been at the point of reconciling herself to the father's unavailability as an incestuous love object, identifying with her mother, and delaying the wish for penis and babies to some time in the future, when she's a grown woman (Freud 1924). How do we understand what the impact of all that externally imposed turmoil did to her oedipal phase?

Supervisor: As you're pointing out, it placed a very heavy burden on her, and it will take a long time in treatment before you can begin to even try to reconstruct what psychic gymnastics she performed and what terrifying distortions she created. What we are seeing is the result of these distortions that live on and haunt her at every turn. But let's go back to the contribution of developmental theory and how these contributions can guide us in our work.

Let's talk about object constancy for a minute. We know through the work of Mahler and colleagues (1975) that when development proceeds well, the child more or less reaches a stage of object constancy by the age of 3. Remember, all that means is that the child can retain a positive representation of the object even when experiencing such negative affects as anger, frustration, disappointment, or envy. The implication here is that self-constancy has to be pretty firmly established in order for the child to maintain a constant representation of the object. In other words, the establishment of self-constancy requires the same developmental evolution as is required for object constancy. We are not talking about two separate processes here. We are talking about a single, highly complicated process that involves various psychic forces interacting and shaping each other. We have the drives powering psychosexual stages and we have their corresponding anxiety levels (Freud 1905). We have structural development with id and ego differentiating and allowing for the ego to begin to function in its particular progression. First the ego takes in or registers tiny bits of internal and external reality. With this process in motion, memory traces begin to form and these in turn facilitate such beginning ego functions as memory, recognition, anticipation, and intentionality. Under ego functions we place adaptive functioning and defense. Inextricably, concurrently, and synergetically, the process of internalization proceeds and powers the development of object relations and identity formation. I placed object relations and identity formation at the end of the list because we were talking about the separation-individuation process and I wanted to underscore all that goes on in the first three years of life in order for the separation-individuation process to culminate in the establishment of self and object constancy. In other words, we can view the establishment of self and object constancy as the most reliable indication that the separation-individuation period has gained a measure of stability.

Here is where we are lacking some essential information about Cleo. We don't know how her separation-individuation process dovetailed with her psychosexual development. For instance, we know that ideally the father acts as catalyst in helping to bring about the child's psychic separation (Abelin 1971). Mr. C. was already drinking and making scenes by the time Cleo was 2. But was he an adequate enough father before he drank and when sober to play this growth-promoting role in Cleo's development? Did she have a reasonably satisfactory separation-individuation process, one that culminated in some measure of self and object constancy that was later severely upset by the cumulative traumas caused by parental violence? Were oedipal issues maturationally imposed on this child whose development had not kept pace and had not resulted in providing her with a firm and stable feeling of identity? What would her identification with her mother be like if her mother was primarily experienced as the father's victim rather than the object of strength and envy that typifies the oedipal rival (Nagera 1975)? And how would the oedipal girl's normal hostile aggression toward the mother find expression (Parens 1990) without causing overwhelming guilt when it appeared to her that the mother was being violently destroyed, as if the child's wishes actually had the power to harm?

To put it simply, we do not know whether what we see in Cleo is primarily the result of regression, or developmental deficit, or a combination of both. We have to be mindful of what we do not know, and rely on what we do know. We know that when she is in her bed at night she cannot hold on to her good object unless that object is physically present. What does that tell us?

We know that going to sleep requires a form of regression, regression in the service of the ego (Kris 1952). This seems to be precisely what Cleo cannot do unless one of her objects is physically present. What happens to her? She becomes flooded by terrifying fantasies. That tells us that repression is inadequate in protecting her from unconscious fantasies. The simple and ordinary regression that facilitates falling asleep is no simple matter for Cleo. In her case, regression weakens repression, and her ego is not adequate to handle her drives. The presence of another person becomes essential for some semblance of safe feeling.

Now let's return to the question that prompted this detour.

The question was, Why can't Cleo know? If we consider Cleo's description of her fears and the content of the fears revealed in her play, we see that her fears correspond to every psychosexual stage: annihilation, loss of the object, loss of love of the object, castration anxiety, and superego anxiety. However, it does seem as though fear of abandonment is a predominant fear.

In the course of treatment we will have to address all of these anxiety nuclei, but for now, we have to concern ourselves with her emotional survival. A little child cannot subsist without a representation of a strong and competent object who will take care of her no matter what happens in her reality and no matter what happens in her fantasy. So perhaps what Cleo can't know is that she experiences her objects and herself as bad and that all of this badness is both the cause and result of her murderous wishes.

Let's think about this for a minute. She has seen her father drunk, abusive, out of control, and violent. That was as overt an example of murderous wishes as you can get, and it was in the person of someone who was, and is, supposed to be her protector. We know that she is keenly aware of teasing and hurting of feelings on the part of her sister and of the kind of teasing and mean behavior that are part of the culture of school life. Of course, that's true for all children, but because of her exposure to her father's violence, she is more vulnerable to any sadistic behavior. That makes her more aware of all that's bad and sad on the news, on the subway, in the park. Most children can block things out. They can hear of a murder on the news and not register the horror of it. Not so with Cleo. She hears everything. Now, given all that, what does she do with her own anger, and retaliatory impulses, and murderous wishes? She has them. Everyone does, but with adequate defenses, such wishes do not generally reach consciousness in such primitive form. They are repressed. For Cleo, such wishes remain on the edge of consciousness, and consequently she feels like a very bad person. So not only is she experiencing the world as terrifying and bad, but she is bad as well.

One of the jobs of treatment is going to be to help her distinguish between thoughts and reality. In this area she still has the grandiosity of a much younger child who thinks that a thought can magically result in real action. Do you see how helpless she is, living as she does in a world that's dangerous inside and out? Her only way out of this terrible place is to gradually come to trust that her therapist is strong, strong enough to help, strong enough to be safe, and stronger than her id wishes.

I have not mentioned the role of superego development in regard to Cleo. Let me briefly review superego development under favorable conditions so that we can be aware of the deficits in Cleo's case.

The superego is the mental agency that establishes standards of behavior through identification with and internalization of standards of parental behavior. As such, it takes on the role of regulating behavior to meet these ethical standards. Through Jacobson's (1964) enrichment of theory regarding superego formation, we have a broadened understanding of both the development and range of superego functioning. We no longer view the superego as being primarily charged by the no-saying function of a powerful and forbidding father, but of being formed out of gradual internalization of libidinally as well as aggressively tinged aspects of both father and mother. These internalizations would then include identifications with aspects of parental care of the child and of parental concern for the child's physical and psychological well-being. If we look at superego development this way, then the standards within the superego include such areas as regulation of mood, self-interest, and self-esteem as part and parcel of the moral and ethical code that it is designated to enforce.

Here we are touching on some critical developmental deficits in Cleo's structure. We are beginning to understand how her object environment shaped her structure. Without object representations of reliable and protective caretakers Cleo cannot feel safe. That's why I earlier stressed your role as that of a strong object. Kind is not enough, understanding is not enough, and empathic is not enough. You need to be all of those and strong as well, because your strength will feel like an antidote to her sense of badness and subsequent need for punishment.

She told you something about her badness in this session. When she talked of Eddy and Mike she told you something about wanting to get rid of the badness inside herself. She wanted to stop being best friends with Eddy, who encourages her "fighting" feelings, and to take Mike, who is kind and caring, as her new best friend. We can take that as a metaphor for an aspect of her struggle, an aspect of which she is dimly conscious. The teacher who eats her favorite food in private and the files in the shower also represent aspects of things that are forbidden and secret and probably "bad," but in a very hazy way. We can't address that material with her yet, but we need to take note of it and keep it in mind.

What I'm stressing over and over again is that with a child like Cleo, the therapeutic process, at least at this stage in her treatment, depends on the power of identification and internalization, rather than on the power of interpretation.

11

The Working Alliance and the Transference

Therapist: Cleo was 10 minutes early for her appointment. I buzzed her into the waiting room but she had a 10-minute wait until her appointment time. When I got to the waiting room she was kneeling on the floor with her back to the baby-sitter and there was complete silence, which I broke by greeting her. Here is how it went between us. ***Hello Cleo.***

Cleo: **Oh? Hello.**

Therapist: She was crouched on the floor, struggling to get her tee shirt over her knees and pulling her arms inside of her sleeves so only her hands showed. She tried to walk toward me in this squatting dwarflike position, but she fell over and began to crawl into my office. Maria never looked up. In a very light tone of voice I asked, ***What's happening here today? First you were kneeling, then walking on the heels of your feet, and now you're crawling.***

Cleo: I'm not crawling.

Therapist: She half stood up, pulled down her tee shirt to cover her knees, and sort of lurched into the office, but just before doing that, she turned her head and looked over to Maria. Maria, of course, never noticed, and I wondered whether Cleo was checking to see if she was going to be chastised. Of course she might have simply wanted to make contact before leaving the waiting room. It's hard to know.

   In the office, she went right to the middle of the floor and said,

Cleo: Let me show you this trick.

Therapist: She began to walk around in circles, in a squatting position, with her tee shirt pulled down over her knees. I said, **When you do that, you look like a little person.**

   She then sat down in her chair and began to swivel around. It was very quiet in the room and I didn't quite know what to say or do with what she had done, and I was still a bit shaken, as I often am, by Maria's total lack of interest in Cleo. Also, I was thinking about what you had pointed out to me last week about the importance of taking this up with Cleo. I said, **You know, when I come into the waiting room to get you, I would not know that you and Maria are together because you never seem to talk to each other, or play, or even look at each other. Why is it that way?**

Cleo: Well, I play my video tape in the waiting room. It was pretty good today. I only had to make one cut. Those actors did really good.

Therapist: **What do you call this video that you are making?**

Cleo: I call it Kittens or Horses, I'm not sure which I like better.

Supervisor: Are you still assuming that she's having a fantasy in the waiting room and calling it a video?

Therapist: Yes. I've gotten so used to her movies and videos as her way of talking about fantasy that I don't even check it out. Maybe I should. In this case though, I was eager to get back to her aloneness when with Maria. I said: *It's good that you can play by yourself, but sometimes a kid likes to have a playmate and doesn't know how to get the person she's with to play with her. Is that what happens with Maria?*

Cleo: Well, Maria was just going to sleep.

Therapist: *How could you tell? Did she say so?*

Cleo: No, but her eyes were looking that way, like she was falling asleep.

Therapist: *If you wanted to play with her, would you know how to ask? Sometimes a kid doesn't quite know how to ask.*

Cleo: Yeah, I know that.

Therapist: She sounded so weary and so resigned that I was startled. Then she said:

Cleo: There's a boy at school, his name is Eric. He wants to play with me, and he follows me around but I don't want to play with him.

Therapist: She began to swivel hard, back and forth, with occasional and 360 degree turns. I said: *Sometimes two people feel differently about each other. One is interested and the other is not. And sometimes you might want somebody to be interested in you but don't know how to get them to notice you. These are difficult situations that we're taking about. They can make you feel pretty uncomfortable.* She was swivelling fast.

Supervisor: I can understand that this conversation would make her pretty anxious. You have never been this direct and focused with her. How did you feel doing that? Did it seem okay to you?

Therapist: I was aware of something new happening, at my instiga-
tion, and concerned about how far to take this. But I was also
aware of the fact that she was not giving me any signals to stop.
I even said to her at this point, *You know, I can't tell*
whether it's okay with you that I'm talking about this. I
just want to remind you that if you don't want me to
talk about this you can just tell me to stop. I would listen
carefully to a request like that and do as you ask.

Cleo: I don't mind talking about this. I know how sometimes that's
a big problem for a kid and a kid doesn't know what to
do. . . .

Therapist: She was talking very softly at this point, and after the last
statement her voice faded so much that I couldn't hear what
she was saying. It was very still in the room and she was
whispering and looking down. A truck passing on the street
seemed very loud. I felt that I was missing something important. I said, *You are talking so softly, Cleo, that I can't*
hear what you're saying, and that truck is making a big
noise, so I am going to close the window so I can hear
better. There, now it's quieter. Yes, I think that we are
talking today about something that's very hard for you.

Cleo: Yes, it is, but sometimes I can just play with my sister.

Therapist: *Oh, it's very good to have a sister to play with.*

Supervisor: You stepped in a little too fast. You could have waited
a while to see where it went.

Therapist: Yes. I can see that now that I read it out loud to you.
Cleo went on:

Cleo: Tina plays with my toys sometimes and tells me that I can't
play.

Therapist: *What do you do when that happens?*

Cleo: I don't know.

Therapist: *Do you tell someone?*

Cleo: Yeah, I tell someone but Tina just says no to me anyway and tells me, "get lost."

Therapist: *It's hard when a child tells someone and they don't listen, and it's hard when you don't know what to do to really get people to listen and to pay attention.*

Cleo: Yes it is.

Therapist: *Let's see if we can figure this out. What could a person do when people don't listen?*

Cleo: They can try again, but sometimes I used to try again and they still didn't listen. So now I don't ask again. I bet those toys don't fight.

Therapist: And she stared at the toy drawer. I said, *Are you ready to play with them?* But she made no move to open the drawer. Instead she stood up and pretended to be fighting, you know, making fighting gestures. I didn't know what was happening and thought that maybe she was continuing our conversation but had switched to pantomime rather than words, so I asked, *Are you showing me that after you've asked once you worry that if you ask again there is going to be a fight?* She didn't answer me and got a worried look on her face and just stood there looking worried. I said, *This is a very different time we're having today. First we were talking and I knew what was going on, and now I don't know what's going on.*

Cleo: What's that over your head? I see a big bug. Maybe it's a roach crawling over your head.

Therapist: *Would you like me to turn around and look?*

Cleo: Yes!

Therapist: I turned around to look and she yelled,

Cleo: I tricked you, I fooled you, I got you to look!

Therapist: *Yes, I did what you asked me to do.*
Cleo then went over to the window and began to stare toward the neighboring rooftops with a look of exaggerated amazement. She said, in a hushed voice,

Cleo: I see two men. They're on top of a building and they look like they're going to jump off.

Therapist: *I wouldn't expect to see anything like that if I was looking out the window. What you are describing is very frightening.*

Cleo: Oh, I think one man is going to jump. I don't know for sure.

Therapist: *What would you like me to do?*

Cleo: Well, it looks pretty bad over here. It's kind of dangerous. I think that you better come over and look out of the window.

Therapist: *Well, you told me what you would like me to do, so I'm going to do it. I'm coming over.*
I walked over to the window and she yelled,

Cleo: I fooled you, I tricked you! I got you to look!

Therapist: And then she started jiggling some money in her pocket.

Cleo: I'm rich!

Therapist: *Oh? You are?*
She took a handful of change out of her pocket and held it out for me to see. I said, *You do have a lot of money, don't you?* I was just making conversation at that point. I was lost. I didn't know where the session had gone and I didn't have the wherewithal to stick with my not knowing and saying something simple about that. Then Cleo showed me that she had three quarters, two pennies, a nickel, and a dime. She put them all on the table and said,

Cleo: I know what these are. This is George Washington and maybe that's Thomas Jefferson.

Therapist: *Those are the names of presidents pictured on the coins, but does that tell you how rich you are?*

Cleo: Yes, it's George Washington.

Therapist: *Do you know how many cents in a quarter?*

Supervisor: Isn't she almost 7 years old?

Therapist: Well, almost 6 and ¾. I couldn't tell whether she really didn't know what these coins were worth or whether she was very anxious and unfocused.

Supervisor: I'm trying to remember what children usually know at that age. It seems to me that most children this age do know the worth of coins, would you agree?

Therapist: No. I think that it varies a lot. Among my children's friends there are kids who haven't gotten interested in money and therefore don't know the worth of coins.

Supervisor: Well, your information is better and more up to date than mine. I'm checking it out with you because it's very helpful to have a general sense of what children generally know at a certain age. Of course, there are enormous variations. But still, within reasonable variations a therapist comes to have certain expectations regarding a child's fund of general knowledge about the world. When a therapist is uncertain in this respect, it's a good idea to check it out with someone who's more up to date.

Look, the important theme here is her feelings about her sister and her identification with her in her actions toward you. She allowed herself to be mean to you for a few minutes, by tricking you the way her sister tricks her. This probably frightened her and she defended against her wish to be mean by an excursion into money. But I'm also interested in assessing her reality awareness. This ego function can tell us something about how individuated our patients are, how alert to the world and to secondary process. Also, money is an abstract concept and it requires a degree of developed symbolic thinking to understand the meaning of money.

Therapist: Well, it turned out that Cleo did not know the cent equivalent of those coins and I volunteered to go over it with her, even though she didn't ask me to. I think I needed to give some structure to the session at that point, to give it shape and order and direction. Cleo calmed down during this structured exercise. She then told me a joke.

Cleo: Do you know why a dime is better than a quarter?

Therapist: *Why?*

Cleo: Because it makes more cents!

Supervisor: So she still didn't get it right.

Therapist: No, and she continued making the same kind of joke with a penny being more than a quarter etc. So, I said, *Sometimes when you're confused you make jokes. I've noticed that about you. Here we just talked about a quarter being twenty-five cents and a dime being ten cents and you know that twenty-five is more than ten, right?*

Cleo: No, it's not. Here's another joke. Why is a quarter more than a penny?

Therapist: *Why?*

Cleo: Because it makes more money. See, I tricked you that time. I said money and not cents.

Therapist: *What I'm thinking about all this is still what I said before. When you feel a little confused, you turn being confused into a joke. I would like to help you when you feel confused, and I could help you, but sometimes you don't let me. Not yet anyway. When you get to know me better, I hope that you will let me help you more.*

Cleo: Once upon a time, there was a little girl.

Therapist: *I wonder whether your story is going to help me know how to help you. How two people can work together when one of them needs some help. Maybe you would like it if we told a story together?*

Cleo: Let's tell a story together. I'll say the names and you tell the story.

Therapist: She then made up these impossible names. Her story went something like this:

Cleo: Once upon a time there was a girl and her name was Jay-Jay-Jay-Goo-Goo-Goo-Gaw-Gaw-Gaw-Kookoo-Lala. . . .

Supervisor: A non-story?

Therapist: Yes. A non-story. I couldn't think of anything to say, but before there was even time to react she asked,

Cleo: Would you like to see me stand on my head?

Therapist: She tried to stand on her head but couldn't quite do it, and I noticed that in between her attempts she glanced at the clock several times. I said, *I noticed that you looked at the clock. You know just how much time we have together. Were you looking to see how much time we have left today?* She continued to try to do handstands. A few minutes later I said, *Now it's 5 o'clock and we have to say goodbye.*

Cleo: Goodbye, see you tomorrow.

Therapist: *I think that you would like it if we could see each other more often.*

It wasn't until I got home that night that I realized that I had forgotten to tell her that I was going to see her mother for the usual monthly appointment. I thought that maybe I should call

Cleo and tell her and find out if she had anything for me to bring up with her mother. But I wasn't sure about calling her.

Supervisor: What weren't you sure about?

Therapist: Well, I don't usually call her. I wondered if it would feel strange to her to hear from me by phone, maybe too big a departure from our usual routine. On the other hand, we have our arrangement about her mother's visits and I wonder what it would be like for her if I just forget to tell her. What does it do to her trust of me?

Supervisor: I have a strong opinion about calling her, and I'm basing it on two factors. One is the same one that you're struggling with and it has to do with being a provider of what we discussed last week, a predictable environment, in other words a very reliable and trustworthy person, somebody she can really count on. In addition to that, I'm thinking about this particular session and the way she portrayed her needs on this day. This is what I would do. I would call her and very simply tell her that you forgot to tell her that you're seeing her mother for one of the regular monthly appointments, and also forgot to ask her whether there was anything that she wanted you to bring up with her mother. I would say that you're calling her on the phone because you think that it's important not to change the way you do things together, and you always discuss this with her in person, but since you forgot to do it when you were together, you want to do it on the phone. I suspect that Cleo will be surprised to hear your voice on the phone and maybe that element of surprise is what bothers you about calling, but I think the overall value will compensate for that. She'll be surprised and she probably won't have anything to say about your seeing her mother and that's okay. It doesn't matter if she's bland about your phone call. What matters is that you corrected an error on your part. You forgot to tell her something important and then you remembered in time.

Now here is what I saw in the session. As an overall summary of the session we see Cleo's endless quest for equilibrium, which takes the customary path of getting closer to you and then darting away, because no place is comfortable, or at least not for long. However, within that general and now very familiar pattern, you did have a period of really direct conversation, which you initiated, in regard to her baby-sitter's inattention, and of Cleo's acceptance of the situation. This led to the problem of how to get people to listen to her. She responded by telling you that she tries, but not more than once, and that she plays by herself, making up fantasies as a way of dealing with her aloneness. She seemed to be able to stay with this very personal, very direct topic for several minutes. Even though she darted away by making jokes and standing on her head, it seems to me that she came and stayed closer to you than ever before. Even her embryonic attempt to tell a story, about a girl no less, seemed remarkably close to home. Never mind that it immediately dissolved into gibberish names. The wish was voiced, and that is a lot for this child. And then at the end, she said that she would see you tomorrow. She isn't able to say that she would like to come every day, or at least more often, or that she wished that she could come again tomorrow. That's too hard for her. So she makes it a semi-joke. But her wish, or better still, her longing to have more of you, comes through very clearly.

What could her wish to have more of you mean? It could mean that a therapeutic alliance is solidifying because her awareness of you as a potential source of help is becoming more apparent to her. It could also mean that a positive transference is developing. It could mean that both processes are in the works. What is the difference between these two phenomena?

First of all, let me just say that I'm using terms that were conceptualized to describe processes in the psychoanalytic treatment of adult neurotic patients, and I'm trying to apply them to a 6-year-old child in once-a-week psychotherapy.

Many articles have been written questioning the validity of using such terms as *transference* (Fraiberg 1951, Reich 1973) or *therapeutic alliance* in regard to child treatment. Many articles have been written taking the position that these terms are appropriate in child as well as adult treatment. My feeling is that while these terms do not fit exactly the same way with children as they do with adult patients in psychoanalysis, they fit well enough to help us conceptualize our work. They add an important dimension to our understanding of a crucial aspect of treatment, that of the object relationship (Blanck and Blanck 1975, 1979, Bollas 1987, Grunes 1984, Loewald 1957), conscious and unconscious, real and transferential, between patient and therapist.

First, let us distinguish between a working alliance (Greenson 1965) and a positive transference. The therapeutic alliance is a primarily conscious aspect of the relationship between patient and analyst and refers to the patient's belief that the analyst is performing a helping function. The patient retains this belief even at those times in treatment when the going is rough and the patient has negative feelings toward the analyst. Transference, on the other hand, is not conscious. Rather, it is the unconscious displacement of feelings and attitudes from early object representations onto the person of the analyst (Freud 1912a, 1915, Moore and Fine 1990). In a positive transference, these displaced feelings would be of a positive nature and obviously in a negative transference they would be negative. I am more interested in the positive transference at this moment because I am trying to distinguish its manifestations from those of the working alliance. That can be a blurry area, one where it's difficult to make that differentiation. The negative transference is easily distinguishable and therefore I'm not focusing on it as much. While the working alliance is conscious and transference is unconscious, both involve early self and object representations.

You might wonder why I'm spending all of this time on such basic and elementary concepts. I think that I need to review all of this for myself because when we don't talk about these concepts in simple terms, we don't always make optimal use of them. I'll come to the point soon.

We know that a therapeutic alliance and a positive transference are not mutually exclusive. They are different but complementary mental processes that coexist at times during the course of treatment. Why is it so important to distinguish between the two? What would this tell us about Cleo? We have known for some time that Cleo wants to come, that she values her sessions, and that they are important to her. We have speculated that she sees you as a potential source of help, and these observations of ours are in the direction of assessing the building of a therapeutic alliance. We can say with some confidence that a therapeutic alliance is forming. I have also talked at times of transferential phenomena, but that's been very hazy. Here is why it's so important. If you are becoming a positively cathected transferential figure, that would tell us that an earlier positive object representation of Cleo's is being displaced onto you. I know that's obvious. I am simply repeating what transference is all about. But remember this. We have often wondered about Cleo's object representations. Why aren't her early good object representations available to her at times of stress? What does that tell us about the process of internalization in her case? We haven't had any answers to these questions. However, if you are becoming a transferential figure, that would tell us that something has freed her unconscious path to the representation of a good early object representation and it is that early object representation that is being displaced onto you. Given Cleo's generally favorable early history and her apparently reasonably "good enough mother" (Winnicott 1953), she must have myriads of memory traces of good and satisfying early experiences that register as memory traces of a good psychic state.

We know that in early infancy, self and other are not sufficiently differentiated to allow for discrete representations of self and object. However, as differentiation proceeds, self and other become distinct entities and with that, impressions and images of these self and other experiences register as distinct representations. Here is where we've been missing vital knowledge of Cleo. What happened to her memory of those good experiences? Is it possible that we are going to begin to learn something about this part of Cleo's inner life? We can only learn about it from the quality of object relations as revealed in her relationship with the therapist.

Now back to the session. How do you think it went?

Therapist: I was worried that I pushed her too much. After all, I imposed a whole subject on her at the beginning of the session, and I did that because you and I had talked about it last week in supervision.

Supervisor: That's one of the problems about being in supervision. We decide what's important when we have our discussions, and then you are eager to do something about it and consequently may lead the patient. In this case though, I don't believe that you really led your patient. After all, she was doing contortions in the waiting room and that statuelike baby-sitter didn't even notice, or at least pretended not to notice. And Cleo even looked at her just before leaving the waiting room. It would have been an error not to bring up the sitter's nonpresence. I think that bringing it up as you did paid off well.

You might have tried to explore the tee shirt over the knees business first.

Therapist: I know. I got a bit carried away with my mission. I noticed that she glanced at the clock during that discussion about getting listened to, and I commented about that to her. I asked her whether she was having feelings about our time going by. I said to her, **_Do you know that people act certain ways because of the feelings that they have inside them?_** I felt as if she might not know that; at least I'm not sure that she does know.

Supervisor: I think that you're right. Sometimes I wonder whether we really understand her use of "videos" and "movies." We assume that it's her system for engaging in fantasy. But sometimes I'm not sure that she knows that she's the author of her fantasies. What we're saying now sounds much more pathological than the way we usually think about her.

Therapist: Yeah, just the way she says these things: "I'm making my video, or I'm watching my video."

Supervisor: She sounds as if she has a little studio or VCR inside her body, or something inanimate of that sort. She doesn't say that she's making believe or pretending. We don't know whether there's some confusion involved in that or whether it's a manner of speech. She's not a psychotic child, but this way of speaking is confusing.

Therapist: Especially when we consider that the initial symptoms had to do with fear of pictures coming alive and taking her away. Yet in these instances that I'm talking about now, the "movie" she creates is a way of keeping herself entertained while she waits for me in that situation with the baby-sitter who is there and not there at the same time.

Supervisor: It's staggering to think how lonely Cleo can feel. Somehow it seems to me that her pulling her tee shirt over her knees the way she did is an attempt to deal with her loneliness. I can't even speculate what that gesture could mean. Could it be a way of gathering herself up, being able to feel herself, her limbs more keenly?

Therapist: Well, it's also a way to get others to look at her, to find a pretext for saying, "Look at me!" One of the problems is that she doesn't know how to get beyond getting looked at.

Supervisor: What you're saying now is that her use of language for real communication is very limited. That's a pretty important observation.

Therapist: Yes and no. Today, for instance, she was able to say that she had a problem in getting people to pay attention to her. She was, as you know, madly swivelling during this discussion, so while the discussion was very hard for her, she did stay with it for a while. I probably should have said something about how hard it was for her to focus on what we were talking about. I'm sorry that I didn't acknowledge that.

Supervisor: How would you have phrased that?

Therapist: I could have said that I thought what we were talking about was hard for her, that I noticed she was speaking very softly, and that I was thinking perhaps that meant that it was hard for her to think and talk about this subject.

Supervisor: But with a child like Cleo, I would not say, "I think that this is hard for you to talk about." I would say, *Boy is this hard!* Do you understand the difference?

Therapist: Do you think that what I suggested would make her defensive?

Supervisor: Maybe that too, but I was thinking of Cleo feeling too separate and too alone in the "hardness" of it. But if you make a more global statement like, *Boy is this hard!* Then you are in it together. She's not so far from you in her struggle. Then you can build on it in small doses whenever it seems right. You can eventually let her know about all the maneuvers she uses when things get hard, for instance her use of distraction and teasing. You can remark that at other times when things are hard she just leaves them behind. You can say things like, *Sometimes when things are hard you tiptoe away and sometimes when things are hard you fly away.*
    I'm trying to think of words that fit and that are uncritical. What I'm also thinking of is how you can establish a place for yourself as someone who understands about hard things and is not afraid to tackle them and help with them. At some point in the future you could say something like this to her: *When you*

***know that something is hard, when you know it in
words as well as in feelings, then it already makes it a
little easier. Knowing things in words is very helpful.***

What I'm thinking about here is to help her identify affects
by being able to verbalize them to herself, on the way to being
able to communicate them to another person. At present, her
affects tend to send her into action rather than into thinking.
Action, in this case, is made up of all the defensive maneuvers
that we've been noting. Thinking, on the other hand, opens up
the possibility of conscious and intentional action. The resignation that we so often see in her and that we find so distressing
is partly the result of her unidentified affective states and her
inability to mobilize herself to get relief. She really does not
know how to effectively help herself or to get help from
another person.

I also have some question about her fund of general information about the external world. For instance, she knows that
coins have pictures of presidents on them, and she knows that
coins have particular value based on the number of cents they
are worth, but this information is not integrated. It remains
very vague. But perhaps the vagueness is adaptive. After all, if
she lets herself perceive clearly, she might see all those dangerous things: violence, people jumping off buildings, and
such. To be vague might seem safer.

Therapist: It's hard to tell how much she knows. At some point in
the session she added up the three quarters and said that it came
to seventy-five cents.

Supervisor: Oh? Then she did know after all.

Therapist: Yes. I said, ***Oh, you really know your quarters,*** and
she replied,

Cleo: When I add all of this up it makes $3,000.00.

Supervisor: The minute you recognize her accurate perception of
reality, she slips away from you. At some point you are going to

have to address that directly. You could say something like, *What is that? When I tell you that you really understand something, then you have to tell me that you really don't. Is it a little like playing hide-and-seek, with you wanting me to look for you and find you for just a short peek before you hide again?*

12

The Difference between the Separation and the Individuation Processes

Therapist: Here's what happened when I called Cleo on the phone last week. Remember, I'd forgotten to tell her that I was seeing her mother the next day for our usual monthly appointment. That meant that I had also not asked Cleo whether there was anything that she wanted me to tell her mom. So, as we discussed, I called her on the phone to correct my oversight. The baby-sitter answered the phone and told Cleo that I was on the line. Cleo picked up the phone and said,

Cleo: Hello Linda Small.

Therapist: I was amused, and told her that since I forgot to tell her that I was seeing her mom as I usually did during our appointment, I was calling her instead. Did she have anything that she wanted me to tell her mom? She answered,

Cleo: Tell my mother: Wocka-Wocka-Wocka, from Cleo.

Therapist: *That's not something you want to tell her yourself? That's something you want me to tell her?*

Cleo: Yes. That's how I want you to talk.

Therapist: I agreed to do as she asked and we said goodbye.

Supervisor: Since you are au courant about these things and I'm not, do you happen to know whether that has some popular meaning?

Therapist: Yes. It's from a television character, Fozzy Bear from the *Muppets,* or the *Muppet Babies.* She watches *Muppet Babies* on Saturday morning. In fact, she probably identifies with Fozzy Bear. He tells terrible jokes and people throw tomatoes at him because his jokes are so bad. He's terrible as a standup comic, but also so bad that he's lovable. Wocka-wocka-wocka is his punch line.

Supervisor: It's helpful to know that. It makes more sense when you have that background.

Therapist: Her mother knew the program and mentioned that Cleo liked it a lot. Mrs. C. was very upset during our session. She told me that her ex-husband had gone to work drunk and consequently got fired. He called to tell her about it and sounded very agitated and angry during the conversation. He'd gone off for the weekend and was not going to see the children as planned. Mrs. C. was worried about the financial repercussions and the impact of his unemployment on the children. She cried quite a bit and it was difficult for me to bring up the situation with the baby-sitter since she was feeling so distraught. I brought it up toward the end of the session when I thought she had gained enough composure to be able to hear me. She didn't seem too interested in discussing Maria, and said that the children wait for her homecoming to talk about anything important and the baby-sitter just gives them dinner, does certain chores, and baby-sits. She did not seem particularly concerned about Maria's lack of interest in the children or of her unresponsiveness to them. I made a strong pitch for someone more caring and involved. During this discussion I learned, to my surprise, that Mrs. C. doesn't get home until 7 P.M. Mrs. C. and her children hardly spend any time together during the school week. That's all the more reason to have an adequate sitter.

Supervisor: Yes, absolutely. Mrs. C. must come home tired after a long day of teaching and tutoring, and the children haven't seen her since early in the morning. They probably need a lot from her at that point in the day and she must be pretty depleted. It's a very common situation, isn't it? So many households are like that these days. I know that you worry about overburdening Cleo's mom, and you're right to be concerned about her situation. But still, you have to be sensitive to Cleo's needs, and it's not that hard to get a more lively sitter.

What are we talking about here? This is not merely a practical issue, so let's be clear about that. We are talking about a mother's failure to provide reasonable care for her children during her absence. By reasonable care I'm thinking of a child's need to be recognized as a live presence, an animate entity who needs connection, stimulation, responsiveness, as well as limits, guidance, and physical care. There is something very strange about this mother allowing such a depressed and vacant person to care for her children for five long afternoons every week. It's a form of neglect, and much as you sympathize with the plight of working mothers and the problem of getting good sitters, it can be done and everyone will be better off when the mother insures a wholesome afterschool situation for her kids.

Therapist: We'll have to wait and see if she pays attention and changes sitters. Now let me tell you about the session with Cleo. She came in drinking soda through a straw and I said, *Oh. I see that you started your snack.*

Cleo: Yes, and I'm going to wear my jacket in your office today.

Therapist: *That's fine. This is your time and you can make these choices.*

Cleo: Oh. Is that so?

Therapist: *Yes. There are certain choices that you can make here.*

Cleo: Well, then how about if you bring out the T.V.?

Therapist:
   I guess you wish that I had a T.V.

Cleo: Yeah.

Therapist: *What would we do if I had a T.V. here?* She sort of stretched out on my couch, took a long sip of soda and said,

Cleo: We'd watch Chip'n Dale.

Therapist: I know this T.V. routine. A lot of kids come home and watch that program. For a lot of kids that program is the transition from school to home. So I asked her, *How would that be for us if I had a T.V. here and we watched together? How would that be for you?*

Cleo: We would just watch together.

Therapist: *How would that feel to you to do that with me?*

Cleo: I watch T.V. with my sister every day after school. She does her homework in front of the T.V.

Therapist: *How does that feel?*

Cleo: Sometimes she makes bad mistakes because she's looking at the T.V. and not looking at her paper.

Therapist: *When she makes mistakes, does that disturb you? Does it interrupt your program?*

Cleo: No. I don't even notice that she's there. I just keep watching.

Therapist: *Well, if we were watching T.V. together, would you not notice that I was there? Would it be like watching alone?*

Cleo: Oh, no. I'd know that you were there.

Therapist: I asked her again what that would be like, but it just wasn't going anywhere and I didn't know what to do with it.

Supervisor: I think that you were trying to explore something important but it had an awkward quality. I'm wondering what was making you go on with question after question? You were struggling and searching for something but you were going against the tide.

I was listening to this dialogue and trying to figure out what you were exploring. Were you trying to find out whether she had a sense of what "companionable" was like? Did she want to watch television with you so that you would leave her alone, or did she want to do something with you that would feel very nice, or very safe, or both? Did she want to be completely passive in your presence? Was she understanding what you were saying to her when you were trying to explore these questions with her? She sounded concrete when she talked about her sister. I'm thinking about a paper by Winnicott (1958) called "On the Capacity to be Alone." In it he discusses the capacity to be alone in the presence of another person as the prerequisite to the capacity to be alone. I'm noting that Cleo never said anything so simple and commonplace as, "That would be nice" or "I would like that." Does she lack the language or the experience itself?

But let's get back to the issue of technique. A string of questions like the ones you described are never helpful. It sounds too much like a drill and it pushes the child away and into an uncomfortable position. It doesn't even sound like you to approach her that way. Furthermore, many children would have stopped you by saying, "Stop those questions." Some of my child patients taught me a long time ago not to ask too many questions. But Cleo doesn't complain about your series of questions, which must make her feel uncomfortable, any more than she complains about Maria, the "not-there" baby-sitter.

Therapist: She doesn't complain at all. I wish she had stopped my excessive questioning. But Cleo doesn't complain. That's one of her problems. I wish I could understand the dynamics of noncomplaining.

Supervisor: It's her form of adapting and it's the best she's able to do at the present, but her resignation and withdrawal are a very sad solution. Maybe you have trouble understanding this aspect of Cleo because it's so sad. She's living with a lot of emptiness around her, and she cannot identify the emptiness. It's her normal world.

   Let's imagine something together. Suppose that Cleo was not in treatment with you now, or at any point in her childhood. Suppose she entered treatment as an adult woman and that the treatment was presented at a scientific meeting. The audience would hear about the immigration to a new country, and the alcoholic father, and the mother as a victim of his drunken violence, and the divorce, and the sister being given certain privileges, and whatever followed. But would the audience hear about the climate of emptiness that she lived in?

   There is probably only one way that the therapist would learn about the emptiness. A smart and sensitive therapist would pick it up in the transference–countertransference manifestations. Chances are that Cleo would not be able to describe the childhood climate of emptiness. After all it would have been her silent norm. But it would probably hang over the treatment situation as a vague presence. The therapist might experience it as a gnawing but hard to identify frustration, a feeling of not quite being able to reach the patient, as if words could not quite bridge the distance between them. It might feel as if the patient could not take in much of what was designed to be helpful and enlightening. The therapist might even begin to feel sleepy during sessions, another possible manifestation of apathy in the countertransference (Seinfeld 1991).

Sometimes it's interesting to try to project into the future, just as it's sometimes interesting to try to imagine what our adult patients might have been like as children. Of course I'm speculating, and it's not to be taken too seriously, but I find it helpful to play this way. I find that it makes me feel more connected to the patient when I give myself this sort of freedom to free associate. Of course not everyone works this way.

Let's imagine a somewhat different outcome to this fantasy of mine about Cleo's future development. I bet that it's possible that without treatment now, Cleo's psychic organization following childhood would so disguise and obscure this current condition of emptiness that Cleo as an adult could have a very talented therapist who would fail to pick this up. If the emptiness is not remembered and does not reveal itself in the transference or in the mood or tone of the treatment situation, it could be lost and remain buried in the unconscious. If that were to happen, that hypothetical scientific meeting of mine where Cleo is being presented as an adult would take a different turn. The therapist would present Cleo's history and the audience would probably join the therapist in understanding the etiology of Cleo's current psychic makeup by placing emphasis on her childhood exposure to the violence, and the alcoholism, and the divorce, and the mother's long hours at work, and all the while maybe the emptiness might have been the most insidious of these forces, but one never to be uncovered, identified, and worked on.

It's good to treat children. It gives us a proper sense of humility about the complexities of development. When and how does Cleo get psychologically nourished? As we learn more about her environment we learn that her mother is emotionally depleted and drained by the realistic responsibilities of her life and routine, and probably by the loneliness of having no mate. The father is often unreliable and on occasion dangerous. We have good reason to suspect that Cleo is not particularly talented at getting her needs met, which, with how little is available, does not make for a good combination of circumstances.

What happened then?

Therapist: I realized that Cleo was telling me more and more about her life outside of the therapy office and it seemed good to me that she was able to communicate in this way. So I asked her whether watching T.V. with her sister was what she did every day after school except for her therapy day. She said yes, except sometimes she had a friend visit. I asked her what it was like for her to miss her shows on the day that she comes to see me. She said that she didn't really mind missing her shows on therapy day. It was okay. She finished her lemonade, threw out the container and said,

Cleo: My sister likes to draw funny pictures. If she saw this container she would copy this funny picture of a cat and a dog.

Therapist: *What made you think of that right now?*

Cleo: That was a joke.

Therapist: *There is that word again. You often call things you say a joke. I think you call things a joke when you don't know the answer to a question I ask. Do you think I'm right?*

Cleo: My tummy is very full from that lemonade.

Therapist: *Is that a comfortable feeling, to have your tummy so full?*

Cleo: Yes. It feels good.

Therapist: She then reached into her pocket and took out a package of bubble gum and started to open it. I noticed that I was getting irritated and thinking that artificial lemonade and bubble gum were pretty poor snacks to give a child after a long day at school. I said, *What do you think, Cleo, do you really need that bubble gum right now?*

Supervisor: Oh, my! What were you thinking of to say that?

Therapist: Well, here's what happened. I said, *You know we have 45 minutes together for our appointment, and when we're together I want to hear every word that you say. Sometimes when kids chew bubble gum, they get so involved in chewing that it's hard to hear what they say. So if you really need the gum, have it, but if you think that you can wait until after our appointment, it might make it better for our time together.*

Cleo: I can wait.

Therapist: She put the gum away and she talked a little about the various shows that she watches on T.V. Then she told a joke and I said, *Oh, I just remembered that I told your mom your joke-message when I saw her yesterday, I told her, "Wocka-Wocka-Wocka from Cleo," and your mom said, "Oh yes, that's Fozzy Bear. Cleo likes that show a lot."*

Cleo: My mom likes that show a lot too, and I am a joker like Fozzy Bear. Do you know why the chicken crossed the road?

Therapist: *One time when you told me the joke the answer was, "to get the Chinese newspaper."*

Cleo: Oh no. This time that's not the right answer. Try a different answer.

Therapist: *To get to the other side.*

Cleo: No, that's not right either. It's to get the bear. This is the way chickens talk.

Therapist: She made squawking noises, and then said,

Cleo: I'd better get that chicken.

Therapist: She went over to the drawer and began looking for the toy chicken. She took out the bag in which I keep animals and called into it,

Cleo: Oh chicken, are you there? Talk to me!

Therapist: She held the bag up to her ear and pretended to be listening attentively. I asked her what the chicken was saying.

Cleo: The chicken says that she isn't going to come out and play.

Therapist: *Why not?*

Cleo: Well, she's a dancing chicken. She's going to dance.

Therapist: Cleo took out the chicken and danced around the room with her and then said,

Cleo: This chicken is going to commit suicide.

Therapist: *Oh my goodness. What happened? Would you ask that chicken what's making her want to commit suicide?* Cleo pretended to ask the chicken and said,

Cleo: Somebody is making her do it. The dog is making her do it.

Therapist: And she took the dog out of the bag and placed the dog next to the chicken on the table. I asked her how the dog could do that, how a dog could force a chicken to hurt herself.

Cleo: He's barking at her and chasing her and barking.

Therapist: Then she dropped the whole thing and got on the couch and sat, crossed her legs, and rocked herself in what looked like a masturbatory type of movement. I've noticed that she has done that several times in the past few weeks. And then she tried to "trick" me again. She yelled out,

Cleo: Oh, I see a big water bug crawling over your floor!

Therapist: *Are you trying to trick me like you did once before?*

Cleo: Oh, no. There really is a water bug crawling across your floor. It's right next to your chair now.

Therapist: *I know that you like to fool me sometimes but I know my office very well and I've been here a long time and I have never seen a water bug in this room, or the bathroom, or the waiting room, or anywhere in this office apartment. So it's very hard for me to think that I will see a water bug here because my experience tells me that I have never seen a water bug here, but if you still want me to look I will look.*

Cleo: No, you don't have to look. What's that over your head? I see a big fly.

Therapist: *Would you like me to look?*

Cleo: Yes, there it goes.

Therapist: I looked up at the ceiling and said, *I don't see a fly. Often with a fly you hear a buzz. I don't hear a z-z-z-z-z, and I don't see a black dot flying around.* I talked a little about how helpful it is when you have experience and can check out what you see and don't see and what is real and what is not. Cleo listened and nodded.

Supervisor: What a wonderful exchange. You took what could have been one of those empty vacant dialogues and turned it into something really useful.

Therapist: It felt very good, it really did, and I went on and said,
Sometimes it's very hard for children because they don't have a whole lot of experience and sometimes children see something and tell the grownups and the grownups tell them that they're wrong and that they didn't see what they thought they saw. Then sometimes children don't know what to believe, their own eyes or the words of the grownups who told them that they're wrong. Or sometimes a child will think something is

dangerous and the grownups will say that it's safe, or sometimes the opposite will happen and the child will think something is safe and the grownup will think that it's dangerous. So one thing about being an adult that's really helpful is having all of that experience that helps to check things out, what's real and what's pretend or not true. That sort of thing. And it's helpful for a child to use and remember her experiences so as to be able to check things out.

Cleo: Well, I know that because I have a therapist.

Therapist: She was lying on the couch and the word "therapist" came out so muffled that I didn't catch it at first and I said, ***Pardon me?***

Cleo: Psychiatrist?

Therapist: Then it clicked that she had said "therapist" and I said, ***I didn't understand you the first time and I think you said "therapist." And if you did, that was right, because I am not a psychiatrist, I am a social worker therapist.***

Cleo: Oh, good. You aren't a psychiatrist, you're a therapist. It's a good thing that I didn't get a psychiatrist.

Therapist: ***Why is that?***

Cleo: If you get a psychiatrist they make you take all these tests to see if you're lying.

Therapist: And I thought that it was a good thing after all that I didn't have a psychological done on her.

Supervisor: Don't you think that she's talking about a court psychiatrist and a lie detector test?

Therapist: I didn't think of that. I am always worrying about not having referred her for psychological testing, so that's what popped into my mind. It's very possible that you're right. After all, she watches all these crime programs with suspects in criminal cases being given lie detector tests. I just thought of psychological tests.

Supervisor: It could be either. We just don't know.

Therapist: So I said to Cleo, *What would make someone think that a child is lying?*

Cleo: Children lie all the time.

Therapist: I didn't handle this well. I said, *That's not my experience.*

I realized later that Cleo lies all the time. She says that things are fine when they are not fine. But it was too late and I didn't know how to undo my statement, and Cleo went back to her chicken and her dog and I reflected again how helpful it is when you know something well and then you can judge whether something is safe or dangerous and whether there is reason to feel scared or not. I told her that it was helpful to know the whole story and not just little bits of it. Then it was time to go.

Supervisor: This was a very important session, wasn't it?

Therapist: It was a very comfortable session.

Supervisor: There was something very touching about it. You were able to provide her with an organizing experience in this session. You laid out a clear picture of how certain things work. You conveyed that logic and experience combine to shape judgment. It was so nice the way you used yourself and your experience of your office apartment to conclude that it would be unlikely to see a water bug. But you attributed this reasoning ability to adults and only vaguely suggested that children can do it too. I would revise that part and present children as fully able to reason. It's more accurate.

You could keep two matters in mind that need to be clarified and communicated to Cleo. The first one is that your experience and judgment are now available to her. She vaguely knows that already, but you could confirm her beginning awareness of this, and let her know that this is something that she can now count on. The second matter is that you will help her with the process of using what she knows and doesn't know to make life easier and safer. You can affirm that children too can think and evaluate things and do not just have to accept anything they are told as the truth.

Therapist: So you think I should stress the autonomous quality of her reality testing and judgment? That she can rely on herself more? But isn't that promoting her already precocious independence?

Supervisor: Yes, that would be, and of course we don't want to do that. No, what I had in mind was that you will work together. That you will lend her your strength in this regard, as she's developing her own tools to be stronger. I think that it's very important for us to think of these two components of growth, keeping separation-individuation theory in mind. You want to help her keep a balance between relying on her self and relying on her objects. You don't want her to have to choose one or the other. We know that Cleo has had to lean too heavily on trying to rely on herself, consequently finds herself in dangerous situations, and experiences acute separation anxiety. I am describing precocious individuation here. The implication here is that individuation is getting ahead of separation, while ideally these two processes should keep pace with each other (Edward et al. 1991, Mahler 1971, Mahler et al. 1975). This imbalance is one of the developmental derailments that we hope to repair in the course of treatment. We hope that she will come to perceive you as someone dependable, someone on whom she can rely, and that the experience of being able to rely on you will become internalized. It is the mental representation of this positive experience with a reliable object that becomes one of the vehicles that fuels the separation-individuation process. Remember that the mental representation of a reliable object has the corollary representation of a reliable self.

I am doing a little theoretical review of very familiar stuff. It always helps a little to bring that kind of knowledge to the fore when we have a treatment situation that it fits and yet doesn't fit. After all, Cleo is already 6½ years old and we are talking about very early development, which probably did not proceed smoothly enough for Cleo. We are struggling with how to help her recover from some fundamental developmental deficits. I don't want to sound reductionistic here. Separation and individuation are not like two ends of a balancing scale that can equalize by adding a bit to the lighter side or removing some from the heavier side. We cannot undo and redo Cleo's separation-individuation process because human beings are not constructed that way. But we can offer her an opportunity to experience and internalize a constant reliable object and that can go a long way toward changing the course of future development. It would result in significant structural change.

Therapist: The distinction between separation and individuation is helpful, and I will keep it in mind. Back to Cleo. She did stay with this theme. She told me that her friend Jimmy told her that his mom had met Davy Jones. She said that she knew that was a lie because Davy Jones was dead. She was letting me know that she does know how to use her judgment.

Supervisor: That's terrific. So she's already letting you know that she can have a reliable object representation and a reliable self representation as well. She can have them together and does not have to choose one or the other. She wants you to know that she has some of your attributes and can use them, in this case to test reality, just as you do.

Now we have a whole other issue to deal with and that's the matter of lying. This is a delicate subject that opens some therapeutic possibilities. I'm thinking about what she said about children lying all the time. That was in response to your awkward statement about your belief that children don't lie. It's extremely important for children not to experience their therapist as gullible, for that is not an attribute of strength. Nor do you want to impart the impression that you don't believe her, which is probably what prompted you to say what you said. So there is that ideal positioning of being strong and savvy as well as receptive to what she tells you. This combination of traits will come across in an organic way through what you are and how you respond to her and understand her. You will find ways to convey to her that you do not see the world in black and white and that you are curious not only about what people say but about their motivation as well. Eventually, you will be able to work your way into commenting on her lies. You will be able to introduce the notion that when she says that she's fine, when in fact she is not at all fine, that's a kind of a lie, a special kind of a lie. There are mean lies that are meant to hurt people's feelings and to scare them or make them feel afraid, and there are other lies that don't hurt other people. There are lies that have to do with pretending that you don't need anything from anyone when you really need help. Sometimes children lie about needing help because they think the grown-ups can't do it, or don't want to, or will get mad if you ask them. Those aren't mean lies. They are lies that leave you very lonely.

These are the sort of things you will eventually be able to say to Cleo, when given the opportunity, and of course in small doses. She has no idea that so many of her lies are designed to protect the object representation. These are adaptive lies and they preserve the object representation, but at the cost of the self representation. These are costly choices and they can lead her into a masochistic direction (Glenn 1989, Novick and Novick 1987).

Eventually you will even be able to tell her that she needs help with her aloneness. What do you think?

Therapist: I think I can see all this happening in the future. It feels as if treatment is beginning to take shape. It makes me feel more hopeful to think of our work this way. And I think she will like this direction. I could see things happening in this direction already in her telling the story about Jimmy and his mother. When she told me that she didn't believe the story, she was very animated and expressive. She put her hand on her hip and demonstrated how she had faced Jimmy and said, **Oh yeah! You think that I don't know that Davy Jones is dead?** She seemed so pleased with herself for not being gullible.

Supervisor: There are several more matters that come to my mind that are going to have to be presented to Cleo in future sessions. One is the proverbial notion that you are there to try to get to know her very well, so that when she tells you something that's a lie, it's important for her to let you know that she told a lie. Then, together you can learn a lot about what made her need that particular lie. Of course, you will also need to find out what she means by a lie. We are assuming that she means what we mean, and she might have a different notion of what lying is all about. Then, I think you can start working on the notion of being together.

Therapist: I'm drawing a complete blank. How would I do that?

Supervisor: Well, take today for instance. She brought up watching television together and you were trying to get to the notion of being "together," but it sort of sank, and I speculated that she didn't have the concept of what companionable is like. By the end of this session it appeared that I was wrong about that, and that she does have a sense of what companionable is, however embryonic it may be. Maybe she hasn't learned how to identify it yet, or maybe she recognizes it but doesn't have the language to express herself. You can help her in this regard. The sessions do provide her with a companionable experience and she is beginning to take this in, and based on today's session she appears to be more able to stay with it and make good use of it. So very simply and very subtly you can say things at opportune moments about what is going on between the two of you.

Therapist: Like what for instance?

Supervisor: Well, think of the whole dialogue at the beginning of the session about watching television together. With hindsight, we see you were too far ahead of her. You wanted to explore her perception of being together. She struggled to respond and talked about watching with her sister and you tried to explore that, and still she stumbled around and expressed herself concretely.

Perhaps we were not listening well enough. When children do not have the language of adjectives and adverbs for their affects, then communication is impeded. In this instance Cleo used comparison to express herself. She compared watching T.V. with you to watching with her sister. It's a young and concrete way of expressing herself, and in your responses to her I think that you scrupulously left out adjectives and adverbs because you didn't want to lead her. But in retrospect it might have been okay to just ask her, *Would that feel nice, our watching T.V. together? Would you enjoy that?* And maybe you could even say, *If we ever watched television together, one thing that would be nice about it is that we'd be seeing the same thing at the same time and if there was something funny, we'd both laugh and if there was something sad, we'd be sad together. But we don't need a T.V. to do things together here. The kinds of things we do together here work better for getting to understand important stuff about you and how not to feel scared.*

Therapist: That makes sense now that I think about it. What about the bubble gum? I was uncomfortable about being a prohibitor.

Supervisor: So was I for the first minute, but then you explained it so nicely in terms of needing to understand what she says that I admired your handling of it.

All in all, today's session was very important and indicative of headway in the treatment process. You made so many therapeutic choices, but there was nothing hit or miss about the choices you made. You stuck with the object relations aspect of the treatment and did not get distracted into entering territories that would overwhelm rather than clarify. For instance, her mention of suicide has to be noted as an important concern that will need to be addressed and explored, but she is not ready to do that yet. You are respecting her pace and staying in step with her. You did not get seduced into prematurely exploring something that's beyond her and that might lead her into that world where people in paintings become live and threaten to come and take her to hell.

13

A Turning Point Session: The First Sure Feeling

Therapist: As soon as Cleo heard my office door open, she began walking toward me so that we met half way between my office and the waiting room. She was pulling down her lower eyelids and looking down. I said, ***Oh my, what are you doing to your eyes?***

Cleo: **Nothing.**

Therapist: She was walking in a kind of exaggerated stiff-legged, robotlike gait. She walked over to a mirrored door in my office, looked at herself with her eyes pulled down, and said, Whew, and plopped herself down in a chair.

Supervisor: What was the quality of the eye pulling? Was it rough?

Therapist: Not particularly. She was making a grimace. She spun around in the chair a few times and then said,

Cleo: Guess what I saw on the way home from school yesterday?

Therapist: *I have no idea where to begin to guess about that.*

Cleo: I'll give you a hint. It was horrible and awful.

Therapist: *Oh my. How do I begin to even try to guess about a horrible sight?*

Cleo: I'll give you more hints. Fall, push off building.

Therapist: *Are you telling me that you saw something get pushed or fall off a building?*

Cleo: Old woman. Man push.

Therapist: *Are you telling me that you saw a man push an old woman off a building?*

Cleo: It was very very scary. I saw it with my own eyes, I saw it with my whole body. You can even ask my baby-sitter if you don't believe me.

Supervisor: She walked in pulling on her eyes and then told you this story. How were you feeling? Did you believe her? Or did you think that she was playing her tricking-fooling game?

Therapist: I didn't know what to believe. I was hoping that she was trying to trick me. I didn't want to think that she might have witnessed such an awful scene. So I said, *Are you telling me that this is not one of those times when you try to trick and fool me?*

Cleo: No. I really really saw it with my eyes and my whole body.

Therapist: *You know, what's happening here between us is very hard right now. Yes, this is very difficult. You just told me that you saw something so awful, so frightening and terrible that I don't even want to believe that it's true. But you're telling me that it really happened and that this is not a time when you're playing that tricking and fooling game. That reminds me of last week when we were talking about children lying. This is complicated. My job is to get to know you very well so that I can understand you and help you. I believe what you tell me, but I also know that you sometimes like to fool me. I just don't always know when you want to fool me and when you are telling me a real story. This is such a terrible story that it's a little hard to believe. I'm talking about the trouble that I'm having understanding this.*

Cleo: Even my friends saw it and I don't want to talk about it.

Therapist: *Well, part of you does want to talk about it, and that's the part that told me about it. And maybe another part doesn't want to talk about it. What do you think would happen if we talked about it?*

Cleo: I'm afraid that if I told you more about it that there would be more scary dreams. I already have enough scary dreams that I can't talk about.

Therapist: *It usually helps to talk about things. Could you at least tell me where this happened so I can have a picture in my mind of where you saw all this?*

Cleo: I was coming home from the shoe store on the bus I always take home from school. The shoe store is near school and I was with Maria, and there were other kids from my school on the bus, and I saw an old lady on a roof and this man was pushing her. She was a crazy lady, and she was shouting and yelling and this man had her by the arm and was pushing her. Somebody on the bus told Maria that she was a crazy old lady. Now look at me. I said that I'm not going to talk about this and I'm talking about it.

Therapist: *Well, maybe part of you needs to talk about it and it's hard to stop. If it feels very bad to talk about it right now, can you stop yourself?*

Cleo nodded yes and began to talk about the height of some

of her friends at school and that she was the tallest in her class. She said,

Cleo: One friend comes up to my chest, and another friend comes up to my nose, and another friend is a midget and only comes up to my middle. I think he's a real midget. That's what people call him and that's what he calls himself but I don't know if it's true. And there's a girl who bothers me a lot. Her name is Kitty and she's friends with these other girls who all drive me crazy about being partners. Sometimes they ask me to be their partner and then they complain all the time that I'm not a good partner and I don't even know what they want. I hate to have them for partners. This girl Kitty is so bossy. And my mother keeps making me go to all these funerals. I hate to go to funerals. Too many scary things are happening to me. Everyone in my family is dying. Well, really two people, my uncle and my mother's aunt died. My mother told me that her aunt was very bossy but that's not what made her die. She was very bossy and very dressed up in fancy clothes all the time. I had to go to her funeral.

Therapist: *Did you know your aunt? Did you think she was bossy?*

Cleo: Yes. She was a fancy, bossy lady. She told everyone what to do. I hate when people are bossy. Sometimes when people are bossy it makes me feel like a monster. Kitty is so bossy that one day she got me so mad that I pushed her. I did, I just got mad and pushed her.

Therapist: She stopped speaking and began to spin in her chair and I said, *Sometimes when children get very mad, so mad that they push somebody, the feelings inside feel like monster feelings. Those are upset and angry feelings and these feelings can feel very strong, but the child is not a monster.* I paused for a minute and scratched my arm and she pushed up her tee shirt sleeve. Bending her arm to show her muscle she said,

Cleo: My friend makes a muscle like this.

Therapist: *Did my scratching my arm make you think about your friend's muscle?*

Cleo: Oh, no.

Therapist: For a moment she talked some more about the comparative height of her classmates and then said,

Cleo: My sister told me not to have any bad dreams because they make you act like a monster.

Therapist: *What does she mean, do you know?*

Cleo: Well, when you get scared you do bad things.

Therapist: I said two wrong things to her at this point. I was too direct. I said, *Is that the case for you?*

Cleo: No, that doesn't happen to me.

Therapist: *Maybe your sister is confused about this idea. She thinks that upset feelings and ideas make people act a certain way.*

Supervisor: She's not so wrong. In fact she's pretty accurate.

Therapist: I see what you mean, but for Cleo it's taken so literally that I felt that I had to undo it. Actually I was feeling so protective of her that I didn't even consider that her sister was pretty astute. I said, *You know, talking about your dreams is a very helpful way of getting to understand you very well. I didn't know that you were afraid to talk about your bad dreams here. This is definitely something that I could help you with. Maybe if you talked about your dreams to me you would feel safer than just keeping them to yourself. To me, dreams are a useful way of understanding fears and upsets and worries.*
  She was very squirmy while I spoke and when I paused she

said that she needed to go to the bathroom. When she returned she said,

Cleo: I'm glad that's over, and it didn't growl at me.

Therapist: She was referring to one day during the consultation period when the toilet made an unusual funny noise and we remembered it together and she added,

Cleo: I thought it was growling at me.

Supervisor: Did she say it with a straight face?

Therapist: Yes, but then she laughed. She can really have a poker face. She can carry that off well. Then she told me one of her jokes.

Cleo: Why did the cow cross the road?

Therapist: *One time you told me that the cow crossed the road to get the Chinese newspaper.*

Cleo: No. That's not the right answer. Guess again.

Therapist: *I can't guess but I can remember and I remember that another time you told me that the cow crossed the road to get to the other side.*

Cleo: No. That's not it either.

Therapist: *I can't think of anything else that you've told me. Is there an answer that you would like me to say now?*

Cleo: No. Just guess.

Therapist: *I'm all out of guesses.*

Cleo: The cow crossed the road because the chicken wasn't there.

Therapist: I thought that was pretty funny and I laughed and she laughed with me, and then her face became very serious and she said,

Cleo: Many bad things have happened to me.

Supervisor: Just like that?

Therapist: Just like that.

Supervisor: Were you stunned?

Therapist: Yes, I was very surprised. She went on,

> Cleo: Many bad things have happened to my sister. She got her arm broken and then she got her tonsils out and she got shots from the doctor. You know, my doctor calls me "Cleo-Cleo-Cleo." He does that because when I was a baby I used to yell so loud when he gave me a shot so he used to say "Cleo-Cleo-Cleo" to try to show me that he was friendly and he still says my name three times even though I don't yell anymore.

Therapist: She was enjoying telling me about how loud she yelled and that the doctor found a special way of saying her name. Then she mentioned that her grandfather was visiting and she explained that he wasn't really supposed to come now but he came because he just couldn't bear to stay away from them any more. He missed them too much. She said that she and her grandfather were watching television together, so I asked her what it was like to watch television with her grandfather and she said,

> Cleo: I really like to watch baseball. I like to think that it's me up there at bat hitting the ball. I like to watch the men running around the bases.

Therapist: *So when you watch T.V. with your grandfather, it's as if you're watching the game and playing the game at the same time. Do you also think about your grandfather being there with you?*

Supervisor: Did I miss something, or did she go from the hard time that she and her sister have been having, and the shots, to this about T.V. with her grandfather?

Therapist: That's right. The pediatrician led to the grandfather.

Supervisor: She's really free associating, so at times it seems disconnected, but not really. She experienced warm feelings when talking about the pediatrician and the good feelings were the bridge to the grandfather.

Therapist: Well I must have known that intuitively because it seemed to me as if she had brought up some element of the theme we discussed last week, the state of feeling companionable. It was there with the pediatrician and it was there with the grandfather. I tried to explore it further and asked, *You said that you like it best when your grandfather is there watching T.V. with you. I imagine you sitting there with him and watching the game and pretending that you're playing it. . . . But what is it like for you when he's there with you? What is it that you like so much about it?*

Cleo became very quiet and got a serious look on her face and said,

Cleo: I like it because it feels like he's there to protect me. It feels like he's there to protect all of us and it feels good.

Therapist: *I wonder how it feels to tell me all of this. Your face has a very special look when you talk about this.* I was not happy with this awkward question and she didn't say anything, so I said, *I can tell by the look on your face how important this is to you.*

Supervisor: That was good. I imagine that you were pretty moved by what she told you. Maybe at first you didn't know what to say, but the next opportunity it would be good to convey to her that it's very important that she knows this good safe feeling.

Therapist: That she recognizes the feeling of being protected?

Supervisor: Yes. This is the first time that she really sounds sure about anything. She isn't being slippery or elusive. She's assured and direct. It's an absolute first, a real turning point in the treatment process. I don't know that she could have located that feeling in herself if you had not been exploring this with her. It's a tremendous achievement. You helped her to look at what she was feeling. Let me say this more completely because it's important to understand the process. You helped her mobilize her observing ego at the very moment that she was experiencing a strong positive feeling. She was then able to put that feeling into words. Chances are that it would have been harder for her to do this with a negative feeling. Usually she expresses negative feelings very fleetingly. They feel too dangerous. From this session you learned that she believes that bad dreams can make one act like a monster. Negative feelings are in the same general category for her as bad dreams. But go on. What happened after that?

Therapist: It gets even better. I said, *It's very important that we're talking about this together. Now that I've gotten to know you pretty well, I know that you feel so many things, like sometimes you feel really scared, and other times you feel lonely, and sometimes you feel really nice like when you watch T.V. with your grandfather. These are all such important feelings, and it's going to help you to feel safer if you have somebody to talk to about all this. I know that sometimes you can feel very lonely if you have nobody to talk to about all this.*

Cleo: Boy you can say that again! My mother works all the time and my sister does her homework and usually my grandfather is far away. Have you ever had parrot juice?

Therapist: I was a bit thrown. I can never get used to her quick shifts. She went on to explain that her mother had put one of those box juices into her lunch box and it was parrot juice and it tasted awful. She said,

Cleo: It comes in a three-pack so I'm stuck with it for three days and it's disgusting. The picture on the box says "Tweet-Tweet-Tweet."

Supervisor: Do you know whether there really is such a juice?

Therapist: I assumed that she wasn't making this up. It's probably some new drink that's supposed to sound tropical. At least that's my association.

Supervisor: Would a manufacturer really name a drink "parrot juice"? To me it sounds like a squashed parrot.

Therapist: That's what Cleo said. She said that it tasted like a squashed parrot. Here is where I got some new information about her. Her mother is very nutrition conscious and won't let Cleo have Hi-C, which is what many of the kids in her class have. She wants but is not allowed to have it because it has sugar in it. She told me that she traded with a boy for his Hi-C and when he took a drink of her parrot juice he said that it was disgusting and wanted his juice back, but she had finished most of it, and when he tried to grab it from her she held it up high, and since he's shorter than she is, he couldn't reach it. I told her that that was one way of getting the juice she wants, and another is to let her mother know what she likes and dislikes and to be very clear about it so that she doesn't get stuck with something she hates.

   She then told me that they had a science project at school and it had to do with making bubbles, and here she got very garbled and said that if you go too fast making bubbles they break. I read into this that she was talking about the treatment process and said, *If I ever go too fast for you, you can tell me that and I will slow down.* She looked at me very seriously and didn't say anything.

Supervisor: Did you think that she understood what you were saying?

Therapist: Yes, but I can't tell you why. It just felt very natural at the time. When I went to write down the session, I realized that it was my free association that prompted my statement.

Supervisor: I don't think that it matters too much whether you had a conscious and formulated reason for saying what you said at that moment. Look, you told her that you will accommodate to *her* pace and adapt to *her* needs. Just think of how good that must sound to her. She is not accustomed to people offering to stay in pace with her. Try to imagine how your offer of partnership might sound to this child who has strained so hard to make do on her own. I imagine that your words must convey something new and hopeful. Through them she can sense a climate of caring, and with the caring comes the sense of safety that she needs to experience in order to get her bearings.

Therapist: That's the end of this session, but I want to talk more about my comment. I'm thinking that if an interpretation is not well timed, then it builds resistance. That's my worry about saying something that I'm so vague about.

Supervisor: A therapist doesn't always say things perfectly or know exactly why she or he makes a particular intervention or interpretation. If you're unsure of your reason, don't automatically assume that you were wrong. In this case, if we review the themes of the session, you might get some insight into your timing. I think it was well timed.

Therapist: Well, she was talking about something going too fast and breaking as a result, and I linked it to the treatment.

Supervisor: But that's precisely the way things work in this process. As you follow the trend of her associations, you are using, both consciously and unconsciously, the principle of contiguity. And so is she. If we reviewed the way the communications followed each other, we would get an associative chain. This would have been true from the beginning of Cleo's treatment. The connections were there, but they were so obscure that we were unable to decipher them. Let's follow today's themes and see what we can do with them.

She began with her pulled-down eyelids, then told of the woman on the roof, and then darted away to talk of her tallness and the height of her classmates. Next came the part about people in her family dying. Then she talked of her fears of losing control and pushing in reaction to anger at bossy people, and to bad dreams turning people into monsters. Her trip to the bathroom and joke about the toilet growling was followed by jokes about the cow crossing the road. Then she was back to bad things happening to her and to her sister, followed by good feelings about her pediatrician and her grandfather, and imagining being up at bat. She was then able to identify the good safe feeling she has with her grandfather and her need of you. Then came parrot juice and the fear of going too fast and bubbles breaking. It doesn't sound quite as disjointed when we do it that way, does it? She is shifting between what's really on her mind, and when that gets to feel too dangerous, to distractions in the form of fairly insipid jokes. She stays with her real concerns for longer periods of time, doesn't she? Also, she engages you more in the process. Two months ago she moved between danger and chaos and pretty much left you out. Today is quite an improvement, isn't it?

Now I would like to go over the material she presented in this session from a different point of view. Let's take a look at what we really mean by "dangerous." Let's talk a bit about the unconscious fantasies revealed in the themes of this session.

Today, she conveyed in an unmistakable way her fear that her anger will overwhelm her and that she will do something dangerous, or more accurately, murderous. Remember, she talked about a woman being pushed off the roof, and soon after told you that she got so mad at her classmate Kitty that she pushed her. This child is terribly afraid to express anger because she fears that once acknowledged it will get out of control.

Also in this session she expressed her fear of bodily injury and penetration. Here is a point where oedipal and preoedipal material converge. It's important to keep in mind that while our theoretical base is indispensable in organizing our thinking, what we see in actuality is not as neat as the theoretical presentation. So the convergence of phases and stages has to be deciphered and understood, so that we may judiciously select our focus. In bringing up her fear of broken limbs and injections, she is revealing oedipal issues around castration anxiety (Freud 1924, 1925a). Add that to her fear of the damage that her anger might cause and we have oedipal murder and retribution through castration. But this can also be preoedipal fears of bodily damage and rage at the preoedipal mother.

Then she mentions two men she enjoys, the pediatrician who gives her shots but is also nice to her, and her grandfather who protects her. The pediatrician gave her a special pet name because she was so loud. That's one form of exhibitionism. Then she presents that interesting fantasy of herself as the ball player that her grandfather is watching with her. Another exhibitionistic fantasy. This could be a little confusing because this fantasy is more what one would expect from a boy than from a girl, but then we have to remember that this is what her father most admires in her, her physical prowess. Her fantasy of herself at the bat could also be viewed as a wonderful condensation of drive, ego function, gender attitudes, compensatory defense, adaptation, oedipal longings, and nonmurderous aggression (Parens 1979, 1990).

Her sister is mentioned as a female companion, but is also a displaced oedipal figure. So now we have the murderous wish, the punishment in the form of castration, the acknowledgment of the love object, and the description of the seduction attempt. But we also have the longing for love, admiration, and mastery.

And then at the end of the session her anger at her mother is expressed via the foul-tasting juice that she finds in her lunch box. How angry she must be at her mother for not being a better protector and for not providing her with a father who is a reliable protector. We talked several weeks ago about how burdened the oedipal process is for a child with Cleo's history and present circumstances. Now we get more insight into her struggle with all this. The mother finally appears as the witch rival who puts poison in the lunch box. We get a view into the primitive anger toward the mother, an anger so great that it might be possible to lose control and push her off the roof. And the weaker the parents are, the more alone and unprotected the child is, and the more at the mercy of her drives.

We can't use any of these insights into Cleo's unconscious fantasies at this point in her treatment. The fact that they are unconscious would make them of no use under any circumstances. But what would happen if we didn't know our theory and were unaware of the fact that unconscious material has to reach a preconscious state before it can register and respond to interpretation? If we didn't know that and tried to make interpretations based on these fantasies, it would only frighten this already terrified child.

Therapeutic restraint is one of the crucial aspects of astute timing. It's important to recognize some of these unconscious themes. It gives us a vivid picture of the forces that Cleo struggles with on many levels. And this sort of exploration on our part enriches our work. But we have to keep some of this insight to ourselves lest we prematurely introduce material that would either cause our patients additional stress, or make them think that we have some mighty weird notions.

There is something else to consider. Cleo isn't particularly accustomed to having lengthy conversations with another person in a basic, ordinary, reciprocal way. Her style is frantic and pretty solo. In this session she was able to be more companionable with you then ever before, but still, she never asks anything of you except oblique stuff, like wanting you to guess.

Therapist: I know, and that's what I was trying to address when she asked me to guess what she saw. I was trying to convey that I had no base to start from and that I couldn't do it, but I wasn't comfortable with my handling of that request. It comes up a lot.

Supervisor: It does, and I have strong feelings about it. It seems to me that it provides the therapist with an important opportunity to define the difference between "the therapist" and the rest of the population of the world. When my child patients ask me to guess, I always tell them that guessing is something I don't do. I don't mind sounding a bit prissy about it. I tell them that it's against my rules as a therapist to guess. Often they try to cajole me into guessing, assure me that it's only one little guess and they will never ask me again, but I always stand firm and say that guessing is against the rules of my work. I explain that if I agreed to guess I would be saying that I'm trying to read their minds. Reading minds is not at all what my work is about. Sometimes, though, I explore their wish to have me guess. For instance, I might ask children how they would have liked it to come out if I were the kind of a person who agreed to guess. Would they want me to guess right or to guess wrong? But in the main I just say that guessing is okay for other people, but this is therapy, this is something different from all other situations, and guessing is not part of what I do.

I find that most children are pretty delighted by the notion that we cannot read their minds. It affirms their sense of boundaries. In the case of some psychotic children though, the idea that you cannot read their minds can be terrifying because they cannot stand to feel so separate. With a psychotic child, you have to find ways not to make that too terrifying. With most children, the no guessing rule is pretty acceptable and useful.

Therapist: Yes, that's the way I feel about it, and I tried to convey that to her. In fact, at one point in the session, and I forgot to mention this, I told her that when you know somebody very well and that person gets a certain facial expression or sounds a certain way, you have a clue as to what she might do or say because you recognize something that has happened before. Then your guess is still a guess, but you have something to base it on.

In retrospect I see that I was reluctant to say "no" to her. When I consider the total picture, I think I would prefer being very clear about it with her and setting those firm boundaries between therapy and the rest of life. And besides, what would

I be gratifying in myself or in her by indulging her wish that I guess?

Supervisor: That's a good question and you can give it some thought. While we're on the subject of clarifying for her how things work in therapy, let's talk a little about clarifying other areas of confusion, for instance dreams. At the next opportunity perhaps you could do a little more with that. For example, I don't think that she knows that she is the author of her dreams. It's always a great surprise to children when it's put to them that way. When you ask them, "Do you know that you make up your dreams?" most children and many adults know it on some level, but don't know it in a really conscious way. With Cleo, it sounds a little as if she feels programmed when she's having a nightmare. In this session she conveyed the feeling that if she regards her nightmare as an awful consequence of sleeping and doesn't talk about it, then she simply suffers the scariness of the experience, but if she talks about it, the nightmare will expand and get so real that she will be transformed into something monstrous. She said something like that today. Never mind that she attributed this to her sister. She believes it and wanted you to know that she believes it. She could even believe that a nightmare is a terrible video that was put into her head while she was asleep. That could be an attempt to undo the violence she heard and saw in the middle of the night when her father still lived at home. It would be a child's solution to dealing with the loss of object representations of good and reliable parents by condensing and combining the actual live nightmare of her father's violence with the stuff of her dreams.

How about telling Cleo that a dream is a story that she makes up while she's sleeping? A bad dream or nightmare would be a story about thoughts and fears that she has that are so big and so awful that she would not allow herself to think about them during the day. But at night, the part of her that can stop herself from talking or thinking about these things isn't as strong as it is during the day. At night she has a much harder time stopping the appearance of these feelings. That's a pretty good explanation to give a 6 ½-year-old about dreams.

She needs this kind of clarification from you, and today she gave you a strong signal that she's ready to move deeper into herself and her life. She told you that she and her sister have a hard life. She really took a chance on letting you in more.

Therapist: I wish I had a better idea of how to develop that.

Supervisor: Well, for one thing, you have a point of reference to return to the next time Cleo mentions something hard. You can say, *Remember when you told me that life can get hard? This is the kind of thing you meant, right? This is another of those hard things in your life.* This intervention can accomplish several things. You are building a history of your time together. You remember what she tells you and you add to it when she tells you more. This builds a climate between you where she feels taken seriously, and ultimately she will begin to take herself more seriously. So, if you think about it, this very simple type of intervention can have cumulative impact of great importance.

Therapist: What about her associations? Should I just keep commenting about how she leaves one thing and goes to another?

Supervisor: Eventually you could probably start saying things like, *Now that I'm getting to know you better, I'm beginning to understand the way your mind works. You tell me that somebody gets pushed off a building and that is so awful to think about that you skip to how tall your friends are, because you want to get away from the scary thing you saw. But it doesn't work and you tell me about people dying because you can't get it out of your mind.* I'm not suggesting that you should have done that today. It's just an example of one way of addressing her defensive maneuvers when she tries to get away from something disturbing and fails.

Before our time is up, I do want to ask you how you understood the part about the woman being pushed off the building. Did Cleo say that she saw the woman fall?

Therapist: No. She just saw the man grabbing her arm. I don't know what she saw.

Supervisor: But suicide is on her mind. This is the second week in a row that she's mentioned it. Last week, didn't she try to fool you into looking out the window at someone who was going to jump off a roof?

Therapist: Yes. My goodness. Could she be having such feelings?

Supervisor: We don't know what this means. We know that it's on her mind and that she has let you know about this fear. It certainly is something that you will have to watch.

This has been such a rich session. Something important has crystallized. Cleo is becoming an ally to the treatment. She's turning into a real patient.

14

A Setback Session

Therapist: I think that Cleo has very acute hearing because she can hear me open the door to my office and it's really a very quiet door. On this day I opened my door and ducked into the bathroom to throw something in the wastebasket, so there was a delay of several seconds in my getting to the waiting room. I saw her get up and then slowly back into her chair. When I got to the waiting room she began to rise and then sat down again and said,

Cleo: Who are you?

Therapist: *I'm Linda Small. I'm your therapist.*

Cleo: Oh, okay then.

Supervisor: What was her affect like? Was she smiling or anything?

Therapist: It wasn't clear. She was pretty neutral. I tend to be optimistic and thought that maybe she was a little playful, but I could be completely wrong.

Supervisor: I'm trying to envision this scene. From listening to your description it's hard to imagine that she isn't just playing with you. I wonder what makes you unsure? Even a poker face wouldn't explain why she leaves you confused. Can you describe her affect?

Therapist: She had a kind of "Who are you?" look. Quizzical perhaps, I don't know how to describe it. When she came into the office I asked her, *What was that? Were you not sure of who I am for you today?*

Cleo: That was just a joke.

Therapist: She then sat down in her swivel chair and I said, *You know, we haven't seen each other for seven days, and that can feel like a long, long time.*

Cleo: No. I wasn't thinking anything like that. I was just making a joke for you.

Therapist: *Well, let's try to understand the joke. Okay?* She nodded and looked at me intently, waiting. *How did you feel when you saw me today?*

Cleo: You know, just regular-like.

Therapist: This time her tone was clear and the implication was that it was good to see me, something regular and good. So I said, *So maybe the joke is that you're glad to see me but then pretend that you don't know who I am? Is that the joke? That when you're close you go far away?* I felt myself sounding very lame and not having this go over too well. Then she replied,

Cleo: I'll tell you another joke.

Supervisor: Let's stop here for a minute and figure out what's going on. You were straining to make sense out of her behavior, to connect cause and effect in her feelings and behavior. Generally, when you do that, she turns you off and doesn't want to have anything to do with it, right?

Therapist: That's true.

Supervisor: And you consider it a very important part of your work as her therapist to put some sort of order into her responses, with the ultimate goal of helping her to get to know herself better. So at some point your observation becomes an interpretation directed at her dynamics, and you might say something like, *I've noticed that whenever I let you know how I understand something that you say or do, you let me know that you don't like that very much.* Or maybe you need to be more tentative and prepare her for an interpretation of this sort by letting her know that you've noticed that she might not like it (Pine 1984). You could say:

   I'm going to say something and it might be one of those things that you don't like to hear.

Therapist: Right, I never made one of those interventions and the session was just awful.

Supervisor: One of which of those interventions?

Therapist: One of those organizing kinds of statements like the interpretation and the preface to the interpretation. I just kept saying things like she wanted something from me but she didn't know what it was so she kept pushing me away.

Supervisor: We've got to be sure to return to this. It's important. Right now we have to consider how hungry she is for her time with you and that it might be hard for her to see you once a week for 45 minutes. She probably wishes you were there all the time. I'm basing this thought on the beginning of the session and that tricky reaction she had to the delay of a few seconds, between the opening of your office door and your appearance in the waiting room. It was almost as if she lost you and tried to cover up the sense of loss by saying, who are you? You are so predictable that when you do the slightest off-course move, like a delay of 3 or 4 seconds between the sound of the opening of your office door and your appearance in the waiting room, that's already enough to upset her anticipatory reaching for you. She had to swat you for your unexpected delay of 3 or 4 seconds. Her being able to swat you is pretty good. She's not feigning indifference or going off into fantasy. She's expressing her anger and we've talked about how afraid she is of that. Maybe she's getting a bit less afraid.

Let's talk about this minuscule exchange from a different perspective. According to our theory, the infant's first ego function is memory, and memory facilitates and promotes the next two ego functions, delay and anticipation. I'm coupling the second two functions because they're aspects of the same process. It's possible to delay the urgency of a need when the mind can anticipate the fulfillment of that need. The mind can only anticipate the fulfillment of a need when it remembers an experience of having had that need met. The simplest way to imagine these psychic developments is to imagine observing a tiny infant waking up and instantly screaming until the nipple is in his mouth, and then sucking intensely. Now imagine a return visit to that same infant, say four or five months later. His behavior would be significantly different if his development has been proceeding well. Chances are that this same infant will now wake up hungry, wait a while, then cry. His mother will be able to call to him from another room and her voice will be enough to quiet him down for another short while. If he has become accustomed to hearing her footsteps heading in his direction fairly soon after her verbal greeting, hearing those footsteps will be enough to calm him for another few seconds, because he will associate his mother's voice and her footsteps with comfort in the form of bodily contact and food. In other words, he will have developed the ability to wait because he will have a memory of the many good experiences with his feeding mother and will be anticipating a repeat of that experience of pleasure and satisfaction with her. Terese Benedek (1938) calls this attitude *confident expectation*. But even with confident expectation, if he has to wait too long, his discomfort might become greater than the sustaining memory, and he will cry again. Of course without repeated experiences of satisfaction it's very hard to wait at all.

We have to be a little careful here since it is far-fetched to compare Cleo to a young infant. She is a 6 ½-year-old girl with speech, motility, and altogether incomparably greater resources available to her for dealing with life and life's frustrations. Yet I find it sometimes helpful to think in terms of very primitive states when trying to explain a puzzling phenomenon. I'm thinking here of a type of regression that can occur in an instant, triggered by a very strong affect. I'm not talking of anything pathological here, but of an ordinary and familiar occurrence, a response to a powerful affect. Think of the intense fear one experiences at the instant of recognition that a car crash is inevitable, or the primal delight one can experience for a moment upon hearing a beloved but seemingly forgotten tune. These experiences transcend time and we rediscover buried but not forgotten early self representations. I think that for Cleo, the 3 or 4 second delay in getting to the waiting room was somewhat akin to the experience of the baby. She might have been anticipating seeing you with very great pleasure, and the opening of your door was like the mother's voice and footsteps in my description of the hypothetical infant. The delay of even a few seconds was a terrible letdown and humiliation. I suspect that she must have been surprised by the force of her disappointment. It was almost too much for her and she had to wipe you out by pretending not to recognize you. I suspect that your delay was particularly frustrating at this point because she wants more of you. We have to remember last week's session and how much closer she was able to get to you and how much she might wish that you were her grownup friend, her mother, somebody who is there a lot, and not the provider of one 45-minute session per week.

Therapist: When we think of it that way, it's less hard to imagine that a few seconds could so discombobulate her, but it must be so, because the whole session was disjointed. She then told me a series of jokes. As usual, they were in question form, and when I would ask her how she wanted me to respond, she would say that I should just respond and say whatever was in my head.

Supervisor: That's amusing. She sounds like a little analyst.

Therapist: But I think that you're right, that she wants me to be just a regular person with regular responses. Somebody who will just guess, and never mind all that understanding stuff. Then she gave up telling me jokes and tried to trick and fool me by pretending to see cockroaches on the ceiling, and so on. I asked her what she wanted me to do about the cockroaches on the ceiling. She told me to look at them and when I turned to the spot she was pointing to she yelled,

Cleo: I tricked you, I fooled you!

Therapist: *You know something? That just reminded me of something we were talking about a couple of weeks ago that I wasn't clear about. It has to do with children lying. Your wanting to trick me reminded me of it. Remember, I said that I didn't know that children tell lies? Well, that was silly of me. What I really meant was that children very often don't start off wanting to lie, but sometimes they get too scared to tell the truth, or they want something very badly and they end up lying because they think that's the only way they can get what they want.*

Cleo: Oh, like my sister and her makeup. I have a secret with her about that but I guess I can tell you because you can't tell my mother if I don't want you to, right?

Therapist: *Right!*

Cleo: Well, my sister is not allowed to have makeup, and she has it hidden away and pretends that she doesn't have any and she told me and I swore not to tell my mom. Sometimes my mom finds a lipstick in her room and asks her about it and she always tells her that it belongs to a friend who left it at our house by accident. Then sometimes my mom looks at me with a question on her face and I just look away.

Therapist: ***Well, that's a lie so Tina can do what she likes and be the boss of herself. That's a kind of lie that children tell.***

Cleo: Yeah, like my friend Sam. Sam told Jeff that he had this great collection of baseball cards, and so Jeff went to his house and found out that he didn't have any cards, not one.

Therapist: ***Oh? Now that's a hard kind of a lie, when you want somebody to be your friend and you think that they won't think you're good enough, so you pretend to have something interesting that they will like, just to get them to be your friend. What a mess for Sam. Maybe Jeff would have wanted to be his friend even without baseball cards. That was a sad lie. And then there are mean lies.***

Cleo: Yep. I know about mean lies.

Therapist: ***So I just wanted you to know that I know something about lies and lying.***
    Then I said something really clumsy about still getting to know her and how important it is to me to know when she's fooling me, which is a kind of lying, and when she's telling the truth. She listened with a blank look on her face and I was feeling awful about sounding clumsy and inane. She then asked me some math question.

Supervisor: You skipped over her saying that she knows about mean lies. Is that why you felt you were clumsy?

Therapist: Goodness. No, I didn't even notice that. I was worried that she might think I was viewing her story about the roach as a lie. I was worried that I sounded stern and judgmental. And I also thought that I sounded vague and general. I wish I had said something about her, like that sometimes she tells me that she's fine when she isn't fine and that's a very special sort of a lie.

Supervisor: Lying is a delicate matter and it's hard to talk about it elegantly. It's going to take a while to get across to her that you are interested in her lies. Try to take it out of the good and bad realm. She needs to know that her lies are valuable in the therapy situation. Tell her that there is a lot to be learned about the kinds of lies people tell, for instance in the lie her friend Sam told. It tells you that Sam doesn't think that he's wonderful and that people would want to be with him. If you and she tried to understand some of her lies, it would be interesting and helpful. You could also tell her that since sometimes you don't know whether she is fooling or telling the truth and it would be good if she could tell you, but if she can't, you will let her know whenever you aren't sure. You probably do that anyway, right?

Therapist: Yes. Whenever I'm not sure, I tell her that I don't know whether she's pulling my leg or serious. In fact something like that happened in this session and I forgot to mention it. She was chewing gum at the beginning of the session and at one point I couldn't understand what she was saying because of the gum. So I said, *Remember last time when I asked you not to chew gum because then I can't understand what you're saying?*

Cleo: No. I don't remember that.

Therapist: But she spit out the gum that instant and said,

Cleo: I didn't want it anyway. It was red hot gum and it was burning my mouth.

Therapist: This was at the very beginning of the session. I then asked, *I'm not sure about that gum and how you feel about it. If it was important to you to have it and if it made you feel more comfortable, would you tell me?*

Cleo: **Oh, it's all right. It was red hot cinnamon gum and it was starting to burn anyway.**

Therapist: So, she not only gave it up, but made it bad and burning so I wouldn't worry about it.

Supervisor: You started off asking her if she remembered last week's request that she not chew gum. She said she didn't but quickly got rid of the gum. Look at how jumbled everything got here. We can assume that she did remember your request about not chewing gum and felt terrible being caught at chewing gum anyway. She then behaved as if your request was a command that she give up the gum. She made your request into something hard and angry and not what you were asking of her.

Therapist: Right. I wanted to know whether she needed the gum to feel comfortable. When she chews gum, she sticks a whole wad in her mouth and goes "chop chop" so loud that I can't understand what she's saying. I want to be able to understand her, but her comfort is even more important. I hope that came across.

Supervisor: I think you got into trouble by asking if she remembered. It would have been much simpler to say that while her gum is probably delicious, you can't understand what she says while she's chewing, and could she stop. Adults usually ask children whether they remember something or another when they really mean "Why don't you remember?", or "Do as you're told." It's generally a thinly veiled reprimand, and if, in this case, it wasn't like that, it was too close for Cleo to distinguish. This reaction to "why" questions is not particular to children. Adults usually respond the same way. It takes most patients a long time to believe that our use of the word "why" is not a reproach but a real question. For instance, if you say to a patient, "Why did you get so angry at your husband's comment?" chances are that your patient will feel misunderstood and reproached. On the other hand, you could say, "Do you understand what it could have been about your husband's comment that evoked such a strong reaction in you?" There is a better chance that the patient might perceive the question put the second way as a pathway to self-exploration. In other words, the same question, if finely tuned, can become an interpretation rather than just a question. I'm talking about technique, tact, and precision all at the same time. When a question is an interpretation it questions not the particular event or reaction to the event but the dynamic, genetic, and adaptive determinants of the issue under discussion.

Now let's get to the session and the subject of lying.

Therapist: After we talked about lying she began to give me math quizzes and then I became sleepy. That's my signal, my reaction alerting me to something going on that I don't understand. I see it as countertransference. I react by trying to create a connection. I don't want to be held at arm's length. I began to ask her things like, *Do you want me to answer this? Do you want me to know the answer? To struggle with the answer? How do you want me to answer?*

Cleo: I want you to answer just the way you would answer what's two plus two.

Therapist: *Well, I know that two plus two is four.*

Cleo: What's four plus four?

Therapist: *Well, I know that's eight.*
And then it became an exponential thing and we were up to 256 + 256 and I said, *These numbers are getting so big that I'm going to need a pencil and paper. Do you really want me to go on with this or is there something else that you want?*

Cleo: I want to see how smart you are.

Therapist: *Maybe there's another way of finding out how smart I am. Do you want me to be smart about math or do you want me to be smart about something else?*

Cleo: This is going to be a game show.

Therapist: She turned the play into a game show and asked me questions in a half-hearted way. Things like who was the first president and how many tens in fifty. I wasn't comfortable just answering so I partly answered and kept injecting remarks like, *You know, you're asking a lot of questions and I'm not sure that the questions you're asking are really the questions you care about. You seem to want something from me. You act as if you want my answers, but I think my answers are getting me far away from you.* We were in fact drifting apart and soon she was playing alone and I was getting sleepy. I made another effort to reconnect. *This kind of reminds me of the beginning of the session when I went to greet you in the waiting room and you said, "Who are you." I think that you must have had several different feelings about me then. I know you said that you felt just regular at that moment, but you must have also felt some other way or you wouldn't have said that you didn't know who I was. I think that for just a moment you really didn't know who I was or how to be with me. Something happened to make you feel bad, to make you feel as if you had lost me, and then you turned it into a joke.*

Supervisor: It does appear as if that delay really threw her off course. As I speculated earlier, she appears to have lost you for those 3 seconds and she must have startled herself with the strength of the feelings that stirred in her. She said, Who are you? Such a dramatic statement, and confusing too because, as so often with her, it borders on the theatrical. Just imagine how much simpler her life could be if she could ask, "Why did you go into the bathroom?" or "How come you didn't come straight out like you always do?" or "I got confused when I heard your door open and didn't see you right away. I know how long it takes from your door sound to seeing your face. What were you doing? Were you trying to trick me?"

Cleo cannot talk that way yet. She's too vulnerable and easily overwhelmed by her fantasies to do that. So she turns to math problems. It's her way of defending herself from feeling overwhelmed. It's adaptive, and does help her regain her bearings. But it makes it hard to stay in pace with her. You tried by staying with the math problem while at the same time trying to turn it into something else.

To conceptualize this situation with Cleo dramatically in order to emphasize a point, let us say that the session operated on two levels. On one level you are together in the room and things are happening between you. On another level she leaves you and climbs into one of her video shows and becomes the producer, the director, the person in charge. She leaves the natural flow of being together and withdraws into a world that has no place for you. Her response to feeling out of control is to take charge and *not* to lean on you and ask for help.

Here is a technical dilemma. The way she leaves you and moves into the game show could be viewed as resistance. But should you tamper with it at this point in treatment?

Therapist: Well, she's using her tried and true way of dealing with disequilibrium and, as you pointed out, she does recover.

Supervisor: How did the session end?

Therapist: Without me in it. She was the hostess of a game show, walking around, hitting buzzers, holding up an imaginary script, and giving hand signals, and I was just there.

Supervisor: Did you say things like, *What's my part? What am I supposed to do here?*

Therapist: Yes. She would tell me to just sit there. I asked several times and each time I got that same answer. And as I sat there I got sleepier and sleepier. And then the session was over and she left in a very compliant way.

Supervisor: How does she greet her baby-sitter?

Therapist: I no longer follow her all the way to the waiting room. I just take two steps in that direction and turn back to my office.

Supervisor: So you don't know if she has make any inroads with Maria.

Therapist: I doubt it. From what I see when I go fetch Cleo in the waiting room, things are as flat as ever. In fact, I no longer greet her. She seems invisible. I don't notice her.

Supervisor: I think that's a mistake. That makes you an accomplice to a terrible situation. When you fetch Cleo you can say "hi" to Maria. And at the end of sessions you can walk Cleo back to the waiting room and at least try to connect with her and thus create some sort of transitional moments for Cleo's arrivals and departures.

I assume that you didn't connect Cleo saying, **who are you?** as a reaction to your delay in reaching the waiting room. With hindsight, had you made that connection, you could have said something to Cleo about the delay, and perhaps about the reaction to the delay. You disappointed her, just as Maria chronically disappoints her. She probably felt tricked by you and then she tricked you in retaliation. The fact that she allowed her anger expression is a favorable sign, a more expressive response than empty resignation.

This session felt like a setback, didn't it? And last week was a turning point up. Still, on this day there were a couple of moments when she connected with you, like trusting you to keep the secret about her sister's makeup, and telling you about her friend Sam. But on the whole, it was more like the old sessions with a very elusive Cleo. She was probably more vulnerable to disappointment after the closeness of last week. It's to be expected. Don't let it discourage you. Let's consider this session a bridge between last week and the next session. It's going to get more and more interesting.

15

Diagnostic Stock-Taking

Therapist: Cleo was 5 minutes early. I could hear her whistling in the waiting room. As soon as I opened my office door she stopped whistling, and when I got to the waiting room she looked stony faced. Maria looked as vacant as ever. I made it a point to say hello to Maria and then turned to Cleo and said, ***Hello, Cleo. I heard you whistling.*** Cleo perked up and kind of smiled, slid off her chair and led the way to my office. I had that feeling I've mentioned before that she thinks she's going to get yelled at, that I'm catching her at something bad. You know, that furtive quality, like the way she stops whistling the minute she hears my door open.

Supervisor: She sounds kind of sassy and playful, and that usually doesn't go with that defensive attitude, but you are there and you sense some fearfulness in her, some uncertainty about what is allowed.

Therapist: I don't know whether she's teasing me like, "You didn't really see me do it" or "I wasn't really doing anything."

There's an edge of some sort, as if she's waiting to get caught. Then when I speak to her in a normal friendly way, she relaxes. I don't know what it is, but there's something there, like playing with danger maybe?

   She followed me to my office and flopped down in her chair and said,

Cleo: Oh, my gums hurt a lot.

Therapist: *Do you have a sore on your gums?*

Cleo: No, they hurt from sucking in because I've been whistling for a long time.

Therapist: *Is it your cheeks or your gums that hurt you?*

Cleo: It's this, the cheeks. I got mixed up.

Therapist: *You know, it's more comfortable when you understand what made a pain.*

Cleo: I agree with that.

Supervisor: She said it just like that, so grown up?

Therapist: Yes, she sounded almost solemn. Then she said,

Cleo: This is a tired kind of day.

Therapist: *What makes this a tired day for you?* She swivelled around in her chair a bit and said,

Cleo: It's raining and it's gray out and I had to get up at 7:30.

Therapist: *Is that a different time than usual for you?*

Cleo: Well, no, but it was hard to get up.

Therapist: *When did you go to sleep last night? Was it later than usual?*

Cleo: I went to sleep at nine like I always do.

Therapist: *Did you have trouble falling asleep?*

Cleo: No, I went to sleep right away.

Therapist: *Well, maybe you're tired from all the hard work you do in a day.*

Cleo: Oh boy, yes! Schoolwork . . . and then that recess!

Therapist: *Is recess tough for you?*

Cleo: Yes. The kids boss me around a lot and tell me what to do and then they get into these fights and make me watch and I don't want to so I sneak away when they aren't looking at me but they always find out and yank me back. Boy, I don't like that. I hate that!

Therapist: *What kind of a game is that, to watch kids fight and to force other children to watch?*

Cleo: Oh, they just like to horse around. I don't mind.

Therapist: *You know, this is one of those times that's puzzling. You say you don't mind, but before you said that you do mind. One of those statements is true. They can't both be true. So this is one of those times that maybe you don't really know the truth about how you feel about it. What do you think about that idea?*

Cleo: Would you like me to tell you a joke?

Therapist: *Now? You're thinking of telling me a joke now?*

Cleo: Yes.

Therapist: *You know something? I've noticed that when we're talking and I'm noticing and understanding something important about you, then you want to tell a joke. You sort of move away from me.*

Cleo: No, I don't.

Therapist: She responded by putting her arms up, you know like giving up, like the surrender gesture. She was laughing as she did it. So I said, also laughing, *All right, I guess we understand each other.*

Cleo: Why does the horse cross the road?

Therapist: *Why?*

Cleo: He goes to find the chicken.

Therapist: Then she just went on and on telling jokes and I just listened and made no interpretive remarks. She was enjoying herself and seemed unusually comfortable. At one point I chuckled and remarked that she really loves to tell jokes. And she said,

Cleo: Yeah, but last year I never told jokes. Last year I didn't even talk much. I cried a lot though. In my house where I live there's a baby on the fourth floor that cries a lot and people complain about him all the time. When I was a baby I cried real loud, real, real loud.

Therapist: I asked her who had told her about her loud crying, and I commented that she seemed proud of having been a noisy baby. I somehow connected it to her pride in the joke telling . . . that she had moved from being a noisy baby to a joke teller. She said,

Cleo: Yeah, I just took that crybaby and pulled her out and plunk, threw her in the garbage.

Therapist: She demonstrated this by pretending to pull the baby out of her mouth with two fingers and flinging it into the wastebasket. I said, *Well, it's good that you can feel strong, but let's not throw that crybaby part away. It's important to hold on to all the different parts of you. It's important to help the crying part of you. When things are sad it helps to be able to cry. Sometimes when things are sad it feels good to* know *that we feel sad and then it can even feel good to cry.*

Cleo: Did you know that I can tie myself up in a pretzel? Would you like me to show you?

Supervisor: I bet you weren't one bit sleepy so far.

Therapist: Not one bit so far. Later, I got twinges of it as she spent quite a bit of time tying herself up into a pretzel, but it wasn't that debilitating stupor I sometimes feel, and I was surprised when it came. This had been such a rich session so far. While she was tying herself up into a pretzel she was also wriggling and squeezing her thighs and I asked her if she had to go to the bathroom. It was like the movements I noticed some weeks ago. They could be masturbatory or they could be holding back going to the bathroom, or, of course, they could be a manifestation of both. I have no way of knowing. So when I asked her about the bathroom she said she didn't, and I explained that I had noticed that she was wiggling and that's what made me ask. It felt clumsy. She just continued turning herself into a pretzel.

Supervisor: How did she do that?

Therapist: She lay down on the floor and did various acrobatics. She was very agile and limber and I made an admiring comment, *Wow! You can really do that!*

Cleo: You know, I got hurt at recess, look at this.

Therapist: And she pulled up her pants leg and showed me a scrape. We talked for a minute about how it had happened; she had run and fallen. Then I had to talk to her about our next appointment, which fell on a holiday. I told her that we would reschedule, but first I needed to know about her week so as to find a good time for us. I asked her when she had "after-school" activities. She said that she had a music lesson on Thursday and nothing any other day. I said, *I think that it's very important that we see each other next week even though we can't have our regular time. I'll call your mother tonight to arrange another time. Do you want to speak to me when I call her?* She said that she didn't. Then

I said, *Another thing that's coming up next week is that I'm having my regular monthly meeting with your mother. Is there anything that you would like me to say to her?*

Cleo: No, I can tell her 'most everything. No, I don't have anything to ask her. Everything is really fine with me.

Supervisor: What a serious and down-to-earth response. I'm stunned by the difference between that and her more typical, obliquely humorous responses. She was sounding straight about this for the first time. What did you think?.

Therapist: Well, I did notice that she didn't say "tell her wocka-wocka," but I don't think that it sank in that it was such a major change. I was also aware of having left more time to discuss this. I tend to ask her on the way out, which is a mistake.

Supervisor: It is a mistake to treat this question as a practical matter. It's anything but practical, and, as you see, it has the potential of eliciting some very important communications. But even at the beginning of this session Cleo was able to be simple and conversational with you in a way that seemed new and different. She wasn't talking about fantastic stuff and leaving you confused. She was talking to you in a matter-of-fact way.

Therapist: I forgot to mention that she drew during this session. After she finished turning herself into a pretzel she sat down at the desk and drew. And she included me in the drawing activity. First she drew a big circle and said,

Cleo: Oh, this is interesting. I wonder what this is going to be?

Therapist: And she turned it into a guitar and told me that her mother plays the guitar. She sat there and colored it in, and it was during that time that we talked about the rescheduling and about my seeing her mother. When she was finished I told her that I would put it into a folder for her and have her name on the folder and put it into my closet. She raised no question about taking it home. You know, this was the first time that Cleo drew during a session since around the evaluation period. She did so with pleasure, and I think it felt like an organizing experience for her.

Supervisor: Two weeks ago we had what we considered a turning point session. Then last week seemed like a setback. And today she seemed the most comfortable we've ever seen her. There's a lot of movement taking place. It's too bad that the summer interruption approaches. We'll have to give the planning of that interruption a lot of thought.

Before we end for today, let's talk about the last three sessions. Let's give them names so as to be clear about which is which. Let's call two weeks ago the Turning Point session, last week the Setback session, and today just today's session. Now, let's review what was so special about the Turning Point session. I'm looking at my notes.

1. She told you that she believes scary dreams can make her act crazy-dangerous, and that anger can drive her out of control.
2. She told you that terrible things are happening to her and to her sister, like people dying and broken limbs.
3. She told you of two good relationships, her friendly pediatrician and her loving and protective grandfather.
4. She admitted her loneliness and her need of you.
5. She told you of something poisonous between herself and her mother, using the parrot juice as a metaphor.

This adds up to Cleo telling you a lot about the forces that move her, the good and the bad of her life. Or, to put it into a psychoanalytic framework, Cleo talks of her struggle with the positive and negative affects that she experiences.

I'm focusing on this because it could imply that Cleo possesses more developed psychic structure than was evident before. Her struggle is beginning to sound like an intrapsychic one, rather than one between herself and her external environment. She is not fighting demons and disasters in these sessions. It shows us that she can sound remarkably similar to an adult patient who comes to a therapist and says, "Let me tell you about my life, the things I love and the things that terrify and frustrate me." I'm talking about a capacity to take hold of things in herself, talk about them, and make observations about herself.

Now let's use the image of a door that Cleo places between the two of you in order to control the degree of closeness and connection between you. In the Turning Point session, she allowed that door to stay open for a good long time, the longest ever since she first began treatment. In the Setback session she kept that door open just a crack most of the hour with just a couple of slight widenings as, for instance, when she included you in the secret about her sister's makeup. For most of that session though, she was very guarded with you.

Today she opened that door again. She whistled in the waiting room, clearly wanting you to hear her before you saw her, and this wish to make her presence known and to show off had a rich phallic, aggressive timbre. She had a humorous reaction to your resistance interpretation; remember how her arms rose in a gesture of surrender accompanied by laughter. She was reflective and conversational about ordinary things: feeling tired, the weather, the rough kids at school. She talked about how much better she feels than last year. She expressed some ambivalence: her rage and sorrow on the one hand and her passive and compliant wishes on the other. She brought a nice part of her mother into the session, the guitar-playing mother, a provocative image but we don't know what it means to Cleo. She even told you that she can say 'most everything to her mother now and that she is fine. She's feeling less angry.

There was also that very interesting dialogue about being forced to watch "children fighting." What a fascinating slip that was, and she took it right back fast. She must have felt *forced* to watch her parents fight and at the same time was probably terribly drawn to watching these violent primal scene-like episodes. Can you now imagine a time when she will actually be able to talk about what she witnessed?

Therapist: I didn't even hear the connection between watching the schoolyard fight and her parents. It went right by me.

Supervisor: That's okay. It'll come up again. The therapist is so often the last to register these things. Haven't you noticed that at case presentations, whether at an ongoing seminar or at a scientific meeting? The members of the audience notice a thousand things about the patient of which the presenter is unaware. And it's sometimes much easier to notice things when one is not in the room with the patient. Not being with the patient makes quite a difference. That's the way it should be. If in addition to everything that you notice: tone of voice, facial and body expression, the temperature in the room, your own psychic state, and so on, you also registered everything that your supervisor and audience notice, you would feel bombarded. Freud (1912b) told us to listen to our patients with "evenly-suspended attention." This recommendation regarding the technique of listening is brilliant and always applicable. To return to the point I made about a connection between watching fights at school and witnessing parental fights, if Cleo had reached the point where it was possible to talk about her experience with her father's violence, you would know it. What I noticed today was that she was getting just a little closer to being able to talk about it in the future.

There is one last thing I want to mention today. I know that you've worried a lot about not having had psychological tests, and I have had to remind you that while they're nice to have, you had some good reasons to not ask for them during the evaluation period. At the time of the consultation, Cleo's mother was alarmed and upset, and you felt that the request for psychological tests would have placed too great an emotional and financial strain on her. You considered the mother's distress as an important consideration and I think you were correct in your assessment, particularly since we knew from the beginning that Cleo was bright and competent in most areas of her life. While we didn't think that she had neurotic structure yet, which is what we would hope for in a child her age, we didn't think she was psychotic. We pretty much saw her somewhere on the border of neurotic, with a tendency to regress pretty severely under what would appear to us to be moderate stress (Rosenfeld and Sprince 1963, 1965). Last week was a good example of that. I'm referring to the Setback session.

So, even though we have never formally given her a diagnostic designation, we have talked diagnostically throughout our supervisory sessions. As we move along, we are getting to see a broader and broader picture of this very interesting child. As we see her change, our diagnostic thinking about her will be constantly reevaluated and revised. The most important reason for having a diagnostic hypothesis is its connection to technique. Our primary concern is still to help her feel safer and less angry. That's already happening very nicely. At some point in the future we will need to help her reconstruct some of her traumatic experience so as to be able to help her correct some of the distortions (Furman 1971, Greenacre 1980). We can be sure that her story about the parental violence in some way involves her as a participant and instigator. The reason I say this so categorically is that our knowledge of early development is very clear about the egocentricity of little children. Children always feel responsible for what happens around them. It is only when and if we grow up that we learn that most of what happens in the world had nothing to do with our having willed it or wished it. Cleo's feelings of guilt have played an important part here, have exacerbated her sense of danger, and have kept her in that chronic state of worry about her safety (Sandler 1987).

16

The Therapist Has a Setback

Therapist: I had my monthly session with Cleo's mother and got some important information. I learned that Cleo never felt afraid in the country house and that her father rarely came there. No drunken scenes ever took place there. That was new information.

I also learned that the father had just that week found new employment, this time working for a pharmaceutical company, and he seemed pretty pleased with that. Mrs. C. said that he would have pretty good insurance coverage after a 6-month probationary period, and that as soon as that was in effect, he would be able to help pay for Cleo's therapy. She said that he had been very irregular in his contact with the children and that she hoped the new job would have a settling effect on him. She said that Cleo refused to discuss any feelings she might have about her father not calling her or seeing her on a predictable basis. I suggested that she didn't have to feel that she had to promote discussing this issue with Cleo. I said that Cleo's need to preserve whatever good she might find in her father was probably very powerful, and that her mother's well-meaning wish to help her unburden some of the disappointment he might cause would probably not be welcome at this time.

A very important piece of information was in regard to the lessening of Cleo's fearfulness. She can now stay in her room by herself and play and does so out of choice and with comfort. She can also walk around the apartment comfortably. I don't know whether you remember that when she first came to see me, she refused to walk from one room to another unaccompanied and refused to stay in any room by herself. So some of those presenting symptoms have abated. She still needs her mother to sit with her while she's falling asleep, although she knows that her mother will leave as soon as she's fast asleep. Also, she is no longer afraid of the paintings on the walls. A lot of good changes are taking place.

Supervisor: Did the mother sound pleased?

Therapist: She didn't reveal that. She sounded matter of fact about the reduced fearfulness.

Supervisor: Let's note that. It's startling that she would not be very pleased about such dramatic changes in Cleo.

Therapist: That's true. She just seemed to be rushing through telling me all of this information in a kind of businesslike manner. Then she told me that the children were going to be in the country house for all of July and all of August.

Supervisor: Were you surprised?

Therapist: Yes, very. I expected one month, but not two. I knew that the grandparents come in the summer and stay with the children, but I didn't realize that they stay in the country the whole time. Also, the mother has a summer teaching job so she will only see the children on the weekends. They will probably not see their father at all during those two months.

Supervisor: Goodness, that's a lot of changes and separations. Does Cleo know that she isn't going to see you, or her father for that matter, for two months?

Therapist: I forgot to ask the mother that.

Supervisor: It's important to know that. Otherwise you might tell her and it really is something that her mother should tell her. If you tell her first, you are taking over her mother's function and that's not wise. Cleo might go home and say that Linda Small told her that she will be away July and August, and the mother might really resent having her place usurped. That kind of error can intensify the rivalry that so often develops between mother and therapist.

Therapist: Well, it's too late. I've already told her.

Supervisor: Did you tell her or ask her? Did she know about the plans?

Therapist: I just told her, and at first I couldn't tell if she knew or not, because she didn't let on. When I asked her straight out she said she did know.

Supervisor: It's so typical of Cleo not to let on. She doesn't have a normal kid response like saying, "I know that" or "Nobody told me," or some expression of what she thinks about it. Most kids her age are dying to tell what they know. She, on the other hand, pulls back at such moments, shuts the door and leaves you and perhaps herself in the dark as to her feelings.

Therapist: How well I know that feeling of being in the dark. Today was a strange session. It began in a funny way. The patient before her opened the door to leave, and at that moment Cleo was coming out of the bathroom, which is right next to my office. So Cleo just walked into my office. I was right at the door, but I was startled because I hadn't quite registered her presence and here she was in the room. There was something territorial about the way she entered my office before I asked her to come in. I said, *Oh, here you are. You look like you got a lot of sun.*

Cleo: I had extra recess today and it was just great.

Therapist: She described a lot about running and playing and she looked animated and flushed as she spoke. I said, *That's good to hear, because I remember that last time we talked about recess it wasn't great. It was a hard time for you.*

Cleo: Well, this time it was great because I didn't have to play with anybody. I could just play with my friends.

Therapist: That really confused me and I wondered whether she could mean that she had made up a video with imaginary friends. I asked, *What friends are these?*

Cleo: Josie and Robert and Mike and Sarah and Matt and Julie.

Therapist: *That's a lot of names I never heard you say before. Who are all these children?*

Cleo: They're kids in my class that I can play with. They don't make me do things I don't like to do, like play games I don't like or watch fights.

Therapist: I was puzzled about this aspect of her school life, but then I know so little about her life at school. She has just started talking about it and her mother never mentions it. I guess I should ask and probably speak to her teacher. Then Cleo said,

Cleo: I want to finish my guitar. I was thinking about something I want to add to it. Can you get it out of your closet?.

Therapist: *Sure. I guess you were thinking about that guitar.*

Cleo: Yes, I was thinking that I want to add something to it, but I forgot what you call it. It's something you put on it so you can put it over your shoulder.

Therapist: *Do you mean a strap?* Cleo nodded and I handed her the folder with her drawing of the guitar, and said, *Sometimes when you aren't here, you think of our time together and of what you're going to do when you get here?* She was sitting and drawing the strap for her guitar. She didn't answer. I asked, *What would you like me to do while you're drawing?*

Cleo: Nothing. I just want you to sit there.

Therapist: So I did, and when she finished, we put her drawing back in the folder and back in the closet. I then said, *You know, I saw your mom yesterday.* She nodded.

Supervisor: This is a small point, but a useful one. Try to put things more in question form like, *Did you know, or did you remember. . . .* Do you see the difference? It engages her more and imparts the sense that she has more control, that she can do her own remembering.

Therapist: Yes, I can see that.

Supervisor: It's also more personal because you're referring to an exchange that has taken place between you. That it's something that took place between you is the important part of the communication. She doesn't let you know when she remembers something like that. Another child would say, "You told me," and revel in remembering and letting you know that she remembers. This is the flat part of Cleo, the passivity that we keep encountering, and yet in many ways she is not passive. But go on with the session.

Therapist: I told her about the summer plans. She did know them and seemed surprised that I referred to her summer place by name. It's Lakeville. She said,

Cleo: Yes, that's the name of my country place. Say it again.

Therapist: *Lakeville. Your mom told me the name. You look a little surprised that I know it.* I waited a minute to see if she had anything to say about it, but she was silent, so I went on, *Your mom told me that you would be there all of July and August and that your grandparents were going to stay with you.*

Cleo: And my mom will come out some weekends.

Therapist: I was stunned. Why would her mom only come out some weekends? She wasn't doing it to accommodate the father's visits. He was not going to see the children over the summer. I had assumed that the mother would be there every weekend. I make too many assumptions about this mother because she's loving and kind in many ways. But there is also that cut-off aspect, the part that doesn't act pleased that Cleo is so much better, and that allows that inadequate baby-sitter to take care of her kids.

Then Cleo asked if she could make another picture and I said, *Sure you can. Remember that when you're here you can pick and choose what you do.*

Cleo: Oops, I took more than one piece of paper.

Therapist: *That's fine. You can take as much as you need.* She began to draw and said,

Cleo: Oh no. I messed up. My horse looks more like a duck.

Therapist: She turned the paper over and said,

Cleo: I guess I'll draw a duck

Therapist: And she began to make the webbed feet and the body and head, and then she said,

Cleo: Oh, now the duck looks like a billy goat. I'll put a beard on it. Good, now that's a billy goat.

Therapist: *How did you get from a horse to a duck to a billy goat?*

Cleo: I don't know. I just did.

Supervisor: Was there anything in the pictures that really looked like those animals?

Therapist: Well, she ended up making the billy goat look goatlike, but the others didn't really get formed enough to look like anything. They were very unfinished looking when she switched their identities. I was trying to get her to be more reflective about her thinking processes, but I ended up just sounding more like a nag. I said, *Sometimes it's helpful to think about how you got from one thing to another. It helps you to not get jumbled up.* She was drawing another picture and didn't respond. I decided to get off my track and said, *This is a different day of the week than the day we usually see each other. Did it seem like a long time since we've seen each other?*

Cleo: Yes, it seemed like a long time and it was a long time.

Therapist: *It was three days longer to wait than we usually wait between appointments because of that holiday. That means that next time it might seem like a short time because we're going to meet again in four days.*
　　She was quite involved in her drawing so I asked her if she wanted to tell me a story about her picture.

Cleo: The billy goat wanted to go home. Oh, wait a minute, I have to draw a tree. Okay, now I have the tree. So the billy goat wanted to go home. Oh, wait I forgot to draw a monkey. I'll put him up here on top of the tree.

Therapist: She was coloring with great speed and energy. The tree was an evergreen with pine cones all over it and a hole in the middle. The monkey sat on top holding an orange ball. The background was all black. When she was finished she said,

Cleo: The billy goat wanted to go home. The end.

Therapist: *That's a very short story. What will he do when he gets home?*

Cleo: He's going to eat and sleep and in the morning when he gets up he's going to play the violin.

Therapist: *Oh, like you. I know that you play the violin.*

Cleo: I have a concert coming up next week.

Therapist: *How do you feel about that?*

Cleo: I don't feel any way about it.

Therapist: *What is it like to play the violin?*

Cleo: It's a very hard instrument to play. This is the way the billy goat would play.

Therapist: And she picked up a magic marker and started conducting with it and sang the song that she was going to play at her concert. Then our time was up, and while we put things away she talked about the games she had played at recess. She seemed animated and enthusiastic and said she was tired from playing so hard.

   I felt as if the session was choppy and I couldn't engage her much. I felt as if I was working hard but not well. Out of step a lot I think.

Supervisor: This time it felt as if you were thrown off course from the beginning. For instance, when you said something about a longer interval between sessions, I thought you were going to lead into the summer interval, but you didn't.

Therapist: I think that I was so preoccupied by learning that Cleo's mother was not going to the country every summer weekend, and of the very long break, that I was not attuned to Cleo. I was disoriented. Not sleepy but absent. It started off so differently with her practically darting into my office before I had a chance to go fetch her. I can see that something is going on countertransferentially that I'm going to have to figure out.

Supervisor: That makes sense. Something was definitely different about you. For instance, when she darted into your office from the bathroom and really startled you, instead of addressing that, you made some sort of social chit-chat comment about her suntan. That's so unlike you and certainly wrong technically.

That one incident at the start of the session got you on a false track. You can probably figure it out.

I think you should ask Mrs. C. to bring Cleo at least once during the summer. Lakeville is not so far away, and a 2-month interruption at this point is far too much. And next week we'll talk about some other ways to keep in contact during the long interruption.

Has it occurred to you that you might be quite upset? You've worked hard with Cleo and care deeply about her well-being. It's hard to have this interruption, especially when you see the start of some promising developments. This is one of the terribly frustrating aspects of child treatment. Our work gets interrupted at the worst times. Forget the myth of neutrality in regard to this sort of situation. Our neutrality helps us in our work, but we are not talking about doing our work here. We are talking about *not* being able to do our work.

17

A Second Turning Point Session

Therapist: Cleo is never more than 2 or 3 minutes late, so when it was 10 minutes past her time and she hadn't arrived, I checked my answering machine and found a message from her mother that must have come in just as I had stepped into the office kitchen for a couple of minutes. Mrs. C.'s message said that the baby-sitter was on vacation and that she had forgotten to tell the substitute sitter about the appointment. Cleo would be there at 4:30. She arrived at 4:52 with the substitute baby-sitter who was very apologetic about their lateness. Cleo came right in, sat down in her chair and twirled around. Her face was neutral. I asked, ***I wonder what you think about all this?***

Cleo: How much time do we have left?

Therapist: ***I see you looking at the clock and I am too. There's not much time left, is there?***

Cleo: Eight minutes.

Therapist: Her manner was almost brusque. I again asked, *I wonder what you think of all this?*

Cleo: Well, one good thing is that I got to watch *Duck Tales.*

Therapist: *I know that you like that show a lot.*

Cleo: Did you ever see *Treasure Island?*

Therapist: *The movie?*

Cleo: The old Walt Disney movie.

Therapist: *Yes, I've seen that. What interests you about it?*

Cleo: Do you remember that crook . . . What's his name? Long John Silver. He's a crook, right?

Therapist: *I wonder why you're thinking about a crook.*

Cleo: Well, a crook is somebody who steals things, right?

Therapist: *This is a puzzle for me. Here you are very late for our appointment, and we have very few minutes together, and you are talking about crooks. I wonder if that's something like the feelings you have about missing most of our time today? Like something was almost stolen from you?*

Cleo: It was very bad to miss my therapy today.

Therapist: *I think that if I didn't ask you, you wouldn't tell me the bad part. You would just tell me about watching* **Duck Tales.** She started to tell me a chicken joke at that point and I said, *Do you see how you change the subject when I get a little closer to understanding you? Someday we will understand why you find that hard, and then it will get easier for you to be understood, and to understand yourself.*

By then our time was up and I said, *You know, our*

time is almost up, but I have a little extra time today,
and if you like, you could stay 10 minutes longer until
5:10? Would you like that?

Cleo: That would be good. So what did the cook say to the lobster?

Therapist: *What do you want me to say?*

Cleo: Say, "I'm going to cut you up."

Therapist: *I'm going to cut you up.*
Cleo began to laugh hysterically and said,

Cleo: No! No! You said the wrong thing!

Therapist: *What should I do now?*

Cleo: Say that you give up.

Therapist: *I give up.*
By the way, this was the first time ever that she was willing to tell me what to say, to write my lines for her script. Of course I followed her directions. When I said that I give up, she got a puzzled look on her face and said,

Cleo: You know what? I don't know the answer either.

Therapist: *I'm still wondering about how you feel about*
what happened with our time today. Could you tell me
what happened at home? Did you remember that it was
a therapy day for you?

Cleo: Oh I remembered. I threw all of my toys on the floor. I yelled. I screamed, "Where's my therapy?!" I even threw my lamp over!

Therapist: *Oh my! And what happened?*

Cleo: I had to clean it all up.

Therapist: *I mean what happened that you got here?*

Cleo: Well, my new sitter called my mother, and my mother asked to speak to me, and I told my mother that everybody forgot my therapy, and so she told my sitter to take me here.

Therapist: *Well, you made it happen didn't you? You cried and yelled and threw things and said what you wanted, and you got people to listen to you.* I was smiling when I said all that, so she could see that I was glad for her.

Supervisor: It's so good that you said that. It's worth being 37 minutes late if in the process she learns that she can get listened to. She discovered that she has executive power, that she doesn't have to fold up and adapt and make do with whatever is thrown her way. She discovered that she can make demands. So what if she had to resort to primitive means like throwing and screaming. She has a lot of catching up to do in this area. Many kids her age are already pretty skilled at getting heard about important matters. Cleo's repertoire is limited in this regard, but on this day she allowed herself to be led by her desire to see you. Her time with you was so highly valued that she was moved to act to ensure having her session with you and she was effective in getting her way. The next time she might take action without getting so upset. She might call her mother herself.

This is a great forward step for Cleo. Later, I want to get back to discussing this more fully. Another fascinating aspect of all this is that you fished so very persistently for her reaction to almost missing her session. It's possible that if you hadn't been persistent, she might not have ever told you all that she did to keep her appointment with you.

Therapist: I know. I'm also struck by the fact that this dialogue took place in the last minute of the 10-minute extension that I gave her. Had I not given her the extension, she might never have told me. It's so rare that I'm in a position to extend a session. It seems that a lot of arbitrary factors converged to make this session so significant.

When our time was up she walked to the door, turned around and stuck out her hand to shake mine, and said,

Cleo: Glad to see you, even if it was for a minute.

Therapist: I put out my hand to shake hers and said, *Yes, it's good that we got to see each other.* And she left.

I felt moved by the session. She really acknowledged the closeness between us. I suppose that she needed to touch me and found a grown-up way to do it by the handshake. I felt fine about that. What do you think?

Supervisor: I think that was the only thing to do and the perfect thing to do. Were you worried about physical contact between the two of you?

Therapist: Worried is too strong a word. I was a bit uneasy. I knew that a handshake wasn't like holding her on my lap or hugging her. I have very definite feelings about refraining from physical contact with children as well as with adults. But this was a handshake and that's something that we even would do with an adult patient at certain points, like termination for example. A handshake is physical contact with a formal cast to it. It doesn't seem inappropriate and infantilizing. But still, I become uncomfortable about any departures from the norm, like allowing food in the office, or asking her not to chew gum, or pointing out that she needs a Kleenex.

Supervisor: Understandably, you become uncomfortable about anything that might seem maternal or seductive. The abstinence rule (Freud 1915) is such a basic guiding concept in our work, and it's important to examine our work from that perspective. We don't gratify our patient's id wishes, nor do we gratify our own at the expense of our patients', and so, of course, seduction of any sort is to be avoided. In line with the abstinence rule, being maternal is not what our work is about. But where do you draw the line between being friendly, caring, welcoming, and being seductive and maternal? Not to have shaken her hand at the end of this session when she invited this gesture would have been a rejection and a bad error. Cleo knew that there was something to celebrate and the handshake was a symbol, but a symbol that would have lost all meaning had you not participated.

What a wonderful session! Here is a little girl who has been living in a state of fear for a long time, and now, in the past few weeks, something new is taking shape in her life. There's a new force, an anchoring of sorts, that makes her feel more grounded and less adrift. What she feels anchored to is her memory of something valuable and promising, something in her therapy.

Let me explain why I say her therapy rather than her therapist. Of course her therapist is at the core of this force and its central generator. But "therapy" is a more global concept than "therapist." It includes the countless experiences she has in that room with you but also all that precedes and follows her sessions. I really mean everything.

Let's try to imagine what her arrival at your office might be like for her. There's the trip to your building, pushing open the downstairs door, the elevator noises on the ride up, walking down the hallway to your outer door, ringing your bell and the anticipatory experience of waiting there, hand on doorknob, waiting for that buzzing sound that marks your response to her call, your unlocking of the door for her entry into the waiting room. Just think of the tension of waiting for that exact moment when she has to synchronize pressing your doorknob one second after hearing your buzz . . . or the door will lock again. And then there are those weighty minutes of listening for the sound of the opening of your office door and your footsteps and your face and voice and finally being in that room and sitting down in what she now considers her chair. And that's just the transitional experience of getting to you. Add to that all the hundreds of affective experiences that follow and coalesce and have become something vitally important in her life. She doesn't even know what this highly charged something is, but today when she almost missed her time with you and discovered the magnitude of how urgently she wanted this *experience,* she called it her "therapy."

Therapist: I guess one component of how she views this *experience* would be with "confident expectation."

Supervisor: It's interesting how our theoreticians come up with complementary ideas that stress different aspects of similar processes. Benedek talks of *confident expectation* (1938), and Mahler of the *mothering principle* (1968), Bollas writes of *the transformational object* (1987), and Loewald refers to a therapeutic *differential* (1960). All of these authors are referring to complex processes leading to an awareness that something helpful is being offered, but there is a difference of emphasis among these terms. Some refer to processes that occur initially in early development whereas others describe phenomena that are particular to the treatment situation. I would say that Benedek's confident expectation is a normal developmental landmark that indicates that good ego endowment and a good object environment have combined to allow the infant to remember and therefore anticipate having his needs met. Mahler uses the term *mothering principle* in those cases where severe pathology has interfered with or inhibited the awareness of a caretaking and caring presence, and this awareness is either sparked for the first time or revived by the treatment process. Bollas, like Benedek, refers to an ordinary occurrence in normal development, that of the mother's attunement to her infant as enabling her to transform the infant's states of distress into states of comfort. However, he describes this phenomenon as one that may occur in the analytic situation when the patient wishes and experiences the analyst as the transformational object. Loewald refers specifically to treatment in his concept of therapeutic *differential.* He refers to the integrative work experienced by the analysand during the course of an analysis. The analyst's function as interpreter leads to the patient's higher levels of organization and self-knowledge, and the patient becomes aware that the analyst is the source of this attuned and growth-promoting work. Loewald does imply that the seeds for this experience might lie in the mother–child model.

To get back to Cleo, one of the reasons I'm so encouraged by this development is that for the first time we are witness to Cleo's overcoming her tendency to accept whatever comes her way with fatalistic resignation. This type of characteristic response is usefully conceptualized by Hartmann as *autoplastic adaptation* (1939). As you probably recall, in autoplastic adaptation, the person internally rearranges himself to adapt to external reality, while in *alloplastic adaptation,* the person expects external reality to be rearranged. Most of us, of course, employ both types of adaptation. In those cases where one or the other is used pretty exclusively, there is a serious problem. With alloplastic adaptation as the predominant type, you would see antisocial, highly egocentric, and psychopathic behavior. With predominantly autoplastic adaptation you would see a form of passivity that could result in a variety of pathological outcomes such as, for instance, the formation of a *false self* (Winnicott 1960), narcissistic character structure, and/or masochism. From early on in this case I've been concerned that Cleo might be heading in the direction of a masochistic character structure.

My concern has been based on my observations of her current functioning and on what I know of her history. Let's look at the very negative facts about her history first, and view them as a likely background for troubled development. We know that as a very young child she witnessed parental violence, including her father's out-of-control sadism and her mother's victimization. We have wondered how this might have exacerbated the violent and exciting primal scene fantasies that are ubiquitous in all development. Then we have her relationships with her parents: she has a dangerous but exciting relationship with her father who wants her to do daring physical feats, we have her increasingly puzzling and bland relationship with her mother who is there and not there for her. These relationships with her parents do not combine well to give her a solid foundation.

But why talk about masochism here? I am so far simply describing a far from ideal set of factors that do not appear to have anything to do with masochism. What concerns me here is what she's done intrapsychically with these very important factors in her life. Her passivity, for instance, her lack of complaining about as deadening a baby-sitter as Maria, and her tendency to withdraw rather than fight are examples of autoplastic adaptation. If this kind of adaptation serves the preservation of the object connection at all costs, then there is insufficient cathexis of the self representation and some blurring of reality. I am making assumptions that some aspects of Cleo's preoedipal development and current psychic structure might be protomasochistic (Loewenstein 1957, Glenn 1989). Novick and Novick (1987), in a paper called "The Essence of Masochism," attribute three factors to the epigenesis of masochism. Cleo fits the first two: a disturbed environment and difficulty in expressing aggression. The third criterion is difficult to assess since it pertains to the particular mode of instinctual gratification. All we know at this point is that it appears that Cleo relies on an autoplastic mode of dealing with internal and external stimuli, but we don't know how that will develop.

The incident today gave us the first glimmer that she now values something enough to fight and yell and demand, thus overriding that tendency toward resignation. Let me put it more strongly. She wanted something today, and she was able to yield to that need and allow her aggressive drive to find expression. She was not so identified with the aggressor, in this instance the forgetful mother, that she had to kill off her own desire, surrender to her fate, and behave as if it didn't matter. Today we witnessed some alloplastic adaptation for the first time. This could be a splendid arrival for her.

Therapist: I was also very impressed that they brought her, even for just a few minutes.

Supervisor: Yes, I think that many parents would not have bothered. It's going to be interesting to see what happens now. Cleo
found out that she can have quite a bit of power. How is she
going to deal with that in the future?

18

Giving Gifts and Planning Separations

Therapist: Cleo was early and had been in the waiting room for 10 minutes when I went to greet her. She was sitting next to an older man. He nodded to me but didn't say anything, so I just said hello to him. In my office I said somewhat playfully, *That wasn't Maria.*

Cleo: No, that was my grandfather.

Therapist: *I noticed that you were sitting right next to him. You never sit so close to Maria.* She didn't reply. She was wiggling around, playing with her fingers and whistling. I asked what she was thinking and she said,

Cleo: Nothing.

Therapist: *By now you know that I often ask you about your thoughts and feelings. I do it because I know that it*

would be helpful to you to know what they are. Then you'd be able to think about them more clearly and that would make you feel more sure of things.

Cleo: Oh, I'm feeling sure.

Therapist: ***Oh? About what?***

Cleo: I don't know.

Therapist: ***You're sure about "I don't know"?*** And we both laughed.

Supervisor: That's a nice exchange, but before we get involved in the session I want to mention Cleo's grandfather. I know that you're being very careful not to lead your patient or impose your own thoughts, but I'm thinking about not having mentioned her grandfather more directly and not having introduced yourself to him. Just because he seemed to feel awkward and didn't greet you verbally doesn't mean that you have to be so minimally responsive to his presence. It would have been very appropriate to introduce yourself, just say hello and who you are, and that would have given him the hint to do the same. It might have been nicer for Cleo to witness this exchange. It's more normal behavior. It would have made it more natural for her then to bring up her grandfather, why he might have brought her, and what happened to Maria.

Therapist: You're right. I get mixed up about neutrality, and professionalism. I worry about acting as if this is just a regular social situation.

Supervisor: Well, just use ordinary courtesy as a guide. Even though this is not an ordinary social situation, you can still behave with ordinary courtesy and not compromise the special quality of your role and function. The so-called neutral analyst, who has neither grace nor good manners, is a sorry caricature of neutrality or professionalism. Ella Freeman Sharpe said it so clearly and simply in one of her papers on technique (1930): "If we are of simple purpose and without pose, we shall be human and blest with common sense" (p. 30). She goes on to say that we should treat our patients (when they are not on the couch) with the tact and courtesy that we would extend to a formal guest. That is a level-headed recommendation and applies well to the situation under discussion. Courtesy, when sincere, is just the outward manifestation of good object relations.

Therapist: That makes good sense. I'll try not to act so stilted in an effort to seem professional. In fact, what you say is a relief to me. I know the caricature that you're referring to and dislike it as much as you do.

Cleo continued spinning and whistling and counting on her fingers, and I said to her, *I see you're counting on your fingers.*

Cleo: No, I'm not. I'm practicing sign language. This is an L in sign language and if I move it this way it's chicken feet and now it's an egg. I'm going to draw you an egg. Can you get me my drawing things?

Therapist: I got her folder and she sat down to draw and asked,

Cleo: Did you see a movie? I can't remember the name. It was about flying saucers.

Therapist: *I don't know if I saw that movie. I don't remember a movie about flying saucers. Last time you wanted to know if I saw the movie* Treasure Island.

Cleo: No, that's not the one I mean.

Therapist: *What did you want to tell me about this movie?*

Cleo: Oh, I don't know. It was just kind of dumb and boring and I just can't remember what it was called.

Therapist: She was drawing with concentration now and looking at the page and I asked her, *What would you like me to do while you draw?* She didn't look up but sort of mumbled to herself.

Cleo: I'm going to mix these colors. I'm going to make a stripe here. No, here, and a dot.

Therapist: *You haven't answered my question about what you want me to do while you draw.*

Cleo: Flump up and down on your head.

Therapist: *How do I do that?*
    She stopped drawing and made standing on her head gestures.

Supervisor: Was she smiling or laughing, and were you, or was this all done straight?

Therapist: It was sort of serious, I think, but I wasn't sure whether she was telling me to go fly a kite, so to speak, or whether she was giving me advice on how to keep myself busy. Cleo does have that knack of acting deadpan, and it's hard to tell. Anyway, I said, with a touch of humor, *As your therapist, there are some things I do and some things I don't do. I listen, I ask questions, I remember, and I try to help us understand things. I do not stand on my head.*

Cleo: A crazy therapist would.

Therapist: *Am I a crazy therapist?*

Cleo: No. That's why you aren't standing on your head. Oh well, back to drawing my egg. This is an Easter egg but I'm going to throw it out.

Therapist: *Why is that?*

Cleo: I don't like Easter eggs. Some people eat them, you know? Ugh, it must be awful with all that runny yellow stuff. Some people eat the runny stuff.

Therapist: She was confused and thought that Easter eggs are dyed raw eggs and she talked about how she wouldn't want to eat an

Easter egg sunny-side-up because all the dye would get into the egg. I told her that she sounded as if she wasn't sure about the insides of Easter eggs, and I clarified this by telling her about hard boiling eggs before dying them. Then she said,

Cleo: Yes, I know that kind of egg. It's hard, but hard like a rubber ball, sort of bouncy hard. I hate those rubbery eggs. And now for another picture. I think I will make eighteen pictures today.

Therapist: *Eighteen? That's a lot of pictures. What will your next picture be? Do you know yet?*

Cleo: An animal.

Therapist: She was drawing energetically, and I looked over to see the picture and said, *Oh, I recognize that animal. It looks like the one you made last week. The one you turned into a duck, and then into a billy goat.*

Cleo: Last week I didn't draw anything. I got here too late to draw.

Therapist: *Oh, that's right. Last week was the time that your mom forgot to make arrangements to get you here, but you found a way to remind her and got here for a little while. It was two weeks ago that you were drawing here.*

Cleo: This one is going to be a camel.

Therapist: She drew a camel and then bars, so that it looked like a camel in the zoo. I asked, *I wonder what made you think of a camel at the zoo?*

Cleo: I went there with my dad.

Therapist: *Oh?*

Cleo: About 17 weeks ago I went there with my dad . . . Well, I don't really know how long ago. It was Easter vacation. Now for the next picture I need these toys.

Therapist: She got out the Playmobile Park and said,

Cleo: I'm going to copy these people. No, I'm going to trace them.

Therapist: And she laid one of the Playmobile people on her paper, traced the outline, and asked,

Cleo: Guess which one I'm going to trace next?

Therapist: *Now here is another thing about my being your therapist. I'm not going to stand on my head and I'm not going to guess. Remember, my job is to help you feel sure, and guessing is not useful for our work. It's okay in other places with other people, but I'm your special helper in figuring things out and so I have to skip guessing. But if you describe what you're drawing, I'll see if I can recognize it.*

Cleo: This is a place where parents take kids to play and they can get on a board and pump and go up and down.

Therapist: *That sounds familiar. That could be a playground with a swing. Are you drawing a playground with a swing? May I look at your picture now? Well, now that I see your picture I know that you did draw a swing. You described it so clearly that I was pretty sure I recognized it from your description. You know, it's interesting that you're thinking about places where children go with their parents. It reminds me of summer vacation.*

Cleo: That's what I'm thinking about too. I'm thinking about my country house.

Therapist: *What have you been thinking about it?*

Cleo: I've been thinking about not seeing my therapist.

Supervisor: Were you surprised?

Therapist: Not really, because it was on my agenda, and having had that very short session last week I was getting concerned that we weren't going to have enough time to prepare for that long summer interruption. I felt that I was forcing the issue by bringing up the summer vacation. Now that I'm reading the session to you, it strikes me as amazing that she was so direct about missing me. I asked her, *I wonder what you were thinking about that?*

Cleo: Just that.

Therapist: *I wonder if there have been times when you didn't see people who are important to you for a while, and then you see them again.*

Cleo: No.

Therapist: Then she was very quiet, just drawing and looking at her paper. The whole session had a very quiet tone to it from the beginning. I was thinking about this quiet tone, and reviewing the session so far to see what I could deduce, if anything. I thought about the fact that she had come with her grandfather and that I had had no idea that he was due to visit. I thought about how little I knew about the family. Mrs. C. very rarely let me know what was going on at home and if I didn't ask the right questions I was left in the dark. I let a little while pass before I spoke and then I said, *You know, Cleo, you seem very quiet today.*

Cleo: Well, it's because I'm happy that my mother is back from her trip.

Therapist: *Her trip? Your mom was on a trip?.*

Cleo: Yes, her school asked her to go to California for 6 days. It was to see a science fair for teachers. She met me at the bus stop today, just to say hello. Then she had to go right to her school and couldn't bring me here. But she'll be home for dinner. So my grandfather brought me here.

Therapist: *I didn't know that your mom was going on a trip. I wonder whether your being quiet had anything to do with your mom going away and coming back?*

Cleo: Well, I missed her a lot when she was away and I'm glad she came home.

Therapist: *So you just had an experience of not seeing somebody very important to you for 6 whole days, and now she's back.* She went on drawing and said,

Cleo: Oh, I wanted to put a sandbox in here and I forgot. I'll do it now. There's room. And I'll put an umbrella over the sandbox. Oops. It came out all wrong. It looks like a gerbil.

Therapist: *Like a gerbil?*

Cleo: No, I don't mean gerbil. I mean that other word for that thing you get at Hanukkah. Do you know what one of those things are called?

Therapist: *A dreidel?*

Cleo: Yes, that's it. I guess I made that mistake 'cause they sort of sound a little the same, like they sort of rhyme a little bit.

Therapist: She finished her picture and then it was time to clean up.

Supervisor: How full of separation this session is: her mother, the upcoming separation from you, and even wooden Maria is gone.

You got some important ideas across about your role with her. You also covered some very basic stuff about cause and effect thinking, including the difference between recognizing and reasoning on the one hand and blind guessing on the other. That kind of educational discussion is useful with a child like Cleo who tends not to make connections and consequently often doesn't know how something came about. It shores up her ability to use her ego functions more effectively, which is such an important prerequisite to doing more analytic work.

It's very difficult to explore one's inner space if the world of reality is not governed by some measure of reason and logic.

Now let's talk about the forthcoming separation and what you can do to make it easier for her. You're going to have to bring it up actively since we have only two sessions before she leaves. We would like her to have a sense of continuity about treatment even though it will be disrupted by the long summer vacation.

Therapist: Well, I did try to open that up. When she finished her picture I said, *Now let's put that picture in the folder the way we always do. This folder is a good safe place to keep your pictures together. Will you remember that when you're away for the summer? Will you remember that I'm making a special place for them in my closet and that they'll be waiting for you here when you get back?*

Supervisor: That's definitely the type of thing you need to say, but it can't wait till the end of the session now that you only have two appointments left. You do have to tell her that the two of you have to plan ways to make the separation easier for her. Tell her that two months is a very long time not to have appointments. Ask her whether she has any ideas. If she doesn't, at this point I think you could make some suggestions, for instance asking whether she would like an exchange of letters or postcards. I would get very specific here and find out whether she prefers one to the other. A letter is more private but a postcard has a picture. You can help her to think this through. Also, you need to know how well she can read and write. Are you going to write to each other or are you going to be the one to do the writing? If she writes to you, does she have to dictate her letters or can she do it herself? Sometimes I've addressed envelopes to myself and stamped them in the child's presence. Then my young patients could just send a picture or a couple of words they know without involving the parents very much. Sometimes I've planned with the child the specific postcard or note cards to be sent, and I've purchased them and shown them to my little patient before the vacation. Then I say something like, "Every time you get a card with a bear family on a picnic you will know that it's from me." This is particularly useful with children who can't yet read. They recognize the picture and know that it's from me. That gives them a sense of ownership and may add a dimension of value, a narcissistic enhancement to their self representation. Sometimes the picture they've chosen before the vacation has some very direct bearing on what we've been working on in treatment, and then the card gives our correspondence a quality of something familiar, therefore all the more valuable.

Let's try to think of the purpose of staying in touch, even though it seems pretty obvious. Let's conceptualize it as an element in the totality of the treatment relationship. You have become an important person in Cleo's life and we can assume that her object representation of you is varied and includes you as someone to be counted on, someone who is capable of helping her feel safer, someone who cares about her, and has special ways of helping her feel less helpless. All in all, you are a highly cathected person. The vacation can represent a diminution of your power. After all, you are not able to prevent the vacation. It's out of your hands. So in a way, to Cleo, going away for two months might feel as if you're abandoning her, and Cleo really can't afford to feel abandoned by you. It took her all these months to stop dodging you at every turn, to be able to say that she will miss you, to acknowledge your value to her and your importance to her life. So you have to be ingenious and creative in finding ways to stay in touch with her during this separation. You have to keep the connection alive. Just remember that the method isn't particularly significant, but the intent is, and so it's important to find a way that's simple enough not to become burdensome for either one of you. If you're going to have telephone contact, make it at a time that doesn't put you out too much or restrict her life or that of her family. If you're going to write, the letters don't need to be more than a sentence or two.

Therapist: What would I say? After all, I'm not going to talk about myself and I don't know that much about her life in the country.

Supervisor: You could say that it's Thursday, "letter to Cleo day." You're sitting in your office at your desk with the white surface and writing to her. You're thinking about her and wondering how she is. It's been a week since she left and it seems like a long time. You could mention intervals between letters and between appointments. You could say that it's hot in New York, and you wonder whether it's hot in Lakeville. You could mention things that she said about the summer. Has she gone swimming yet? Just the most ordinary commonplace things will do. If you've changed anything in the office, you can mention it, no matter how trivial. You bought new Magic Markers and she'll get to see them when she has her midsummer appointment. The wobbly leg on the little plant table has been fixed. That sort of thing will do. It's your common meeting ground. It's your history together. It's all she needs and it's a great deal to receive.

Therapist: So the theme is constancy. The content of the letters focuses on our connection. I can achieve that by bringing to the fore that I'm the same person in the same place and that we are separated by time and distance. Finally, the interval of time that separates us is limited and shrinks daily until she is back in New York City and we are back to seeing each other again.

Supervisor: Exactly. The letters represent your steadiness, your reliability, and your capacity to think about her when she's not physically present. That's why monotony is fine. You don't need to do anything particularly clever. Remember that repetition is very soothing and reassuring. Think of children's books and their reliance on simplicity and repetition. Rhyming is in that same category of what is soothing because of the predictability of the repetition of sound. The authors of children's books and good storytelling adults know this. The origin of the principle of repetition in children's books and stories is not by any means obscure. Just try to tell a young child a story and then try to tell that same child a different story the next day. Chances are that the original story will be requested and if you try to change any of the details, you will be corrected by your young listener.

I realize that I sound as if Cleo is even younger than almost 7. I slipped into feeling that way because of our topic. Important separations cause regressions in most people and I'm antici- pating that to be the case here.

To get back to making plans, remember to plan the exchange of letters with Cleo. She might have something important to contribute. It's good to engage her as a participant in this planning. Her active involvement allows her to exercise some of her ego functions. The investment of her creative energy can go a long way toward reducing the kind of resignation we sometimes worry about in Cleo. Try to let her decide as much as she wishes about specifics. Should you always write on the same day? Should this be so for both of you? That would make the intervals between letters very predictable. Should you always write in a particular color pen or on a particular color paper? That would make it clear who the writer was before even opening the letter.

Now, the other matter that should be taken care of right away is arranging that Mrs. C. bring Cleo in for an appointment at the midpoint of her vacation. You should try to arrange this immediately, before Cleo's next session. You would be better off doing it in person, but if that isn't possible, you could do it on the phone. Time is of the essence here. Be free to be pretty insistent that this be done. It's not a very big deal to bring her in to see you. It's a two-hour trip, that's all. If she were very far away and bringing her in to see you was a real hardship, we would have to manage. Under the circumstances, why accept such a long interruption when a midway appointment is rea- sonable? When that's done, you and Cleo can make a little calendar that contains all this information: the day of the separation, the letter-writing days, the date of the halfway appointment, the dates of your vacation, her birthday, and anything else that the two of you come up with in the next two sessions. She can take the calendar to the country and have all this information at her disposal. Then you must plan with Cleo what you're going to do about her birthday. Have you thought about it?

Therapist: Yes, I was thinking of sending her a card. I'm a bit confused about gifts for children. I don't know whether it would be appropriate to send her a present. What do you think?

Supervisor: Let's think about it as another of these issues like allowing a child to eat in the therapy office, or speaking to the child's teacher, or introducing yourself to the grandfather. These are issues that a child therapist has to address over and over again. Well, here's a guiding question to ask yourself: Will this further the child's treatment? I don't mean to imply that we always know the answer in advance. Sometimes we think that something is indicated and it causes unexpected trouble. For instance, it can be very helpful to speak to a child's teacher if the teacher is a reasonably mature person with good judgment. But it's possible for a teacher to misuse the contact with the therapist and be indiscreet or treat the child differently after learning that he or she is in treatment. So it's unwise to initiate contact with the school automatically. Do it if it seems highly important. I find that often it causes more complications than gains, but on some occasions it's been enormously helpful. We've talked about this in regard to Cleo. So far you haven't talked to the teacher, even though you wish you knew more about her school life. I haven't encouraged you to do so because I'm familiar with the potential for complications and so far it hasn't seemed critically important. But let's get back to the idea of a present. What is your gut feeling about it?

Therapist: As you know, I worry about those very protective feelings that I sometimes get about Cleo. I question the wisdom of sending her a gift because it might be perhaps . . . too gratifying? Then I think of how important birthdays are at that age, and how a gift is such an intrinsic part of a birthday celebration. So of course I want to send her a gift. But I'm the therapist, not the mother or friend. Then I begin to wonder whether the gift might be gratifying my wish as well as hers and compromising the uniqueness of the treatment relationship.

Supervisor: You're asking yourself the right questions and they're hard to answer. Child treatment is complicated by the constant appearance of these gray areas. Let me give you some very simple principles that I use in my work and have found effective.

When working with young children, children under the age of around 10, I explore the issue of gifts. I do this in regard to birthdays, or Christmas, or Hanukkah, and at the time of the summer break if it's to be a long one. I discuss the issue of presents well in advance and ask the children whether they wish that I would give them a present. As you might imagine, most children say yes, but some children say they don't know or don't care. The unsure or indifferent children graphically reveal an aspect of their problem by giving such a response, and that often can lead to some very productive work. The children who say "yes" also become engaged in a very interesting process, since I make it very clear that the present has to become an aspect of therapy, and not a conventional gift that a nontherapist might give. The child has to choose the gift. That way the therapist never has to guess what the child wants, nor is the gift ever a surprise, since surprises are not a part of therapy. Then there is the question of money, and here you have to use some discretion since you don't want the gift to be very expensive or elaborate. In giving a gift to a child patient, you're also communicating something to the parents, and that has to be a factor to be considered in your plan. You would not choose something that would be burdensome for the parents, such as something messy, like a chemistry set, for instance. Nor would you give a gift that would make you look superior to the parents, such as giving a book that the parents had promised to give and then had failed to deliver. That would be tactless and competitive. If your young patient asked for such a present of you, it might be an opportunity to explore with the child why he was giving up on getting it from his parents. As you can see, I'm alerting you to some of the complications of gift giving as well as to some of the important treatment areas that it can open up.

I have some other principles that apply to gift giving. Since a gift from the therapist represents an aspect of therapy, I don't like gifts that are flimsy or poorly made, or that get used up, like bubble bath powder or food. A gift from you should be made to last, since we assume that you will pick something that the child values and wants to keep. Sometimes there's a particular therapy toy that the child is attached to and not allowed to take home because it belongs in the office toy pool. Getting the child a duplicate of that toy can sometimes be a good present. The main thing right now is to work this out with Cleo and to help her figure out something that she would like and that represents your work together. Then when she receives this package from you sometime this summer, she will remember your discussion. You can make reference, in an accompanying note, to the process of arriving at the idea of this gift.

I also mentioned that the summer separation is a time when I consider giving a young child some small gift. Do you have any thoughts about that?

Therapist: Well, I'm thinking of transitional objects.

Supervisor: I'm glad you thought of that because I know that this could sound as if I'm attempting to create a transitional object, and I want to be sure of correcting that impression. Winnicott (1953) developed this valuable concept and we should stick to his idea and not muddy it up and weaken its original meaning. A transitional object arises out of very specific conditions and has distinct characteristics. Cleo is past the age where the correct meaning of transitional object applies. Furthermore, the transitional object is always chosen by the child alone. I'm talking about something quite different. I am trying to develop some devices to help ease the difficulty of separation by boosting the good memories of the object representation, of the self representation, and of the representation of their connection. When object constancy is more reliably established, all this is not necessary. Cleo loses her connections under stress, so in her case it is important to have some way of bolstering her during this interruption. But I want to stress that a device to aid the transition is *very* different from Winnicott's very complicated and specific concept, the transitional object.

Since you and Cleo are doing all of this preparation for the summer break in such a limited amount of time, I would suggest making a calendar with her, as I had mentioned earlier. It can contain all the important dates during the summer: her birthday, your vacation, a letter-writing schedule, the midsummer therapy appointment, the date of resumption of treatment, and whatever other events she would like to include, such as the specific weekends that her mother plans to spend in the country. I thought of the last item because I was so startled that her mother went away for 6 days and didn't let you know. I wonder how Cleo had been prepared for this recent separation. She never mentioned it to you.

Therapist: I'm going to call the mother tonight and set up a midsummer appointment for Cleo, and I'll remind her to let me know of future trips or any other unusual changes of routine.

Supervisor: What we've been discussing in terms of planning the separation is so different from anything we would do with our adult patients, or older children, or even children of Cleo's age who have a different history and different needs. In Cleo's case we're relying on concrete modes of keeping the connection alive. We are not relying on interpretation at this point in her treatment because she is not yet able to use interpretation in regard to loss. Remember that disappointment and loss cause her such anger that she kills off her good object representations and feels bereft. Eventually, as she gets stronger, interpretation will be the more effective therapeutic tool. What you are doing now is preparing her for that eventual shift into treatment that allows for intrapsychic work.

19

Discussing the
Summer Vacation

Therapist: I was able to arrange to see Mrs. C. prior to my session with Cleo, and to discuss the summer plans in person. I told her that the summer break was a very long one and that it would help the continuity of Cleo's treatment if she would bring her in once during the summer. She was willing to do that and we scheduled it at the end of July, a halfway point. I again asked about the father's visitation pattern and plans and was told that he was very unpredictable. Mrs. C. is always very vague when she talks about Mr. C. As far as I could understand what she was saying, his pattern seems to be one of being attentive for a few weeks and not showing up for the next few weeks. Mrs. C. said that she no longer counted on his plans materializing and always had alternate plans should he fail to show up.

Supervisor: I can't get any sense of her affect from your tone.

Therapist: I think that's because I'm duplicating her lack of affect. She was stoical, with a touch of resignation. That's typical of Mrs. C. She will go along talking and reporting in a dispassionate manner, and then, with no warning, she'll begin to cry. This time she began to cry when she talked about the country house being up for sale, and that people would be looking at it over the summer, and that this probably was their last summer in that lovely house. She said that the children are going to feel as if they're losing their country home.

Supervisor: That's not a feeling. That's a fact. She sometimes seems very nebulous about very specific and real matters. That's why you occasionally feel that she isn't altogether present. Has she told the children about the house yet?

Therapist: She had been putting it off, but she realizes that she must explain that their cousin is going to sell the house and that it of course would not be available to them after it was sold. We discussed what to tell the children and she was willing to tell them the truth. Her cousin finds that he cannot afford to spend so much money on a house he so rarely uses. She said that she would tell them that evening that this will be their last summer in the house.

I asked Mrs. C. about her recent trip, which had caught me unprepared. Mrs. C. was surprised to learn that she had not told me about it. She had known about it for several months. She said that Cleo had not been upset by her absence. In fact, Cleo's grandparents reported that she had taken it quite in stride.

Mrs. C. said that just a week before her trip so much happened all at once. Maria suddenly gave a week's notice, giving Mrs. C. only a week to make child care arrangements for her 6-day trip. She said that leaving the children with a stranger or her ex-husband was out of the question. She was frantic at the thought of having to cancel the trip. She was being considered for a promotion and didn't want anything to spoil her chances. Her parents were not due for their summer visit for another three weeks and they were her only hope. Luckily, they were able to arrange to come early and provide the kind of child care that she can trust.

Supervisor: Was there any talk about Cleo's fears?

Therapist: I had to ask about that, and yes, she is definitely less fearful and can really play well by herself for long stretches. She no longer gets overwhelmed by fear, as in the past. Mrs. C. found her generally much calmer. She still wants her mother in the room when she's going to sleep, but her wanting this has a more relaxed quality, unlike the desperate need of the past. I found out that Cleo will now go to sleep by herself when her mother is away. In other words, her grandparents do not sit with her when her mother is away. That's really big news, and yet this sort of information is always conveyed in an impassive tone of voice.

Now let me talk about my session with Cleo. As you know, this is the next to last session before the summer and I have quite an agenda.

Cleo was 15 minutes late. Her grandfather brought her and said he was sorry they were late. The minute I saw Cleo I realized that I had not told her that I was going to try to see her mother before this appointment, and by not warning her I had broken one of my own rules. So I explained what had happened, and that I had arranged an extra appointment with her mother to help us plan the summer interruption. I ended by saying that I was sorry that I had not told her that I was going to see her mom as I always do. I said, *That means I didn't ask you whether there was anything that you wanted me to tell her or show her.*

Cleo: Oh, darn. I wanted her to see my drawings.

Therapist: *Well, would you like me to have her come again to see your drawings?* She shrugged and said that she didn't know.

Supervisor: You might have been better off asking her, *What should we do about that?* I'm making it more vague because you don't know what she had in mind. For example, maybe she really didn't care all that much about the pictures but wanted to find fault with you because you made a mistake, a breach of contract so to speak, and wanted to rub it in a bit. That would be a good forward step, wouldn't it? To express anger instead of covering it up with indifference? So if that was going on, you wouldn't find out about it by taking the content of her communication so literally. You jumped in too fast and led her in a particular direction.

Therapist: I have that tendency. I try to solve the problem before it's been identified. I don't do that with my adult patients.

Supervisor: Since you don't do this with your adult patients, what do you think makes it more difficult to do this with Cleo?

Therapist: My maternal part comes out more easily with children, and what we're discussing isn't even such a constructive "mommy" part. It would be better if I were to help my own children do some of their problem solving. I guess what I'm saying is that it's harder for me to be neutral with Cleo and probably with any child patient. I'm more protective of children than of adults.

Supervisor: Well, you're not alone. A lot of child therapists have trouble in this area. If they recognize it, then it's not as much of a problem. It's a form of countertransference and needs to be examined, as does any manifestation of countertransference. But when this goes unrecognized, then a problem is developing. Some child therapists become so identified with their child patients that they convey to the child a position of "you and I against the world." I have seen this happen on numerous occasions and with very bad results.

Let me talk a bit about what happens in these situations. First there is the therapist's expression of rivalry with the parents and teachers, which remains unexamined and is therefore given free rein. Then there is the communication to the child that the world is not a safe place outside of the therapy room. In other words, a therapist who becomes overidentified with her child patient is in a position to do severe harm in many ways, including fostering dependency on the therapist and suspicion of the world outside the therapy office. Since the therapeutic situation does have the potential of imbuing the therapist with a great deal of power, this parasitic sort of symbiosis can develop in the treatment relationship. Now just consider how terribly dangerous, no, how impossible it would be for a child to express any anger at a therapist who has become the object of such a state of surrender, idealization, and worship. If we stop and consider just that—a therapist's inability to tolerate a patient's anger—we face a critical obstacle in any treatment. It would be imposing a situation where the child would have to split his object world into good therapist and bad everyone else in order to be able to express anger.

As you know, there are countless reasons why overidentifying with our patients is harmful to the treatment process. It's particularly important to be scrupulously countertransference conscious with children because in many ways we do have more power with them and they can evoke more countertransference than adults. It's something to think about. Of course you don't do any of the extreme things I've described, but still, when you feel that maternal impulse, it is not to be dismissed. It's not a trifling matter. It warrants careful analysis.

Therapist: It's a pretty interesting subject. I have never considered the question of whether it's more likely that adults tend to overidentify with children with less awareness than they might feel were this to happen with their adult patients. I certainly have experienced some of those feelings of being a better parent than the parents of my child patient, and sometimes it's realistically so, but I still do recognize it as an indicator of countertransference and try to understand what's going on within myself. I certainly will not dismiss so lightly what I call my mommy feelings. It's complicated, isn't it? It tells me a lot about myself. These feelings only appear at certain times, times when Cleo might seem particularly waiflike. When she doesn't cover up her affects I feel those protective feelings. So actually it's when she lets me get a little closer that I feel maternal and when she distances me I get sleepy. This is very interesting and a lot to think about. Back to Cleo now.

With time running so short I told her that we needed to sit down together and discuss our summer. I got out my calendar and showed her the pages from July 1 to September 5 when we are to resume. Cleo began to count. She counted all the days.

Cleo: 65 days. That's a very, very, very long time. That's much too long. That's like forever.

Therapist: *Well, that's why I asked your mom to bring you in on July 30. I think it might help a little for us to have an appointment right in the middle of that long long time. What do you think?*

Cleo: That's makes it half of forever.

Therapist: She began sort of flopping around and acting very physically restless and sort of counting to herself. She seemed very distant from me and I asked her, *Is it very hard for you to talk about this?*

She nodded and sort of shrugged her shoulders. She looked as if she was trying not to cry. I said, *Do you have any ideas about what could make that time easier?*

Cleo: What do you mean?

Therapist: *When you've been away from people who are important to you, people you miss a lot, do you do anything to make it easier?*

Cleo: I don't know what you mean.

Therapist: *Your mom was just away for almost a week. And what about your grandparents who stay with you and then always leave for Argentina? What does that feel like?*

Cleo: I miss them sometimes. I miss them a lot.

Therapist: *And what do you do when you miss them a lot.*

Cleo: Sometimes I tell my mother.

Therapist: *And what does she say?*

Cleo: She says that I'll see them again soon.

Therapist: *Do you ever write them a letter or receive a letter from them?*

Cleo: Sometimes my mother gets a letter from them and sometimes she writes to them. Sometimes they send a message for me and my sister. My sister always gets the stamps on their letters.

Therapist: *What do you think about the idea that you and I write letters to each other during the summer? Do you think that might help us?*

Cleo: I have some nice cards that somebody gave me for my birthday last year and I never used them yet. They have pictures of different animals.

Therapist: *Would you like to use them this summer to write to me?*

Cleo: I don't know how to do that.

Therapist: *You could bring your cards in next time and I could address them for you so that they get to me. Would you like that?*

Cleo: Then could you send them back to me every time, 'cause I like them a lot and want to collect them? When you collect things you get to keep them forever like my sister and her stamps. I could write something on my cards like: hello Linda Small. Then you could write back something like: hello Cleo. But you could write a lot more because you know how to write much better than I do. Then you could put the card in a new envelope and mail it to me.

Therapist: *What a good idea! And just think, you'll always know which animal you're getting because it will be one that you picked to send to me first. How often should we do that?*

Cleo: Just like our appointment every Wednesday. I could mail you a card every Wednesday and you could mail it back to me every Wednesday.

Therapist: *Let's see how that would work. You would mail the first card the first Wednesday of your vacation and I would mail it back to you the following Wednesday. So if we do it that way we will each be mailing a card on Wednesday and maybe receiving those cards by the weekend. How does that sound to you?*

Cleo: Good, but I got mixed up. Could you say it all again? A week is 7 days, right? Could I have a piece of paper? We aren't going to have appointments for 28 weeks, right?

Therapist: She seemed very distracted and drew contiguous boxes on her paper and wrote "week" in each box. I said, *Something about this is getting very hard for you and that's why you're getting mixed up. Let me help you. Let me set up our own calendar. We can work on it together. We can start with today. Next week will be our "goodbye for the summer" appointment. Then we can put down all the days that we aren't going to see each other, the appointment in the middle of the summer, and the day we start our regular appointments again in September. Then we can write down on all the Wednesdays: Cleo mails card to Linda Small and Linda Small mails card to Cleo. How does a calendar like that sound to you?*

Cleo: It sounds good. Then I can count how many weeks it's going to be. I wish you could write to me a million times a week. I never got a letter in the country before. We have this mailbox in front of our house and the mail car comes by and this lady puts mail in our mailbox. But it's just newspapers and not letters. Then if we want to mail a letter, we just put it in there and then put up this little flag and then the lady knows to look for a letter to mail. But I don't have any stamps. How will I get stamps? Does the supermarket sell them? My grandfather doesn't know where the post office is. Does the mail lady sell stamps?

Therapist: She was getting a little upset and so I told her that I would have the stamps for her. I don't know if that was a little overprotective. I said, *I will bring stamps to our next appointment. You can remember to bring the cards and I will remember to bring the stamps. Let's count the weeks of your vacation so that we know just how many cards and stamps we need.* By then I had finished making the crude outline of the calendar and I said, *Here, let's start with the first Wednesday of your vacation,* and together we counted ten Wednesdays.

Cleo: We need ten cards and ten stamps. I have to bring ten cards and you have to bring ten stamps.

Therapist: *Right, and could you also bring me your address in the country?*

Cleo: Yes. I'm scared I'm going to forget.

Therapist: *How about my writing a note to you. A reminder note.*

Cleo: That's good.

Therapist: I wrote a note to Cleo that said, "10 animal cards and 10 envelopes and summer house address." I also wrote a note to myself that said, "ten stamps for Cleo."

I gave her her note and suddenly remembered my vacation and that I was going to be away too. So I said, *Let me show you the dates that I'm going to be away for my vacation. Here, I'll draw a line through these two weeks. That means that two of those animal cards are going to have to be mailed to my vacation place. Here, I'm marking on your calendar the two Wednesdays that you'll mail me a card to a different place. How about if I address those cards in green ink and write "green ink" in your calendar on those two Wednesdays?*

Cleo: That sounds good. I don't want to get mixed up.

Therapist: *Does it sound confusing so far?*

Cleo: I have to bring my cards next week and my summer house address.

Therapist: *Right. I have to bring a green pen and 10 stamps and my summer house address. Also, before you come next time, I'll do some work on this calendar to make it easier to keep track of everything. There is one other very important matter for us to talk about. Your birthday. It's on August 15th. Here, I'm marking it down. Is it all right if I send you a different card for your birthday?*

Cleo: Yes. What kind will you send?

Therapist: *Is there a kind that you would like?*

Cleo: There's a kind of card that says how old you are. I like that kind of card but I never got one before. My friend Lily got one like that when she was 7. You could send me one like that every year and I could collect them. This year you can send a 7-year-old card, and next year you can send an 8-year-old card until I'm . . . When do they stop making cards for how old you are?

Therapist: *Not for a very long time. You can get cards like that when you are all grown up. This year I will send you a 7-year-old card. Do you think you might like me to send you a present too?*

Cleo: A present? I don't know what would fit in the mailbox. A small present would fit I think. Do you know how big a mailbox is and what fits?

Therapist: *Yes, I do know how big a mailbox is. But what about the present itself? What do you think you would like it to be?*

Cleo: What happens if a present is too big for the mailbox? What happens to it? Does the mail lady take it back?

Therapist: *If it can't fit inside the mailbox, the mail person brings it to the house. If nobody is home the mail person leaves a note in the mailbox saying that you have a package and that they will bring it back or that you can pick it up at the post office.*

Cleo: But my grandparents don't know where the post office is, so I would like a small present that can fit in the mailbox, but I don't know what.

Therapist: *Could you think about what you would like and tell me next week? But there is something that I have to tell you about a present from me to you. There is something different about your therapist giving you a present from other people giving you a present. My present to you has to have something to do with our work together, something we talk about or do together, something that has special therapy meaning, something that will remind you of our time together. So when you think about my giving you a birthday present, think about it that way, all right?*

We were sitting on my couch and talking with the calendar between us, and she was no longer restless and fidgety the way she had been early in the session. In fact she was very relaxed, and I thought that she liked sitting next to me and working together this way. Then my next patient rang the bell and I buzzed her in and in that instant we both looked at the clock. Our time was up and I was about to say so when I noticed a funny look on Cleo's face. She was still looking at the clock, and slowly she turned and said,

Cleo: A clock just like that would be small enough to fit in my mailbox.

Therapist: *Do you think you would like a clock just like mine for a birthday present?*

Cleo nodded as she got up to leave. I said, *Well, you could think about it during the week and let me know next time.*

Cleo: I know now. I need a clock like that of my own. I'm sure that's what I want.

Therapist: Our time was up and she left carrying her reminder about the cards and the summer address. It had been a very pressured session. She had been 15 minutes late on a day when we had so much to settle before the vacation. I almost felt as if we had no time to talk, but just time to do preparation for separation. I felt rattled. I don't know what was wrong with me.

Supervisor: It isn't so hard to understand why you felt pressured. She had almost missed one appointment through lateness, been late today again, and all this almost on the eve of a long summer break. Plus her mother had failed to tell you of important changes in her life, specifically the 6-day trip to California, Maria's sudden announcement of her permanent departure, the grandparents' arrival three weeks ahead of schedule to replace Maria, the father's unreliability regarding visiting the children. It's hard not to wonder what's happening to your alliance with the mother when she "forgets" to tell you all this and then cries so helplessly over the prospective loss of the summer house. It's hard to know what she's crying about. I'm not making light of losing a beloved house. I'm just wondering what the loss of the house might mean to her. For instance, is Mrs. C. feeling profoundly bereft in a general way and unable to be in touch with that feeling in herself except when she can use a concrete event in her life, such as the loss of this house, as a catalyst and pathway to her affective state? Is the loss of the house a symbol for other losses in her life? There is much to wonder about here.

Then there is the helplessness of her crying, its unexpected appearance in the session, her sense of vagueness about you as a reliable partner regarding her daughter; these are the features that make me wonder about something in Mrs. C. Something faintly unsteady in Mrs. C. manifests itself in these subtle ways, and maybe it's the same something that explains how Cleo got so frightened.

Therapist: Well, I think you're putting something into words for me. I need to understand more about this mother. I think she's learned to use the language of feelings but that she doesn't recognize the feelings themselves.

Supervisor: That's an interesting formulation. If she has difficulty identifying her own affects, then it would be very difficult for her to identify those of others unless they reach overwhelming proportions, like perhaps her husband's violence or her daughter's terror. It can be difficult for little children to recognize and identify their own affective states if their primary caretakers haven't done this for them. I'm talking about something very simple and ordinary here, normal comments that a parent makes to a child. For instance, saying to a child, "You seem a little glum today. Is something bothering you?" or, "You looked so happy when you remembered that today is our picnic day. You were smiling from ear to ear."

I'm talking about all the things that we generally take for granted in the course of our relationships, like noticing, with empathy, in both happy or sad circumstances, the affects of the people we love. Or expressing the emotional responses we experience to the people dear to us.

You're saying, in not so many words, that Mrs. C.'s affective states are confusing to you. She sounds staunch, then she collapses, unexpectedly. Her rhythm is hard to follow. There is no warning before the tears come. No signal, no awareness that she's losing her balance. It confuses you, and when she collapses you begin to feel as if you alone can carry Cleo. But Cleo is going to be gone for over two months, so how are you going to do it long distance? It certainly sounds as if something about her makes you feel that you're carrying the whole weight of things. Perhaps you're beginning to grasp, through your countertransference, an element of emptiness in Mrs. C. Remember our session many weeks ago when I imagined Cleo as an adult being presented at a scientific meeting and the general difficulty over recognizing the state of emptiness that she experienced in childhood. Perhaps we're seeing something like that in Cleo's mother, seeing it through your countertransference in the form of your wish to protect and rescue this little girl. It's important for you to recognize your great sense of urgency as signifying both a realistic concern, and that "mommy" brand of countertransference we talked about earlier.

When are they actually leaving the city?

Therapist: The weekend after my last appointment with Cleo.

Supervisor: So if for any reason you don't have time to finish the necessary summer vacation preparation, you could ask to see her a second time that week, couldn't you?

Therapist: I could ask for an extra session, but why didn't I think of that? Because of that urgent feeling of having to fix everything . . . that countertransferentially propelled rescue fantasy of mine. I did think that it might make sense to see Mrs. C. during the summer, to be kept abreast of what is happening, but again, I experienced that feeling I so often have with her that I don't want to ask too much of her. So what I did was to say that at present I had no reason to want to see her over the summer, but that I did not want to wait until the last week of September. I scheduled an appointment with Mrs. C. the first week of September.

Supervisor: You certainly should see her before that. You should see her before Cleo's midsummer appointment to find out what's happening to Cleo, to her fears, to the sale of the house and so forth. You really should know something about the shape that Cleo is in during the summer. You might even want to refer to some of what you hear from her mother in some of the letters that you write to her during the summer.

I think that the planning you did with Cleo was fine. I very much liked the way she began by tentatively presenting some of her own ideas on how to conduct a correspondence, and how you took her up on her ideas and combined them with your own. It was such a nice partnership; it was wonderful. And then, at the end, your discourse about the birthday present was correct in principle, but I wondered whether it wasn't too theoretical for a little girl. Then, to my surprise, she suddenly found a very appropriate present—a duplicate of your clock. What could more perfectly symbolize your time together and your reliability and continuity than your clock, the instrument that determines when your sessions begin and when they end? Were you surprised?

Therapist: Very. Because while I was talking about gifts I also thought that I was being too theoretical. I was feeling that sense of pressure to get things done, settled, orderly. Then came that fortuitous ringing of the bell by the patient after Cleo who always comes late, never early, and because of the bell we both looked at the clock together, and I believe that was the spark for her idea. Yes, I was extremely surprised. Now I feel a little more prepared for that final session before our summer break.

Supervisor: I have one more cautionary comment to make before we stop for today. You're being very careful and responsible in the way you're planning to keep the connection ongoing during the summer break. You have taken on writing once per week and sending a birthday present. The letter writing will also take place during your vacation. Do you feel okay about that or does it feel like an intrusion? It's very important to plan these things with care so that they meet the needs of the child without becoming too great a burden on the therapist.

Therapist: No, I don't feel burdened by this plan. If I had many children in my practice and had an involved plan with each one, well, then I might find it a bit too much . . . maybe not. Maybe one letter a week to even half a dozen children would still be okay. I could allow one hour a week to do this sort of correspondence. My letter to Cleo will not take more than five minutes. But I get your point. It worked out all right, but it could have crossed the border into too much. Cleo is not very demanding, so it worked out fine. With some children I could end up running around the city looking for a particular card with a particular dinosaur or airplane or something like that. That would be a problem, but this is fine.

20

The Summer Goodbye Session

Therapist: Cleo got to her session 5 minutes early. I could hear her talking in the waiting room and that was very unusual, since the office is pretty well soundproofed. I knew that she must be talking very loud for the sound to carry. I opened my door a bit to listen, and I could tell that she was talking to someone rather than talking in her play. I decided that since I had some free time, we would start early. We had so much to cover in this final session before the summer.

In the waiting room I saw that she was with her father and it was to him that she was talking in that unusually loud way. I remembered our recent discussion about my not properly greeting her grandfather, so I made sure to greet Mr. C. He responded politely and asked me how long the appointment was going to last. Cleo interrupted and said that we were finished at 5:00. Her father said that he would go out and make a few phone calls and be back in plenty of time.

In the office I told Cleo that I had been surprised to see her father in the waiting room with her since it's so unusual for him to bring her to her appointments. She answered,

Cleo: I've been with him all day today. I asked my mom if I could spend the day with him since I didn't have to go to school because today was teacher conference day and so the kids don't go, just the teachers. I only have two more days of school and then I have freedom for two months, freedom from recess and being too hot and not having anything to drink.

Therapist: *That doesn't sound too comfortable. Recess on hot days with nothing to drink sounds pretty unpleasant.*

Cleo: You can say that again! Do you know that this might be the last summer that we have our country house?

Therapist: *Your mom said something to me about that. Can you tell me what's happening with your country house?*

Cleo: Well, it really isn't our country house. It really belongs to my mom's cousin but he always lets us use it and now he decided that he can't pay for it anymore. See, he has to pay for it every month and he says that it costs too much and my mom can't pay for it, so if nobody can pay for it then he has to sell it. It's real bad that it's happening because it means that I can't see my friends anymore after this summer. My very very best friend lives on the same block. We like everything the same, the same jokes, and the same games, and we like to go bike riding together and we even like the same drinks and the same food. This is the last summer I can be with my friends. My mom says that I better be sure to make it the best summer I ever had.

Therapist: *That's very sad news then, about your summer house and your good friends. And it's too bad that we didn't know about it before today. We could have talked about it and maybe I could have helped you in some way. Maybe I still can, even though we have so little time left. After all, today is our "goodbye" appointment.*

Cleo: No it's not!

Therapist: *Oh dear, did you forget that today is our last appointment until your mom brings you in the middle of the summer on July 30th?*

Cleo: No, that's not true. I'm seeing you today and I'll see you next week like I always do.

Therapist: *Oh my. I think you're saying what you would like and I'm saying what is really going to happen.*

Cleo: No. It can't be goodbye when I see you every week.

Therapist: *Oh, I'm beginning to get an idea of how hard all this is. There are so many goodbyes in your life right now. More than you want to think about, and I can understand that very well. And you're right that we are not really saying "goodbye." We are saying "goodbye for the summer." And look, I finished making that calendar we started together last week and I wrote in all the dates that we talked about. Look, here it is. Here is today, June 27th. See, it says on the date box for today, "4:15 p.m. Cleo and L. S. have last appointment before summer vacation." And on the July 30th box it says, "Cleo's mom brings her to N. Y. C. to see L. S. in the middle of vacation." And here in the September 5th box, "Cleo and L. S. begin regular weekly appointments again."*

Remember what we decided about using green ink? Well, here in green ink I marked all the days that I will be on vacation, and the two "green" Wednesdays that you mail me your cards that I addressed to myself in green.

I am showing you all this because I know that it's important for you to know all these things so that you can feel more in charge of what's going on in your life. When you don't know what to expect, it makes it hard for you. When you know just what to expect, it does make things a little easier for you.

Cleo: Here, I brought the ten animal cards and my summer house address.

Therapist: *And I brought the ten stamps. How about gluing them on the envelopes right now? And I have a printing stamper with my name and address on it. We can use it on eight of the envelopes and I have a green pen for the two envelopes that will go to my vacation house.*

Cleo: But before we do that would you write on my calendar on the box for this Friday: "Cleo goes to Lakeville for 65 days?" then on all the Wednesdays write: "Cleo writes card to L. S. and L. S. writes card to Cleo." No! just you write about me going to Lakeville and I will write the part about us writing on Wednesdays.

Therapist: And so we got very busy writing on the calendar, with Cleo asking me how to spell things and making her letters too big for the calendar boxes and then erasing them to make smaller letters, like all kids her age do, and fastening stamps and addressing envelopes, and while we worked this way I said, *You know, we're doing all sorts of things to make not seeing each other for such a long time a little easier, but it's still hard to have such a long time apart. It still means missing each other a lot, but missing each other and knowing that it's not forever. Have you thought about the missing part?*

Cleo: Yes, I've thought about it.

Therapist: *Your voice sounds so tired it makes me think that it's too hard to even talk about.*

Cleo: It's very hard to talk about and to think about. I know that I'm going to miss you a lot because you taught me that I don't have to be afraid. Now when I'm afraid I tell myself to think of you.

Therapist: *Could you tell me about how you do that?*

Cleo: Every night when I go to sleep I think of you.

Therapist: *What happens then?*

Cleo: I feel a little better.

Therapist: *Do you think you'll be able to do that in Lakeville?*

Cleo: Yes. I can do it there too, but I'm not so afraid there. I'm more afraid where I really live. I'm more afraid when I'm here, here at home.

Therapist: *That's something very puzzling that we need to understand. We can talk about it after the summer.*

Cleo: Yeah.

Therapist: *It's very sad to lose that country house. It's even harder to lose a house that you feel safer in than you feel at home.*

Cleo: Yes. I don't know where I'll go next year when it's time to go away from you. Maybe I'll go to Argentina to my grandparents' house. We can write letters the same way to Argentina, right?

Therapist: *We can write letters the same way to Lakeville, to Argentina, and to any place in the world.*

I was very moved by what was transpiring between us. She was able to tolerate so much closeness in this session, and she was expressing herself directly, with the anticipation of our maintaining continuity, and of working and being together now and next year. I was amazed that she could even think of the separation a year from now. I had been feeling so pressured to get all the practical issues regarding our vacation break settled that I had nearly lost sight of the emotional impact of this "goodbye" session. Cleo, on the other hand, was able to hold on to the solemnity of the occasion and be expressive. But she brought me back to what was really important with those amazing words: You taught me that I don't have to be afraid. I was holding that sentence in my mind, and sort of turning it around in wonderment, because I couldn't believe that this little girl could have said that . . . this little girl who told chicken jokes to get away from closeness and feelings. I'm telling you the kind of state I was in as this session was at the halfway mark. Now I'll return to the session.

While we were talking, we were writing. Cleo had stamped my address on eight of the envelopes and was now licking the postal stamps. I had written her country address in my appointment book, addressed the two envelopes for my vacation place with green ink, and was looking through her calendar for special dates to be marked, such as her birthday. It was silent in the room. Suddenly Cleo began to talk quietly.

Cleo: On the first Wednesday, after I write to you, I'll put the letter in the mailbox myself and push up the red flag so the post office lady knows to look inside for a letter to mail. Then I'll get on my bike and ride over to Emily's house. Emily lives on my block and she's my friend. She has a new baby and a pool and her mother is nice. I'll go play with her. We draw a lot. Maybe I'll send you some of the pictures we draw together.

Therapist: *It sounds as if there's a lot of stuff for you to look forward to in Lakeville. It sounds like a nice place with friends and swimming.*

Cleo: And cookouts and picnics and sleepovers and some bad things too.

Therapist: *What are the bad things?*

Cleo: My mom isn't there and my dad isn't there and you aren't there.

Therapist: *Yes, I can see that there are bad things as well as good things.*

We stayed quiet for a few minutes, finishing the calendar entries, and then it was time to stop, and I said, *Now we have to say goodbye in a couple of minutes so let's make sure that we have everything finished and ready.*

Together we checked the calendar and the ten cards in their stamped and addressed envelopes, and at the last minute I stapled one of my professional cards to the back of her calendar so that she would have my telephone number, should she ever want to speak to me. I showed her how I had marked her birthday in my appointment book as well as her address and all the important dates. I said, *Goodbye Cleo. Have a very very nice summer.*

Cleo: Goodbye Linda Small. I'll see you next Wednesday. That's a joke. I'll see you when I see you.

Therapist: Together we walked into the waiting room. Her father stood up and Cleo said to him,

Cleo: Today is the "goodbye for the summer" day.

Therapist: Her father asked if this was "it" for the summer and I told him that it was, but that we had one appointment in the middle of the summer. He stood up and put out his hand and shook my hand and wished me a nice summer and then put his hand on Cleo's shoulder in an affectionate way, and they left. I felt better seeing him act fatherly and protective.

Supervisor: Like a regular father.

Therapist: Yes. I haven't really seen them together. My image of him is colored by my knowledge of his drinking, his violence, his unreliability, his disinclination to have anything to do with her treatment, and that is not a pretty picture. It was nice to see that he had a tender and affectionate side. I realized how protective I was feeling toward her during this session. I was so glad that she had a friend on her block with a nice mother, a pool, and a new baby. I was glad that her father had a soft side. This was a hard session for me. I did not feel like Freud's (1912b) ideal analyst who has the coolness of a surgeon. No, not one bit like that.

Supervisor: How about stepping back a bit and looking at this session as a whole rather than one particular segment or another? What do you think of the session as a whole? How do you think it went?

Therapist: It's a good idea for me to discuss that with you because right now I'm feeling as if it was too rushed and that I was too identified with Cleo and not professional enough. If I think of it as a whole session it looks much better to me. In fact, if I think of it as session number eighteen in the course of the treatment of this little girl who began with me in such a state of fright and guardedness, it seems like a fine session from the standpoint of her growth. I think I was too focused on the part I felt I had to play and not attuned enough to Cleo. The more I look at it the more I see that I was a bit obsessional under the guise of being professional. This session had a regressive effect on me.

Supervisor: I told you that important separations have a regressive effect on people. I didn't mean just the patients. Did you think I was excluding the therapists from being subject to regression at these junctures?

Therapist: Yes. I thought you were talking about just the patients. The therapist should stay level and strong.

Supervisor: Being rattled and feeling pressured does not undo your strength. I still think that you should take a look at what happened in this session. I think you're shortchanging yourself.

Therapist: I'm looking at my notes. First there was her loud talking in the waiting room. She was excited at being with her father and not restraining herself as she so often does. In fact she was very direct about her feelings from the very beginning. She expressed her happiness at not being at school. She talked seriously about the loss of her country house and her nice life there and her best friend. There was a little fooling around about this not being our last session, but she very quickly got into our joint project regarding our communication during the vacation. Then came that stunning acknowledgment about missing me, and that I taught her that she didn't have to be afraid, and that she thinks of me when she feels afraid. Then she talked about the future in a way that amazed me. She sounded as if the future is not some completely unknown, unsafe, and unthinkable region. She sounded as if she could have some control over the future.

Supervisor: I agree that these are extremely encouraging communications. She's beginning to sound like a child with a range of affects. There are good things in her life and there are bad things as well. She can enjoy the good things and bear the bad ones without having to deny them. She can link a pleasurable affect with an action, for instance when she anticipates the process of writing to you, mailing the letter, and then going to Emily's house where she expects to have pleasure and to be welcome.

Therapist: I'm glad we're reviewing the session this way because I lost track of how much we accomplished in the last three or four weeks. Why is there so much growth at the point of separation? It's a paradox, isn't it? You were talking about a separation causing a regression and that makes complete sense, but what we see instead is a spurt of growth. What is that?

Supervisor: Life. It's called life. The therapist regresses and the child has a spurt of growth and mastery. Is that an accident? No, I think that it's all connected. We could speculate about it but we would never be sure. Do you have any ideas?

Therapist: A few weeks ago, when Mrs. C. forgot Cleo's appointment and Cleo had the temper tantrum that mobilized the attention of the adults and got her to her session, that was a regression that resulted in growth. She discovered that she could express strong feelings, that she didn't have to stifle them, and she could get what she wanted and needed. There's been a serious acknowledgment of the difficulty of the separation from me, her therapist. Maybe there was something in the earnestness of my concern for keeping our connection active during vacation that really meant a lot to her. Maybe in my concern I was more accessible to her. Maybe there was more affect emanating from me. Maybe it had a lot of carrying power.

Supervisor: A lot of maybes here. The point is that it worked out well even though you, the therapist, felt pressured and dissatisfied with yourself. Whatever forces converged and resulted in this outcome, the outcome is a good one. Cleo leaves you for the summer a much calmer child than the little girl of 5 months ago. She even has a sense of having a past, a present, and a future. That's quite a stunning achievement.

Now there's another matter we should discuss. What about Cleo's father? You met with him once, and as I recall it was not a very satisfactory meeting, right?

Therapist: No, it was not. He was quite late to his appointment and indifferent to his lateness. In every way, without ever being rude, he made it clear that he had no interest in Cleo's treatment. He never paid my bill that I sent to him three months in a row. I finally wrote him a little note about the unpaid bill and that too went unanswered. I mentioned it to the mother at some point and she said that she would pay it. After all, treatment was her idea and she didn't want me to remain unpaid for the appointment.

Supervisor: Since we haven't talked about the subject of payment before, I assume that it hasn't been a problem except for this one incident involving the father's failure to pay for his single appointment.

Therapist: No, it hasn't been a problem. Mrs. C. pays me by the middle of the month, as I requested during the consultation period.

Supervisor: Tell me, how did it feel not to get paid by Mr. C.?

Therapist: It made me mad and it made me not want to be bothered with him. I never telephoned him about his unpaid bill. I wrote to him, and while I consider that a perfectly acceptable way to have handled the situation, I recognize now that it's also more distant and perhaps a bit more antiseptic. It has the quality of not wanting to stoop to asking for the money. Money does stir up all sorts of feelings, doesn't it? I can hear what a loaded issue it was for me, as if there was something dirty about the money. Now that I'm talking to you about it I can hear it in my voice, I can feel my indignation. At the time, I dismissed it and thought that it was more a matter of being too identified with his wife and with Cleo, and, of course, resenting his ignoring my bill. I realize the countertransferential quality of my anger and that it resulted in my writing him off rather easily. Perhaps his bringing Cleo today and being friendly and wanting to shake hands with me was his way of letting me know that he's more amenable to participating in Cleo's treatment. Maybe I'll give him a call. What do you think?

Supervisor: I'm not sure. It might be good idea. Let's explore it a bit more. If you see him, will you bring up the bill?

Therapist: I think I have to bring it up. If I ignore it, it could be understood as my condoning not being paid.

Supervisor: I agree. What do you see as the purpose of seeing Cleo's dad? We all know that it is good to involve both parents in the treatment of a young child. I'm asking you to explain the obvious because perhaps it's not so obvious.

Therapist: Well, I want to support his fathering role. As soon as I say something like that I realize it sounds pompous and presumptuous. I should say that I need to know more about his fathering experience. I only know about him through his ex-wife, and even then I know very little. I do know that he's unsympathetic to the field of mental health, so it's risky to get involved with him. But I do think that his friendly behavior today was some sort of green light. I don't know why I should see him. We're doing very well without him. I hope I'm not motivated by guilt. It's easier not to see him; therefore I must see him? Help?

Supervisor: You don't know what you might gain by seeing him and you don't have to know. You can't know something like that in advance. It's something to find out, though. Remember, he's a part of her history, the part you know so little about. He is also a part of her present and of her future and you might be of help to him and consequently to her, and that makes it worthwhile to see him and explore the possibility of his being more of a participant in her treatment. If you don't impose an agenda on this potential meeting, no harm is likely to come from your asking him whether he would like to come and talk to you. It might be useful and it might not, but it will not be harmful so long as you really and honestly believe that he has the right to say yes or no to you. If, in your heart, you don't allow him the choice, I would recommend that you leave well enough alone. I say that with full respect for the role of this father in the life of his child.

Cleo's father is not just the man who behaved violently on several occasions and who pressures her to do things that are bordering on scary. He is not just a man with a drinking problem, an unreliable dad who misses appointments with his kids. He is also the father who held her when she was little, who probably read to her, told her stories, explained things to her, and fixed things for her and made her feel safe and protected. He is *the* man in her life, a man with a look and touch and feel and smell and voice. For the rest of her life all the men she will ever look at and befriend or reject, love and marry, will consciously and unconsciously be compared to her father.

That's just the way life is and will always be, psychoanalysis and psychotherapy notwithstanding. That's the way these early object representations inhabit our unconscious and shape all future relationships.

What's my point? That a little girl's father, no matter how absent or unreliable, is still the prototype for her future heterosexual relationships, and without in any way minimizing the incalculable importance of this relationship I still feel that his participation in the treatment is not compulsory. As you said earlier, you've done well enough without him. So really, only call him if you believe that he has the *right* to refuse you.

Therapist: I think I can do that. It's really interesting that Cleo allowed herself to show us off to each other. I wonder what that was about? I was so hellbent on taking care of all the vacation business that I didn't let myself reflect on that part of the session. She did that loud talking in the waiting room and told me that she had asked to spend the day with him. What was that all about?

Supervisor: What are your thoughts about it?

Therapist: Maybe she's fixing us up, making a couple out of us, the couple her parents are not?

Supervisor: That would not be too surprising since you already must at times be viewed by her as an ideal mother.

Therapist: Well, in light of that, I'd better check out whether that's not a fantasy that I share with her.

Supervisor: That would be the kind of checking that's of paramount importance. We've talked before about a child therapist trying to be a better parent than the real parents. That's a very dangerous aspect of our work and we have to check ourselves diligently in that regard. You have just been through a series of sessions with Cleo that surprised both of us by how accessible and close she was with you. On the eve of a long separation she let you know how much you mean to her. You, in turn, have gone to great lengths to find a way to keep the connection going during the physical separation. Everything you've done has been fine and will probably be very valuable to her. You've been very caring and have invested a lot in your work with Cleo. Look, you really feel some strong pangs about letting her go, right?

Therapist: Yes.

Supervisor: Well, it wouldn't be very good if you didn't, and yet you have to be careful because you do. I don't mean careful in the sense of wary, but in the sense of taking care to be aware.

Therapist: I have such respect for the principle of "evenly-suspended attention." It always fits so well, no matter what issue is placed before us: to be aware on all fronts and to allow things to evolve as they will. I really need to develop that ability in my work. It sounds so simple, but it isn't, is it?

Supervisor: No, it's not simple at all because try as we might, we still have our own wishes and hopes and expectations, as well as our blind spots. But we don't have to be perfect to do a good job. We can do a good job with all our imperfections. It's essential, though, that we examine our own work scrupulously. This is a profession that requires a great deal of honesty, humility, and courage. But what a satisfying profession it is, don't you agree?

21

Epilogue

Linda Small took on the task of working with a frightened and traumatized child in once-a-week psychoanalytic psychotherapy. At the beginning, her primary approach was to offer a therapeutic environment that was calm, predictable, and safe—an environment wherein she would stay in step with Cleo, but not too close and not too far away. During those early weeks of treatment, Linda Small was often baffled by Cleo's communications. She had difficulty in deciphering and conceptualizing the material and in finding themes that would illuminate the flow and direction of the treatment process. Cleo's elusiveness was enervating, and Linda Small began to experience bouts of sleepiness that descended upon her at particular moments in the sessions. She identified these as her response to feeling disposable, extraneous, and peripheral. Analysis of this countertransference yielded some insight into Cleo's intense reaction to disappointment, her defense of withdrawal, and her disconnection from her objects.

In those early sessions Linda Small's determination and faith in the therapeutic process had to remain steadfast and outpace Cleo's fear and ambivalence. She persisted and used any and all openings to make an inroad. She created therapeutic opportunities by addressing small and ordinary things like the time and date of appointments and their unwavering regularity, and by noticing and identifying an affect, a response, a wish. She was interested and curious and attentive. She remembered previous sessions and so built a common history. She could now talk to Cleo about the things they remembered together. She could say, "Do you remember when *we* played that game and such and such happened?"

I refer here to the most ordinary aspects of therapy, to those things that often feel to us as if we are not doing anything in particular. But we are. We are both doing something and being something and this has a cumulative affect.

As those early months of treatment unfolded, the therapist always stayed the same. No matter how Cleo spun around in her chair, darted in and out of barely audible fantasies, and did tricks and jokes, Linda Small was steady, and interested, and present. Slowly, and over time, things began to take new shape for Cleo.

When Cleo resumed her sessions after the summer vacation, she brought with her the calendar that she and her therapist had made together. It had clearly become a valued possession. She now came with Katie, a new and lively baby-sitter, and when Linda Small noted the difference between Katie and the former sitter, Maria, Cleo volunteered a memory. When she was 4 years old, she had had a beloved sitter named Lalli, a baby-sitter who was nice because she *played* with her, but then she went away. Soon after that communication Cleo drew a picture of a woman with red hair and glasses, like your red hair and glasses, Linda Small, she explained offhandedly, not consciously knowing, of course, that to be able to acknowledge out loud her therapist's physical actuality was a big event.

A month later, the mother reported Cleo's new attachment to a teddy bear, which now was taken into her bed nightly. Although we know that it was too late in her life to consider this a transitional object in the true sense, it was nonetheless a welcome indicator that transitional phenomena were being employed adaptively. We could understand this new attachment as ushering in the emergence of a less frightened state, one perhaps containing some revived libidinal investment in the self and object representations, some affection, something more hopeful than before.

Several months after that long summer interruption, a second session each week was arranged. While Cleo's father held to his position of nonparticipation, he financed this increased frequency of appointments and in that way expressed his support of his daughter's treatment. The sessions continued in their customary pattern of periods of direct communication alternating with Cleo's characteristic darting away. Linda Small's bouts of debilitating sleepiness also continued to appear in response to Cleo's retreats into a distant realm of inaccessibility. Once, when Cleo noticed and commented on her therapist's sleepy look, Linda Small was able to make an interpretation that addressed the dynamics between them.

There was no long vacation break the second summer. With the country house sold, Cleo went to day camp and continued her appointments throughout most of the summer. But as summer approached, she remembered all the plans that had been made the previous year to maintain contact during that long separation. Together Cleo and Linda Small remembered the cards, the calendar, and the special envelopes addressed in green ink. Perhaps all that talk about remembering triggered a much earlier memory.

Cleo remembered being 2 years old and staying with some married cousins. She remembered being awakened during the night by the sound of glass crashing and breaking, and she remembered the crashing happening over and over again throughout the night. The next morning, when she saw her cousins, they both had cuts all over them. She remembered being very scared and thinking they had gotten cut by the glass.

Linda Small was astonished that Cleo was able to voice and share this memory of violence. It was the first time that she had ever shared a memory that came so close to that terrible period of her life when she so often was awakened by the loud sounds of battle and discord. Linda Small wondered how to respond to this very important communication. Was this a screen memory? Was it going to lead to the recovery of those other memories and the traumatic fear she must have suffered when she was exposed to that terrible time of parental warfare? How does a therapist deal with the opening up of such possibilities with a young child?

Linda Small felt a great sense of awe at this development in Cleo's treatment, and we tried to talk out and explore her discomfort and apprehension. We talked about this for a long time. We tried to stay with Cleo's story of glass shattering in that bedroom, of people getting hurt and cut, and of blood and danger. We tried to reconstruct what a little child could do when she wakes up scared at night. Of course the natural response for a little child is to call her parents for help or run into their bedroom for comfort and reassurance. But what if the source of fright is violence emanating from that room, and the haven of safety is the locus of terror? What does a little child do then? Where is there to go? Linda Small began to gain an awareness of what this preverbal and early verbal experience could do to a young child, the kind of terror and confusion it would create, and how it might result in a 6½-year-old child believing that she should be able to manage dealing with rats and robbers on the subway all by herself. In talking and thinking this way, Linda Small began to grasp how all this insight into Cleo's early experience could slowly be used in the treatment.

We discussed how Cleo could eventually be told that when she was very little and could not yet talk much it was hard for her to understand things, especially things in the night, in the dark. It was hard to understand what she couldn't see and touch and recognize. What made it such a particularly hard time for her was that she was very little then, too little to know how to get help for herself and too little to know how to soothe herself. That left her all alone with her terrible fears. Cleo could be told that little children can't bear to be so scared and confused, and when they are, they usually make up stories for themselves to explain the frightening mysteries around them, and their stories often become so real that they sometimes become more real than the truth of what actually happened. Now that she's older she can make videos and plays and movies and she knows the difference between make believe and real, but when she was small she wasn't sure about these things at all. When she was small, some of the stories that she made up to explain the noise and fighting in the middle of the night were much scarier than the scary enough truth of what was really going on, and yet, somehow, when she was little she managed to contain her fears. Later though, when she was 6, she couldn't contain them anymore. Things just became too frightening for her to bear. Maybe being moved to that big room and being alone there, without her sister, was too great a strain on her. Maybe that was the precipitate to her panic. It was hard to tell for sure why her terror erupted when it did, but then for a long time she could no longer fall asleep because it was the night that she dreaded the most. The night reminded her of the times of crashing glass and sounds she couldn't understand and recognize. It revived the terrifying stories she had made up about people coming out of paintings to take her away because she believed she was bad. Because the night had been the time of feeling the most alone and scared when she was small, anything that reminded her of that lonely terror was more than she could endure and only her mother's presence could quiet her fear of surrendering to sleep, to night, to that vast and terrible unknown.

Linda Small and I talked this way until the deepening of Cleo's treatment began to feel less awesome and intimidating. As we talked, she came to recognize that she had set a tone and established a climate from the very beginning that had made this unfolding of the treatment process possible. As we talked, the language of psychoanalytic theory began to come alive. When approached in this way it had an organic feel. It fit the trends in Cleo's treatment. After a while the therapist found that the deepening of Cleo's treatment no longer felt like some mysterious process beyond her understanding. She discovered within herself a growing comfort and ease in treating a child.

We also talked about how long it sometimes takes before the treatment can move into a new phase, one of a more exploratory nature. In Cleo's case it took a long while for the treatment situation to represent a climate of safety. Only when that was achieved did it become possible for Cleo to be more daring and to look around.

With her reliable therapist at her side she was able to begin to examine her past and her present, her inner life and her external situation.

By the end of the second year of treatment Cleo began to find the world of reality pretty engaging and this became reflected in her play and in her interests. Gradually she became a more typical latency age child, a more conventional little girl in some ways, but wasn't that our goal from the beginning? She could now look forward to a family outing with the expectation of having a nice time, talk about the future, and make plans. But the best development of all was something that would seem pretty commonplace to anyone who didn't know her history. Cleo, like most other children, could now have occasional ordinary bad dreams about ghosts and other demons, instead of the paralyzingly real night terrors of her past.

References

Abelin, E. (1971). The role of the father in the separation-individuation process. In *Separation-Individuation: Essays in Honor of Margaret S. Mahler,* ed. J. McDevitt and C. Settlage, pp. 229–252. New York: International Universities Press.

Benedek, T. (1938). Adaptation to reality in early infancy. *Psychoanalytic Quarterly* 7:200–214.

Blanck, G., and Blanck, R. (1975). *Ego Psychology: Theory and Practice.* New York: Columbia University Press.

_____ (1979). *Ego Psychology II: Psychoanalytic Developmental Psychology.* New York: Columbia University Press.

_____ (1986). *Beyond Ego Psychology.* New York: Columbia University Press.

Bollas, C. (1987). *The Shadow of the Object.* New York: Columbia University Press.

Edward, J., Ruskin, N., and Turrini, P. (1991). *Separation-Individuation: Theory and Application.* New York: Gardner Press.

Ekstein, R. (1966). *Children of Time and Space, of Action and Impulse: Clinical Studies on the Treatment of Severely Disturbed Children.* New York: Appleton-Century-Croft.

Fenichel, O. (1945). *The Psychoanalytic Theory of Neuroses.* New York: W. W. Norton.

Fraiberg, S. (1951). Clinical notes on the nature of transference in child analysis. *Psychoanalytic Study of the Child,* 6:286–306. New York: International Universities Press.

Freud, A. (1936). *The Ego and Mechanisms of Defense.* New York: International Universities Press, 1946.

――― (1965). *Normality and Pathology in Childhood.* New York: International Universities Press.

Freud, S. (1905). Three essays on the theory of sexuality. *Standard Edition* 7:130–245.

――― (1912a). The dynamics of transference. *Standard Edition* 12:97–108.

――― (1912b). Recommendations to physicians on the psychoanalytic method of treatment. *Standard Edition* 12:109–120.

――― (1915). Further recommendations on the technique of psychoanalysis—observations on transference love. *Standard Edition* 12:157–171.

――― (1924). The dissolution of the Oedipus complex. *Standard Edition* 19:173–182.

――― (1925a). Some psychical consequences of the anatomical difference between the sexes. *Standard Edition* 19:243–247.

――― (1925b). Negation. *Standard Edition* 19:235–239.

Furman, E. (1971). Some thoughts on reconstruction in child analysis. *Psychoanalytic Study of the Child* 26:372–385. New York: Quadrangle Books.

Glenn, J. (1989). From protomasochism to masochism: a developmental view. *Psychoanalytic Study of the Child* 44:73–86. New Haven: Yale University Press.

Greenacre, P. (1980). A historical sketch of the use and disuse of reconstruction. *Psychoanalytic Study of the Child* 35:35–40. New Haven: Yale University Press.

Greenson, R. R. (1965). The working alliance and the transference neurosis. *Psychoanalytic Quarterly* 34:155–181.

Grunes, M. (1984). The therapeutic object relationship. *Psychoanalytic Review* 71:123–143.

Hartmann, H. (1939). *Ego Psychology and the Problem of Adaptation.* New York: International Universities Press, 1958.

Jacobson, E. (1964). *The Self and the Object World.* New York: International Universities Press.

Kris, E. (1952). *Psychoanalytic Explorations in Art.* New York: International Universities Press.

Loewald, H. (1960). On the therapeutic action in psychoanalysis. In *Papers on Psychoanalysis,* pp. 221–256. New Haven: Yale University Press, 1980.

Loewenstein, R. (1957). A contribution to the psychoanalytic theory of masochism. *Journal of the American Psychoanalytic Association* 5:197–234.

Mahler, M. (1968). *On Human Symbiosis and the Vicissitudes of Individuation.* New York: International Universities Press.

_____ (1971). A study of the separation-individuation process and its possible application to borderline phenomena in the psychoanalytic situation. In *The Selected Papers of Margaret S. Mahler, M. D.,* 2:169–187. New York: Jason Aronson, 1979.

Mahler, M., Pine, F., and Bergman, A. (1975). *The Psychological Birth of the Human Infant.* New York: Basic Books.

Moore, B., and Fine, B. (1990). *Psychoanalytic Terms and Concepts.* New Haven: Yale University Press.

Nagera, H. (1975). *Female Sexuality and the Oedipus Complex.* New York: Jason Aronson.

Novick, K., and Novick, J. (1987). The essence of masochism. *Psychoanalytic Study of the Child* 42:353–384. New Haven: Yale University Press.

Nunberg, H. (1930). The synthetic function of the ego. In *Practice and Theory of Psychoanalysis,* pp. 120–136. New York: International Universities Press.

Parens, H. (1979). *The Development of Aggression in Early Childhood.* New York: Jason Aronson.

_____ (1990). On the girl's psychosexual development: reconsiderations suggested from direct observation. *Journal of the American Psychoanalytic Association* 38:743–772.

Pine, F. (1984). The interpretive moment. In *Developmental Theory and Clinical Process,* pp. 148–159. New Haven: Yale University Press.

Reich, A. (1973). *Psychoanalytic Contribution.* New York: International Universities Press.

Roiphe, H., and Galenson, E. (1981). *Infantile Origins of Sexuality.* New York: International Universities Press.

Rosenfeld, S., and Sprince, M. (1963). An attempt to formulate the meaning of the concept of borderline. *Psychoanalytic Study of the Child* 18:603–635. New York: International Universities Press.

_____ (1965). Some thoughts on the handling of borderline children. *Psychoanalytic Study of the Child* 20:495–517. New York: International Universities Press.

Sandler, J., ed. (1987). *From Safety to Superego.* New York: Guilford Press.

Seinfeld, J. (1991). *The Empty Core: An Object Relations Approach to Psychotherapy of the Schizoid Personality.* Northvale, NJ: Jason Aronson.

Sharpe, E. (1930). The analysand. In *Collected Papers on Psychoanalysis,* pp. 22–37. London: The Hogarth Press, 1968.

Spitz, R. (1959). *A Genetic Field Theory of Ego Formation.* New York: International Universities Press.

_____ (1965). *The First Year Of Life.* New York: International Universities Press.

Tyson, P. (1978). Transference and developmental issues in the analysis of a prelatency child. *Psychoanalytic Study of the Child* 33:213–236. New Haven: Yale University Press.

Winnicott, D. (1953). Transitional objects and transitional phenomena: a study of the first not-me possession. *International Journal of Psycho-Analysis* 34:89–97.

_____ (1958). The capacity to be alone. In *The Maturation Process and the Facilitating Environment,* pp. 29–36. New York: International Universities Press.

_____ (1960). Ego distortions in terms of the true and false self. In *The Maturation Process and the Facilitating Environment,* pp. 140–152. New York: International Universities Press.

Index